To _____

From _____

A Mother's Love

Best-loved Memories from
Guideposts Magazine

DIMENSIONS
FOR LIVING

NASHVILLE

A MOTHER'S LOVE

This book is printed on recycled, acid-free paper.

Library of Congress Cataloging-in-Publication Data

A Mother's love : best-loved memories from Guideposts magazine.
    p.   cm.
ISBN 0-687-27256-4 (hard : alk. paper)
    1. Mothers—Miscellanea. 2. Mother and child—Miscellanea.
I. Guideposts (Pawling, N.Y.)
HQ759.M895   1994
306.874'3—dc20   93-23324
                                                                     CIP

94 95 96 97 98 99 00 01 02 03 — 10 9 8 7 6 5 4 3

MANUFACTURED IN THE UNITED STATES OF AMERICA

A Mother's Love

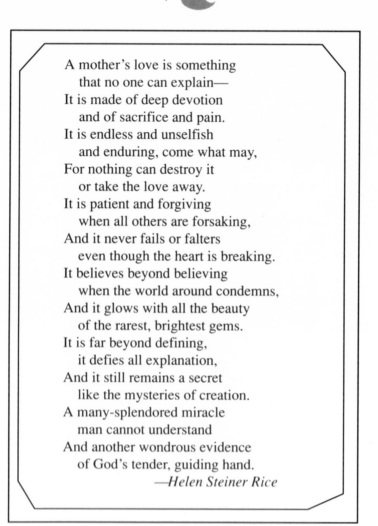

A mother's love is something
   that no one can explain—
It is made of deep devotion
   and of sacrifice and pain.
It is endless and unselfish
   and enduring, come what may,
For nothing can destroy it
   or take the love away.
It is patient and forgiving
   when all others are forsaking,
And it never fails or falters
   even though the heart is breaking.
It believes beyond believing
   when the world around condemns,
And it glows with all the beauty
   of the rarest, brightest gems.
It is far beyond defining,
   it defies all explanation,
And it still remains a secret
   like the mysteries of creation.
A many-splendored miracle
   man cannot understand
And another wondrous evidence
   of God's tender, guiding hand.
                    —*Helen Steiner Rice*

Contents

Foreword / *Marion Bond West*   9

I. GOD GAVE US MOTHERS

The Mother of Mother's Day   13

That's My Mom / *Brock Kidd*   15

Song Across the Years / *Louise A. Driver*   19

Mama's Spiritual Scrapbook / *Elenore Knox*   22

The Day I Grew Up / *Greg Hunter*   24

Message of Love / *Brad Wilcox*   27

Mama Had Always Been There / *Linda Brown*   31

My Mother, Heloise / *Poncé Heloise Cruse*   37

Love Reborn / *Kris Welland*   41

The Person I Call Mother / *Susan McFeatters*   45

Mama's Dream / *Betty McFarlane*   47

Always Mama / *Clara Wallace Nail*   51

Visiting Mother / *Betty L. Mills*   54

Fields of Yellow Daisies / *Carol Kuykendall*   55

II. GOD GAVE US CHILDREN

A New Mother's Reflections on
God's Love / *Kathryn Slattery*   59

Mommy Praying / *Linda J. Burba*   63

First Day of School / *Nancy A. Carlson*   66

I Don't Want to Be a Mother
Today / *Sue Monk Kidd*   67

A Mother's Prayer / *author unknown*   72

The Fullness of Life / *Lynn Colwell*   73

When the Sunbeams Danced / *Frances Adams Schultz*   76

Bubbles and Rose Petals and the
Smoothness of Satin / *Nancy L. Riley*   78

Motorized Mother / *Patricia Lorenz*   82

The Child I Couldn't Have / *Rose Sinclair*   85

Who's My Real Mother? / *Grace Thompson*   89

Ange's Boy / *Marilyn Helleberg*   95

A Foster Mom / *Karen J. Kanatzar*   99

I'll Drive, Mom! / *Carol Kuykendall*   102

Becoming Acquainted at Last / *Lois Williams Theuring*   106

Single with Children / *Patricia Lorenz*   111

What Being a Mother Is All About / *Patricia Brennan*   116

The Lunch Box / *Marion Bond West*   120

Love Will Keep Us Close / *Frances Liming*   125

A Fortune in Memories / *Hope B. Friedman*   126

Foreword

Motherhood is one of the most challenging undertakings in life. Along with being challenging, motherhood is sometimes impossible, wondrous, frustrating, rewarding, maddening, blissful, overwhelming, exciting, depressing, victorious, heartbreaking, and triumphant. A mother may swell with pride and nearly burst with joy one day, only to cry into a mound of unfolded clothes the next day. Unfortunately, the only real way any mother learns how to be a mother is by being one, which often involves years of mistakes and blunders. Fortunately, however, God seems to have created children ready to forgive.

In *A Mother's Love,* you will meet stay-at-home moms and working moms; natural mothers, foster mothers, and adoptive mothers; young mothers who wearily long to crawl back into bed at two o'clock in the morning and older mothers with gray hair and distinct wrinkles in their hands. Most are ordinary mothers, whose names you will not recognize, who perform simple acts of love for their children, such as teaching daughters to braid their hair or writing "You're #1!" on a hard-boiled egg that is put into a son's lunch box on the day of the big football game.

One mother dreams of becoming a writer and prepares a box with an optimistic label that says "Acceptance Letters." Through the years she fills the box with answers to the long, loving letters she has written to family and friends who are hurting or lonely. Another mother is determined not to allow her child, who is entering first grade, know of her own apprehension about "letting go."

A young mother desperately tries to find time to pray during her hectic day. The mother of a newborn with Down syndrome, whose initial emotion is "I can't do it," discovers gratitude and joy. Another young mother recounts that lonely time at two o'clock in the morning spent rocking a crying newborn and feeling as though "the flame of joy that burns so mysteriously inside each mother's heart has simply gone out." (No one has told her that this is normal and will happen many times in different ways through the years.)

A woman who can't have her own child experiences the agony of disappointment and then discovers that God had a special plan in mind all along. An adopted child demands to find her "real" mom, and her adoptive mother wonders, "Will we lose her?"

A wise mom takes a break from her busy chores to lie in a hammock with her son whose world has temporarily toppled. A single-again mother with children to raise alone moves into a deeper, more dependent relationship with God. A mother becomes a child in her old age, and the child becomes the reluctant parent. A mother experiences the grief of visiting her son in jail only to discover that he is vulnerable and in need of her love and understanding, much like he's a little boy again.

As I read *A Mother's Love,* a startling thought hit me: No wonder God wanted his only Son to have a mother!

Marion Bond West

I.

God Gave Us Mothers

The Mother of Mother's Day

SHE WAS NEVER A MOTHER HERSELF. SHE WAS A spinster schoolteacher. She was the daughter of a Methodist minister. At one point she was an advertising executive with a Philadelphia insurance firm. And for fifteen years she devoted her life to caring for her ailing mother.

After her mother's death in 1905, she yearned to find something to honor the memory of that good woman. And then she remembered the picnics that her mother had helped to organize back home in Grafton, West Virginia. They were called Mother's Friendship Day picnics, and mothers gathered at them in an effort to heal the hatred lingering after the Civil War. Then came the idea: Why not a national day to honor *all* mothers?

She wrote to the U.S. Patent Office and obtained a copyright for "Mother's Day." Then tirelessly she pressed her idea on governors, state legislators, congressmen, senators, clergymen, even the White House to get "her" day recognized. At last, in 1914 President Woodrow Wilson signed a proclamation making Mother's Day a national observance.

For the rest of her life she campaigned to keep the holiday from becoming too commercialized. "Give your mother something useful," she once told a friend, "a pair of comfortable slippers, or shoes, new eyeglasses, an eiderdown if she isn't warm at night, or fix her stairs if they need fixing."

Upon her death in 1948, a wreath of forty-three carnations was placed on her grave, forty-three because that many countries celebrated Mother's Day due to her efforts. And why carnations? The carnation is the flower she suggested be worn on the holiday. It was her mother's favorite flower.

And it remains an enduring reminder of Anna M. Jarvis, the woman who gave birth to Mother's Day.

That's My Mom

Brock Kidd

t all began in psychology class. My teacher
was leading a discussion on the modern
day-care system and working mothers. . . .

"Well," the girl in front of me volun-
teers, "my mother started me in day care
when I was nine months old. She had to
work."

I grow totally absorbed in the exchange that follows. One
after another the kids around me share their experiences.
Many have mothers who work outside the home. It
becomes clear that I am in the minority. "My mom," I say
finally, "stayed home with me."

There is a silent pause as the other students turn to look
at me as if I've said something weird. Then the bell rings. I
have to tell you that I am relieved. To be truthful, I am feeling pretty confused.

As I grab my books and dart out of class, I remember
something I haven't thought about in a long time. I'm in
kindergarten, and one by one the kids in my class are standing up telling what their moms and dads do. When my turn
comes I announce, "My dad is a minister, and my mom is a
dancer."

Mom laughs her head off when my teacher tells her.
Later she asks, "Brock, why in the world did you say I was
a dancer?"

"I don't know; I just lied," I answer. What I don't want to tell her is that I am embarrassed because all the other mothers do neat things like work in banks or law firms. My mom? Well, she doesn't do anything, as far as I can tell. She is just a mom.

Back to the present. I clear my head as I walk down the hall. I guess I'm so used to the things Mom does for me every day that I never realize what a gift God has given me in her. Maybe I've taken her for granted.

She had a promising career ahead when she met Dad. But after they married, they went up to the Appalachian Mountains to be missionaries. Then they had me and later my sister, Keri. Mom was too busy to go back to her career.

That night I tell Mom about the discussion in psychology class. "Brock," she says quietly, "this *is* my career, being a wife and mother, and helping your father with his ministry. It takes all of my time. But I feel unbelievably blessed to have been able to stay home with you and Keri."

Later in bed, I lay in the dark thinking. Last Sunday my dad's sermon had been on Ruth.

"In our story of Ruth," he preached, "God shows us what we'll call the Type R personality—R for Ruth. R for people who fulfill commitments to the end. It is these people, people who have learned to serve others, who are truly happy."

I think of my mom again. She's always there, at every one of my games, at school meetings, or at home cooking our favorite food. She helps Dad edit his sermons and with a lot of the public relations work he does for the church, and she often visits the hospitals with him. She's always on the go. But best of all, she's just always there. For me, my sister, my dad. We *are* blessed.

Type R. That's my mom.

6:15 A.M. Breakfast smells are the first thing I notice as I roll out of bed. Bacon, toast, fresh orange juice. Thirty minutes later I'm walking out the front door on my way to school, thinking about the big game. Mom is standing there with my lunch bag in her hand. She begins singing in her off-key way. "It's hurrah for Mr. Touchdown. It's hurrah for Mr. Team. . . ."

I smile as I head for the car. Tonight is the biggest football game of the year for Hillsboro High. We won our district, and now we're in the state play-offs. A victory tonight could take us all the way to the state championship.

There's excitement in the air as I arrive at school. Banners are stretched through the halls. ALL THE WAY TO STATE! they scream. My stomach suddenly tightens. The pre-game jitters begin. As an offensive guard, I worry about my blocking assignments because our opponents are known for their awesome defense. It is crucial that I execute my blocks. This is my senior year.

Finally lunchtime comes. Today the nervousness drives me to sit by myself. I get my lunch bag out of my locker, bypass the cafeteria, and go outside under a tree. I pause as I am about to crack open my boiled egg. There is something written on it. YOU'RE #1! it says, a message from Mom. I chuckle. Yesterday I found a cartoon in the bottom of my bag, cut from the morning paper. I lean back against the tree. I relax for the first time that day.

5:00 P.M. The team meets in the locker room. We want this game badly. In its fifty-year history, our school has never won a championship. Now here we are in the play-offs. Our coach gives us an incredible pep talk. I stare at the twelve green and gold balloons—the team colors—hanging in the air. Mom sent them. I'm ready to rock and roll.

The game is hard fought. We are well into the third quarter when it suddenly hits me like a ton of bricks: We are not going to win this time. The other team is ahead by three touchdowns, and their vaunted defense is like a steel wall. Slowly, to our frustration, they are grinding us down, beating us.

With a weary clap of our hands we go into formation for

the next play. Then a strange thing happens. Over the roar of the crowd one voice rings out perfectly distinct. "Go Brock!" I hear my mom cry.

The final seconds crush down on us. Then it's over. Losing this game is one of the hardest things I've ever experienced. My buddies and I are battling back tears as we head for the locker room. Suddenly I feel a gentle hand on my shoulder. I look up. Mom and Dad are there. My teammates know my mom well. She's cooked many a pre-game meal for us, cheered us on when we were down.

"I left some homemade soup on the stove," Mom says. There are tears in her eyes too. This is as hard for her as it is for me. Yet I stand there feeling very proud. I am very proud of my mom.

Back in the quiet locker room I peel off my Hillsboro jersey for the last time and change into street clothes for the drive home. It hurts.

I sit alone in the car in my driveway for a long time. My last high school game is over, and with it passes a part of my life forever.

I look up now from where I sit in front of my house. Light pours out of the windows. A feeling I can't describe comes over me, sitting out here in the dark and knowing that I can walk toward that light and be home.

I ease out of the car and head up the walk slowly, nursing the stiff muscles that will be sore tomorrow. I drink in the pure night air of autumn and my heart beats a little faster. I walk toward the light. I know that Mom, Dad, and Keri are waiting inside, and that the house will smell like vegetable soup.

Song Across the Years

Louise A. Driver

om is far from beautiful—"nice looking" probably describes her better. Her hair is graying, and the wrinkles in her hands are more distinct, which is not surprising because Mom has worked hard all her life.

When we kids were growing up, we lived in the tiny community of Minong, Wisconsin. Dad and Mom ran a live-bait stand for a living. Because most of the bait we sold was bought by tourists during the summer months, winters were sometimes hard, but Mom was always cheerful.

Mom raised a vegetable garden. Each summer she canned over seventy-five quarts of string beans, besides all the other vegetables, "to make ends meet," Mom always said. Mom used to sit on our porch and snap the beans and sing. I never thought much about her singing. It was just what you heard when you opened the door, or while you watched her washing the dishes.

One day the singing stopped. I was too young to remember an exact day. But all at once I realized Mom wasn't singing any more. She looked tense and tired. Waking up one night and hearing her crying, I knew what was happening. The following day we were told. Our parents' marriage was ending—in divorce.

The day came in June. The truck loaded all our belongings and left Dad's behind. We moved to Rice Lake, where my mom could find work.

She must have been very unhappy and very scared, all alone, with two young children still at home to support. But she just told my brother and me that she loved us and that somehow things would turn out all right.

Even though she worked many long hours, Mom found time to remember the little things. She remembered Easter baskets and orange birthday cakes with blue frosting and animal candleholders and even our old plastic Christmas stockings. Mom probably could have made a lot of new friends in Rice Lake, but we kept her too busy to try.

Mom could never hate. She tried to explain why she thought the divorce had happened and taught us to love Dad. She never would let us criticize or blame him.

Mom helped me through the growing-up years. She rode around and around the block with me when I was learning to drive. She stood up proudly at my honors banquet and graduation from high school. She was always there.

I remember one trying period during those high school years. I was very discouraged. I finally told Mom I had lost God. I explained how he seemed so far away and unreachable that I'd stopped praying to him.

"Are you really looking for him," Mom said, "or are you waiting for him to run to you? For if you are, he has already run. Turn around and meet him halfway." I knew Mom was right. I started to pray again, and as I prayed, my faith returned.

Several years later, I married David Driver. It wasn't an easy wedding for Mom. She didn't want Dad to walk me down the aisle. She said that she felt he had lost his right to do that. I thought she was wrong, and we talked a lot about it. Finally one night as we lay talking in our shared bedroom, Mom settled it. She said she had prayed and the answer seemed to say, "Anne, look at Louise and forget about Merril." After the wedding, Mom told me she had done just that, and it worked. Mom has never interfered in our marriage.

Not long ago, as I stood one night in the bedroom of our two small children and looked from bed to crib, I suddenly found myself praying: "Dear Lord, let my children love and respect me as I love and respect Mom. Help me, Lord, to teach them the things that I have been taught: that there is always a loving mother to call on when everything else seems impossible and that you are always near to watch. Amen."

The next time I saw Mom I told her about that prayer. She didn't say anything. But when we went to Mom's for supper a few nights later and opened the door, you know what I heard? I heard Mom singing.

After all those years, Mom was singing.

Mama's Spiritual Scrapbook

Elenore Knox

here I was, stumped, right in the middle of sorting out and disposing of my mother's possessions. Her furniture posed no real problem, and her clothes we could give away easily, but what was I to do with all these odd little personal items Mama had collected over the years? What about these clippings from her church paper, or this bookmark with The Lord's Prayer on it, or the Rose of Sharon pin her friend had brought home from the Holy Land? These oddments would mean precious little to anybody else, I thought. Even so, I couldn't bear to throw them out.

"I'll make a scrapbook!" I told my husband suddenly. "I'll gather together all these bits and scraps that were meaningful to Mama, and I'll paste them in one giant book."

It took me a long time, but that's exactly what I did, until I had a big book bulging with such things as a letter from the minister who had married Mama; a silver coin showing praying hands and an inscription that read, "With God all things are possible"; "An Indian Prayer" written on birch bark; a cross woven from a Palm Sunday frond—all mementos of God's love. Gradually I began to add items of my own, and whenever I took out the scissors and paste to make another entry, I had the feeling that Mama was there, looking over my shoulder.

And then came that ugly day when my doctor told me I had cancer. Immediate surgery would be necessary, he said.

What a terrible enemy fear can be! Suddenly my faith was gone and despair took over. I loved this life and the husband, children, and grandchildren I shared it with. I didn't want to lose it. First came "I don't believe it." Then "It isn't fair!" And finally, worst of all, "There is no God."

At home that afternoon, my husband came to me as I sat in the armchair staring worriedly into space. Silently he placed the big scrapbook in my shaking hands, and almost involuntarily I opened it. My eyes fell on words Mama had loved, carefully copied from the twelfth chapter of Isaiah: "Behold, God *is* my salvation; I will trust, and not be afraid: for the LORD Jehovah *is* my strength and *my* song; he also is become my salvation" (Isaiah 12:2).

Slowly peace flowed back on a stream of renewed faith. Panic faded. God would take care of me. It seemed as though Mama herself were there, reassuring me once again that God was with me and that everything would be all right.

Two years have passed since then. I am completely recovered. But just to be sure, I keep Mama's spiritual scrapbook handy. It's the life insurance Mama left me.

The Day
I Grew Up

Greg Hunter

 know this may sound strange, but at one time in my childhood I was very much ashamed of my mother. Today the shame I feel is for myself, especially since the reason for my attitude toward her was that she was totally deaf.

Deafness swept over my mother when she was just a little girl. Doctors were baffled. They tried their best to help her, but all efforts failed. It is still unknown to this day why she is deaf.

When I was still in grammar school, we were a close-knit and loving family who lived happily in a red-and-white trailer on a grass-covered hill in the country. Yet the time came when I began to see that my mother was different from other mothers, and knowing that she was deaf and had a slight speech impediment embarrassed me. I stopped inviting my friends over to my house, and I avoided being around my mother whenever we were out in public. She noticed this strange behavior in me, but she overlooked it and loved me all the same.

One Saturday afternoon, though, something happened that changed my foolish attitude completely.

My mother and I went shopping for groceries that day, and I did as I always did whenever we went to the supermarket: I waited for my mother to get her cart and begin her shopping, then I headed for the magazine rack to spend my time reading the magazines rather than being around her when she shopped. She tended to be a little loud at times and cause unnecessary scenes. Just the thought of being around her frightened me, because I did not want people to know that she was my mother.

After an hour or so I finally saw my mother pushing her cartload of groceries to the checkout counter. Knowing that I was safe from embarrassment, I relaxed against the magazine rack. But while the cashier was ringing up the total of the groceries, my mother suddenly could not find her purse. Her eyes widened, her mouth dropped, and she started yelling with her high-pitched voice that she had lost her purse. People turned their heads, staring at her, thinking she was crazy or something. My face turned pale and my body froze in fear that she might call for me.

As my grief-stricken mother stood alone in desperation before all of those people, she looked about, asking people in her squeaky voice if they had seen her small purse. When no one answered her, she began to cry and started to lose control of herself. I remained silent behind the magazine stand, looking anxiously for an escape route out of the store, but there was none.

Suddenly I heard her cry out my name. I wanted to run and hide, but my body would not budge. My mind raced and my thoughts were spinning and becoming more confused; but like a selfish fool, I remained frozen, I slowly turned to gaze at my mother, and I saw her crying more as she searched frantically for her purse. A man tried to calm her down, but she only yelled out, screaming that someone must have stolen her purse. The man kept asking her what was wrong, and she kept repeating that her purse was gone. But he could not understand her.

Suddenly, my heart began to go out to her. I really couldn't figure out what was happening with my feelings, but finally I seemed to realize how uncaring and selfish I had been. I knew I had to drop the ignorant attitude I had carried with me for so long and run to my mother with outstretched arms to prove to her that I did indeed love her and would protect her.

As I raced toward her, I thanked God for helping me see my mistake, and I reached out for the most special person in my life and held her with all my might. Then as my embarrassment faded away, I became aware of something unique and wonderful. This lady who held me in her loving arms was the caring lady who gave birth to me, raised me to be a good person, raised my sister and my four brothers to be good and responsible people, took care of all of us when we were sick, was always there when we needed her, and, most of all, loved her family more than she did her own life. All of this is what made her special.

When the crowd of people finally receded and my mother took control of herself, we found her purse behind a box of cereal in the grocery cart. We both laughed hysterically, happy that this day had brought us closer together.

On our way home, I thought deeply about why my mother seemed unhappy at times. I knew that, deep down in her heart, she longed to hear again. She prayed so hard, wanting to be able to hear the wonderful world and hear, for the first time, her own children's voices. But only God knows what is best for her.

I am thankful for the Lord's help in that weekend incident that occurred so many years ago. I am proud of this courageous woman, my mother, my love.

Message of Love

Brad Wilcox

y lonely headlights searched the fresh snow ahead of me. I fumbled with my top coat button against the cold. Of all nights for this to happen! Dad away in Seattle on business, and my brother Roger at college!

"Don't think about it, just drive." I told myself as the wheels slid sideways on the icy street. I tried to think of a song to fill the rhythm of the struggling windshield wipers. But there was no song in me.

No wonder it had happened. This snowstorm, the same snowfall I had thought so beautiful and pure just two hours ago, was now the white-cloaked villain who had so mercilessly forced my mother's car off the road. Now she lay unconscious in critical condition.

"Are you her son?" they had asked on the telephone.

"I'll be right there!" I had shouted.

Dad didn't know, and Rog didn't know. There was just me in my old heap of a Chevy, and this snow.

A frozen string of tears beaded my cheeks. I pulled the glove from my left hand to wipe my eyes.

Just the other day Mom said these gloves were too small, I thought, as I flexed my cold fingers to circulate the blood. *Are the gloves too small, or are my hands too big?* These hands which just a few hours before were squeezed so lovingly by my beautiful mother.

"That snow looks bad, Mom. I wish you weren't going out tonight."

"I do, too. But some things just have to be done." She reached to squeeze my hand good-bye.

"Aw, come on, Mom. I'm too old for that," I declared, withdrawing my hand, "I'm not a little boy. I don't want to play baby games any more."

"It's just my way of telling you, son. It's our secret code."

"I know, I know," I said with exasperated resentment. "I'm tired of your silly secret code. Three squeezes, one-two-three. I love you," I mimicked in full-toned sarcasm. "Never again, Mom."

The words burned in my mind as I stared blankly ahead. I could still see her hurt smile.

Three squeezes had always been our love language. Because of that simple code, countless cuts and bruises had been healed. How often had we sat in church, hand-delivering our secret message, or walked through the park saying, "I love you," in silent communication?

During my sixteen-year lifetime, Mom and Dad must have invested a trillion hours per year just helping me. Ever since I could remember there had always been thoughtful rewards, and lately, dollar bills for feeding my gas tank or feeding my date. But always delivered with our secret code, the secret code that my hands had, only two hours ago, grown too large to return.

I clutched the steering wheel with one hand. Gripping the old glove in my teeth, I finally managed to fit it back over my chilled fingers. The snow fell lighter now. I was making better time.

I had never faced a problem entirely alone before. Rog had been the dependable big brother who always shepherded me past pitfalls, buying my lunch tickets, picking me up after practice.

I had wanted responsibility, and now I had it! Terrified is a pale word to describe how I felt.

What if she dies! Could anything ever be right again? Suddenly the snow looked sticky and ugly. How I wished I could bury the snow, my head, my hands, responsibility, everything!

The lights of the hospital guided me through the white blackness. My old car chugged, sputtered, and died. With a frustrated shove I freed the frozen door. Wind lashed at my exposed face. A slip on the ice sent me sprawling to the frozen pavement.

I stood up and shook myself. The biting wind hurried me toward the institutional glass doors.

I stammered Mom's name to the receptionist. It sounded foreign. To me, she was always just "Mom."

The receptionist referred to her files. She seemed ponderously slow, but finally faced me. She manipulated the switchboard, then directed me to the elevator.

"A nurse will be waiting on the third floor. I hope everything will be all right."

My rapid steps echoed dully in the endless tunnel of the hospital hallway. Elevator doors closed, trapping me inside, then drew aside again like curtains opening on a stage set. A young nurse entered stage left, taking my arm, including me in the scene.

"Please wait here," she told me. "I'll get the doctor."

I leaned my forehead against the sharp coldness of the window, peering sightlessly into the night. Snow whirled dizzily against the pane.

"Are you her son?"

I turned to find a new character in my drama. Even from my six-foot height the doctor seemed tall. Costumed in surgical green, he was well-cast in his role.

"I'm glad you came so quickly. Since your father is not here, you must be the man of the family."

I shifted uneasily in my wet shoes. Those were the exact words Dad had left with me. I wanted Dad here; here in the hospital where I was born, here with this tall doctor wearing this clinical face.

He led me down the hall. "This is her room. Now remember, son, you mustn't expect her to respond. She may not even recognize you. She is in a semiconscious state and suffering considerable pain."

I pushed the door open and stepped inside. There lay a figure surrounded by machines, strapped and laced with tubes and needles. A transparent oxygen tent encompassed the upper half of the body.

As I stood looking across at that pale, pained face, I realized this was not another character in my dramatic scene. This was my mother!

Mom's eyes opened in an unnatural stare. I stepped across the silence of that small hospital room lit only by street lamps outside the window. I reached out and laid my trembling hand on hers. I knew what I had to do. My message had to be clear. I squeezed—one-two-three. Only God knew how important it was that she understand.

Her eyes flickered. She knew me! A tear ran down my face and dropped upon my hand—the hand that had been too grownup for this baby game.

My hand enfolded hers and passed our secret code again and again until she fell asleep. Through the window I could see the snow falling gently now.

"Thank you," I prayed in marvelous relief. "Thank you for life, and hands, and secret codes."

Mama Had Always Been There

Linda Brown

 slid impatiently into the small car next to my fiancé, Greg. Mama was standing on the sidewalk outside the Brooklyn apartment where she'd raised me, smiling hopefully.

"Good-bye, Mama," I said offhandedly.

When she leaned toward my rolled-down car window to kiss me good-bye, I moved my cheek slightly away—I didn't want her to kiss me.

I'd hoped Greg couldn't see how hurt Mama looked, but his light-blue eyes were glancing curiously at me as we drove away. I sat beside him silently, my back rigid against the vinyl seat, my own dark eyes fixed stubbornly on the shadows that flickered across the windshield.

"Linda," Greg finally said, "I know it was all my idea to meet your mother . . ." I stared stonily ahead.

"And I'm glad I did. She seems very nice."

I still gave no response.

He sighed. "Well, frankly, I've never seen you act this way. You were so cold. I don't know what's gone on between you and your mother, but I do know that there must be a reason for the tension I just saw."

A reason! How dare he judge me? I had years of reason, lists of reasons! But when I turned to glare at him, I saw that his face held no judgment, only quiet concern. His hand left the steering wheel and tentatively covered mine. And slowly, I began to tell him about Mama—and Daddy. . . .

In the 1950s, when I was growing up, my father was a very troubled man. While other children's fathers came back from work in a stream of gray-flannel suits, my father sat on the stoop in front of our apartment building, wearing torn blue jeans and a white T-shirt. He never held a job. He'd just be sitting there, staring into space, his hands cupping a lighted cigarette.

Sometimes I would see the little girl who lived next door running to greet her father as he walked up the block with his shiny leather briefcase, and I would run into our apartment to hide my embarrassment. All my childish prayers revolved around my father: "Please, God, just let Daddy get better."

Mama's frustration grew with each unpaid bill she added to the pile on the kitchen shelf. Sunday mornings were the worst. While Daddy slept through the morning, Mama would throw a coat over her nightgown and run out to buy *The New York Times*. Then her red pen would come out. She'd sit at the white Formica table, with its pattern of tiny boomerangs, furiously circling ad after ad under "Help Wanted—Men." When she had covered the newsprint with bright-red circles, she'd take them to Daddy.

"Here are some jobs you could do!"

Daddy would only burrow more deeply under the old brown blanket. "I can't," he'd whisper. "Not this week."

One time Mama grabbed him by the shoulders. "We have no milk, no bread!" she pleaded.

Daddy stared at her helplessly. "Do you think I want to be like this?"

I believed he didn't. But Mama was too desperate to be sympathetic. Her lips pressed together in a thin line. The next Sunday, when she opened the *Times,* it was to "Help Wanted—Women."

But in the 1950s it was considered a gamble to hire a woman with small children. One night from the hushed darkness of the tiny room I shared with my sister, I heard her praying. When Mama had a problem, she wouldn't use fancy words; she'd just say it straight out to God, like she was talking to a friend who hadn't ever let her down. "I'm a hard-working woman, God," she was saying. "Please don't let us go on welfare. I'll take any job I can get, even if it's for a tiny paycheck. I'll be the best worker they ever hired."

Eventually a friend of a friend gave Mama a secretarial job—and a warning: "I'm taking a chance on you. But if you plan on taking time off for every runny nose and blister your kids get, you can plan on finding another job."

Mama never took one day off. Even when my sister and I were miserably ill with the measles, she made it in to work. When we needed special care, we were trundled off to a neighbor's. I would lie feverishly on a couch there and hear her whisper loudly into her pink telephone, "What kind of mother goes off and leaves her children?" I didn't like this neighbor, but her attitude made me wonder about my mother.

Daddy grew worse and worse. Without Mama there to care for him, he became increasingly disoriented. I'd come home to find the apartment filled with smoke from cooking pots he'd left forgotten on the stove. I'd run around flinging windows open, terrified of what Mama might do if she found out.

One day I came home and found Mama there alone.

"Where's Daddy?

"You could have been killed," she said reproachfully. "He could have set the house on fire."

"Where's Daddy?" I demanded.

"I sent him to the city hospital."

I raced to the door, as if he would still be there, but of course he wasn't.

"He was very sick, Linda. I had no choice. I can't look after all of you." She was, I supposed, trying to comfort me, but I ran away from her, inconsolable. The next day she was back at work, and Daddy had been placed in the psychiatric unit.

When my father was released from the hospital, he didn't bother even trying to come home. His emotional problems and chronic depression made it impossible for him to face the pressures of family life. He lived alone, supporting himself with odd jobs. I blamed Mama for locking him out of our lives.

"You've got to forget the past," Mama would say when she noticed me looking particularly unhappy. But I couldn't forget. And I couldn't forgive her for sending my father away. Not a day went by when I didn't think, *If only she'd tried harder to help him . . . .*

Greg had almost reached my apartment now, and my voice was hoarse. "Has your mother forgiven your father?" he asked.

"No!" I launched into a diatribe on how Mama still spoke against Daddy. "She can't forget the past. She still blames him for things he couldn't help. She can't forgive, she won't forgive—"

"Well," Greg interrupted gently, "can you?"

"Of course I can! I *have* forgiven. I know my father couldn't help the way he was. He never meant to hurt us. He—"

"I meant," Greg said patiently, "can you forgive your mother?"

For many seconds the only sound was the noise of the traffic outside the car windows. Me? Forgive my mother?

"You know, Linda," Greg said, breaking into my thoughts, "I've learned that times come in life when you have to make a really tough decision, a choice that is actually brutal. That's what happened to your mother. The situation got down to no food on the table, and was she going to take care of her husband or her kids? So she made that brutal choice. She had to choose between your father and you and your sister. She chose her children. She chose *you.*"

I turned to look at Greg. What was he saying? *Mama chose me.* I had begun a silent review of all the hurts, but now, unexpectedly, those thoughts faded, and a different sort of memory crept into my mind. It was a morning long ago.

I was sitting on our worn green sofa, sulkily watching Mama rush around getting ready for work.

"You're never home," I said accusingly. "You're never here. You don't do anything for us like a *real* mother. Robin's mother bakes jelly cookies for her lunch box."

"Linda," she said wearily, "I go to work so you can *have* a lunch. I'm tired when I come home; I have no time for baking."

"You have no time for anything!"

"Would you rather see us go on welfare?" she asked quietly.

I wasn't sure exactly what that meant. "Yes!"

Mama grew pale. "Oh, honey, you think welfare's fun? My mama and I were on welfare once. We never had enough food, or clothes, or money for doctors. I just want you and your sister to have it a little easier. But I can't be everything. I get tired, too."

"Well, in real families," I said spitefully, "the mommy stays home."

She winced, but said lightly, "In this family, I'll get fired if I'm late again," and she ran out to catch the train.

The following week I found three large homemade jelly cookies in my lunch box. But I never thanked Mama, never even mentioned that I'd seen the cookies. *How many times, I wondered, had I ignored Mama's efforts to please me?*

Now all the little things she'd done came flying to me. Mama staying up late to restitch my worn-out seams, Mama teaching me how to braid my long dark hair, Mama stepping in when my sister and I had an argument. As badly as I had treated her, it was still Mama who had always been there for me. Why hadn't I been able to see this before?

Right there in the car I did what I had seen Mama do so many times—I bowed my head and prayed, silently. My prayer was for forgiveness—but this time for myself. *And please, God, help me to get rid of my bitterness.*

"Greg, I know this is going to sound crazy, but—"

"You want to go back to your mother's," he finished. He was already smiling, turning the car around.

Later, sitting in Mama's familiar, cozy kitchen, I gave silent thanks. I had watched Mama move about this kitchen a thousand times, but I had always been too angry to feel the strength of her love, the steady warmth of her support.

"Mama?" I said hesitantly, not sure how to begin. "Do you think sometime you could show me your recipe for jelly cookies?"

For a moment I thought she wasn't going to answer, but then I realized she was nodding, and in a voice so low I could hardly hear, she whispered, "You remember those cookies after all these years?"

"Yes, Mama," I said, "I remember."

My Mother, Heloise

Poncé Heloise Cruse

 i, how are you?"

My mother used to walk up to people and say that all the time. Then she'd introduce herself, "I'm Heloise. You know, the lady who writes the helpful hints column. I noticed the shine on that table you're polishing [this to a cleaning lady in the lobby of a posh London hotel]. Could you please tell me what you're using?"

"Vinegar, madame."

"Vinegar!" exclaimed Mom, "Why, I've never heard . . ."

Mom chatted with this stranger as though she were a next-door neighbor while, as usual, I nearly died of embarrassment. But it was a great day for vinegar. Vinegar became a favorite household helper in Mom's column.

That was Mother, uninhibited, friendly, and so eager to learn how to make life run smoothly that she'd ask people everywhere—in restaurants, shops, taxis, on the street— their secret cures and shortcuts for mending life's little problems.

"It's the little things that drive you crazy—the broken heel, the stain, the drop. If you take care of the little things, the big things become manageable."

That was her philosophy, and it became her career in

1959 when she marched into the newspaper in Honolulu (where our family was stationed) and offered to write a "Reader's Exchange" column of helpful tips. "I'll do it free for a month," she told the editor.

Mom had never written professionally in her life, but the editor agreed to let her try, and then watched his paper's circulation increase by more than 30 percent during the next three years. He claimed it was mostly due to Mother's column.

I was seven when Mother started it, and I remember our family—Dad, a captain in the Air Force, my older brother, Louis, me, and Mom—sitting at the dinner table discussing tips sent in by readers.

"Here's a letter that says you can shine silver with tooth-paste. Poncé, run, get the toothpaste! Let's see if it works."

It did. And Mom used it in her column.

Another time, she told us, "A lady wrote that she was about to throw away her daughter's old petticoat, one of those stiff net ones that had begun drooping. Instead, she cut it up and used it for scrubbing pots and pans."

We laughed. Scrubbing pots with petticoats! But Mother went right out, bought some nylon net, and scoured all of our pots and pans. "It works!" she told her readers, and that idea became one of the most successful in her column.

I can see Mom now, pounding out tips on her typewriter in her folksy style as though she were writing to a good friend. And her readers *were* good friends. And she'd tell me, "Homemakers are the backbone of the country. If life becomes a mess at home, it will fall apart everywhere else."

Mother wrote books; she made public appearances. She did radio and TV shows. She worked as a hospital volunteer. She wrote a song. She even did fine paintings. But, above all, she was a homemaker. Her heart was in the home and with the people who kept it.

She understood the irksome nuisances of homemakers.

(She lived with them, too.) And she was tireless in finding their solutions: "Your cottage cheese going moldy? Store it upside down next time." Mom found solutions for everything from taking off garlic skins to putting on a girdle. She taught me that one of the best solutions in life is *persistence.*

I remember yelling from the sewing machine one day, "Mom, I can't get this zipper right. It's full of ridges!"

"Poncé," she told me, "you've got to rip it out, Honey, and stitch it in again. It will never zip that way."

I put it in again. Nothing but bunches and puckers.

"Dear, that's all wrong, Try it again." *Snip. Snip. Snip. Ch-ch-ch-ch-ch-ch,* I stitched around the zipper. "Ugh! It looks awful, Mom."

"Just rip it out and start over," Mother said.

And I did. Over and over and over. It took me seventeen tries to get that zipper in flat. The rest of the garment was ruined from all of the ripping out. But I *knew* how to put in a zipper. And you'd better believe, I never *forgot!*

Mom was like that, persistent, when it came to her relationship with God. She kept her word, just as she did at home and with her readers.

One of her promises is still ongoing, even though Mother died in 1977. It began when I was born. My eyes were so crossed that you could see only the whites. The doctors were doubtful that I'd ever be able to see correctly. Well, Mom *wanted* me to see. She'd gone through five miscarriages before I came along. She'd endured thirty-two hours of labor before I was born. And then I was born severely cross-eyed.

The doctors said it would take five operations to straighten out my eyes, and then they shrugged over the possible outcome. They wouldn't give her much hope.

So Mom said to God, "Please, if you'll cure my Poncé, I'll tithe my income to the blind." The operations worked, and fifteen percent of Mom's income, even from her estate today, has always gone to purchase Braille typewriters for kids who can't afford them.

Always persistent in giving back to God, that was Mom. You see, she wanted her spiritual life to run smoothly, too.

You have to work on the little things—those little spiritual problems inside of you. You iron those out. Then you work on those little messy tasks around the home—those greasy, drippy, dusty, creaky, nagging little frustrations that take away your home's harmony. Day by day, with persistence.

That was Mother's way of making the home. Her way of making it a place of safety, a place of comfort, a place where people could feel joy, peace. A place where each of us could come and know that we belonged, a place where we could be restored and go out to meet the challenges of the day.

Once upon a time, being a homemaker was women's work—proud work. Many people don't feel this way today. With so many women in the work force, being a house-keeper often seems trivial. But I myself believe that we need the homemaker more than ever.

Straightening. Ironing. Mending. Gluing. Polishing. These things go on, day by day. The home is where we start from and come back to, and the homemaker—women, and men, too—remains "the backbone of our country."

Mother understood and loved and honored homemakers; she wanted to make their daily tasks easier; and now, as the "Hints from Heloise" columnist, so do I. I've come to love and revere all those people who are proud to put their ener-gies each day into making the home a glorious place to be.

Love Reborn

Kris Welland

My mother's alcoholism became apparent to me when I was about nine years old. For seven years I watched as her illness made a grayish, skeletonlike animal out of the intelligent, charming beauty I loved. Liquor tore her apart and tore us apart too, my brother and sister and father and me, and all the other people who loved her, which included anyone who knew her.

As for me, I changed as much in those seven years as I thought my mother did. I began to hate her because hating hurt less than loving her and watching her destroy herself. Later I felt that her drinking was directed purposely at the family, and I steeled myself even more against the sympathy that made me vulnerable to soul-ache. I like to think now that had I known what she was suffering, I would have helped her. But I didn't.

I was fifteen when my father carried her limp, gray, emaciated form out to the car and drove her away, and I remember distinctly the overwhelming relief and exhilaration I felt that hot June day. She was going away for good, far away to a rehabilitation center in Minneapolis, Minnesota, and my father was divorcing her. I would never have to see her again. I didn't, either, for almost two years.

During that time, I thought about my mother as little as possible; I was happier than I had ever been before, ignorantly happy. To appease my niggling conscience I read the letters she sent us, full of a love that disgusted me, but I never wondered at her struggle to regain her sobriety, her sanity, and her self-respect.

She won that struggle without my help. When I was sixteen, she wrote to say that she was leaving the rehabilitation center for an apartment and a position as a secretary in an insurance company.

I could not believe she was really well at last. Secretly I resented her licking it without us when she couldn't with us, and cynically, almost hopefully, I expected her to start drinking again within a week. But her letters kept coming; enthusiastically, crisply, she wrote of her activities at work, of decorating her apartment, of skiing weekends.

My mother seemingly ignored the fact that we never answered her letters, and she kept writing until we finally did answer them. Courtesy, I told myself. But the truth was, I had to admire her spunk. After a lot of internal struggle, I accepted one of her invitations to visit, and two days after my seventeenth Christmas I boarded a plane for Minneapolis.

I have never felt so frightened as I did when I stepped off the plane that wintry evening. My mother must have been frightened too, but as I glimpsed that unfamiliar, familiar face in the crowded waiting room, she hurried to me and hugged and kissed me and kept her arm around me as we walked away. I wanted to shrug off that arm—one of the principles of my hate had been that I never allowed her to touch me—but she kept it there, and in my confusion I talked furiously.

We picked up my luggage and stepped out into the shocking cold and the cobalt night. As we drove noisily through the dark and snow, fast along the flat highway, my ego and I began to recover from our fright, and my hauteur and hate came back. I answered reticently, even curtly, her eager questions about my sister and brother, about my friends, about school.

Sometimes with deliberate cruelty I spoke of things to remind her of her losses—of my brother's new tallness, the beauty of our Christmas tree, the family jokes around the dinner table at home—a hundred things that could only grieve and sadden her. Never did I speak encouragingly of her amazing return to health; never was I enthusiastic about the details of her new life in Minnesota; not once did I display a particle of affection.

Yet my mother kept her composure and retained in our conversation both untiring interest and, more remarkably, love. By the time we got to her home I was a little ashamed of myself, which only served to make me nastier toward her.

We walked into the warmth of her apartment and I held my breath. My mother adored daintiness and airiness, and how beautiful she had made that room! Gauzy white curtains floated at the windows, filtering the light onto the snow outside. The floor was blanketed richly in pale yellow, the light blue furniture was decorated with sprays of tiny white flowers, and around the room she had scattered great bunches of daisies in crystal bowls.

For Christmas, tables were adorned with graceful candles and delicate silver angels. The little gilt bell that had tinkled *Silent Night* for us so many years at home was now on her desk, and next to the large window stood a dainty little fir tree, bearing bugles and teddy bears my mother had made by hand. It was all so lovely, so bright and warm and homelike that it caught at my heart.

I stood looking at that room while my mother bustled around putting finishing touches on everything. When she was done she led me to her room, which was as delightful as the other, and exhausted, I got ready for bed. My mother was to sleep on the living-room sofa while I was there, and she too prepared for bed, all the while chattering lightly. I allowed her to kiss me good night before she left the room, and then I climbed into the bed's softness and lay watching the snow swirl against the window. My door was open, and for a long time there was no sound but the *swish, swish* of the icy flakes against the glass. I lay awake for a long time, and inside I was as cold and hard and relentless as that snow.

When I finally began to get drowsy, a frighteningly familiar sound started me awake. It was a soft sound, a sound I had heard often in the night. I got up quietly and padded out into the living room. The fir tree's lights twinkled gently, and in their soft light I saw my mother huddled on the couch, her face in her hands. She was weeping as she had wept many times, alone and in the dark. I stood silently for a moment and watched her, and then my heart couldn't stand it anymore. I went to her and put my arms around her, and from that moment have never ceased to love her.

The Person
I Call Mother

Susan McFeatters

y mother had a very unusual first name—Tirzah—and she was always proud to tell people that it was drawn from the Bible. I never paid much attention to the name itself, for to me my mother was simply my mother —the person who was always there when I needed her.

Of course I knew that she'd had a life before I came along. Nana, my grandmother, had told me tales of Mother's childhood. About how her father had demanded she receive the same education as a boy. (As a result, she was the only girl in her high school chemistry class.) About her romance with my father. (She was barely sixteen, my father an older man of twenty-four, but they convinced both sets of parents to allow them to date.) All the same, I never thought of her as being anybody but Mother.

Then about a year after a job with an advertising agency lured me to New York City from Pittsburg, I got a phone call from home. Nana, whom I adored, was sick. I wasn't really worried. Nana was a tiny wisp of a woman, but like most specimens of that breed best characterized as "a lady through and through," she had a backbone of steel. She'd survived setbacks in the past. The doctors thought she'd survive this one, too.

The doctors were wrong. A day or two later, Nana died.

I couldn't get a flight home until the next day, so I had time to nurse my grief. I felt sad and hurt, but also betrayed and angry. Why hadn't "they" leveled with me and told me she was really dying? How could "she" go off and leave without giving me a chance to say good-bye? That first day, I felt Nana's death only in terms of my own loss.

My father picked me up at the airport. We were quiet on the ride home. When we pulled into the driveway, I got out of the car ready, I suppose, to run upstairs, to throw myself into Mother's arms. Somehow she would make everything right again.

I went in the basement door. At the top of the stairs stood my mother. Only this time I didn't see my mother. I saw a woman. A woman who had just lost *her* mother. Now I ran up the steps. I threw my arms around her, embraced her, comforted her, soothed her hurt and sorrow.

I did some growing up that day, as I began to see my mother as herself—an individual with her own feelings and dreams, not someone God put here mainly to take care of me and my needs.

And when I freed my mother from my narrow view of her, I opened myself to seeing other people in all their richness—not defined only by their roles and responsibilities.

Life is far more interesting when I allow people to be what God—in his infinite creativity—made each and every one of us to be: Unique. As unique as Tirzah!

Mama's Dream

Betty McFarlane

 wish now that I hadn't opened the old cedar chest, for there, under the quilt I'd come for, was the old familiar box with the words "Acceptance Letters" penciled on it. Now the fragrance of roses that Mama always wore drifted faintly toward me and I looked again at Mama's writing box. Memories rushed in and a sense of sadness filled me. Her dream had never become a reality.

Yet as long as I can remember, Mama had always wanted to be a writer. She frequently told us children of the stories she was going to write and where she was going to send them. Most often she would carry a small notebook and, as she hurriedly went her busy way, she would quickly take the notebook out and jot down an idea or two as it came to her.

I first knew Mama was really serious about her writing twenty years or so ago. She sat at the kitchen table with a tear snaking down her cheek as she put on paper how she had just been forced to sell a horse, an old paint, that she loved. We had needed the money for a house payment.

Mama never sent the article anywhere, but after that day I saw a new light in her eyes. "Children," she told us, "your mama is going to be a writer. I feel that the Lord wants me to write stories that others may read so that they might feel encouraged or uplifted or loved." And this time she put her words into action.

First she took a little of our much-needed money and bought stationery and business cards with her name, address, and the words "Writer and Lecturer" on them. She said it was important to handle things correctly and in a businesslike manner; that editors would be more likely to read her work if the cover letter looked proper.

She then cleared a corner in the basement, made a desk by putting a door across two file cabinets, and borrowed an old typewriter from Grandpa. But what I really remember most was the box that she fixed and carefully placed on the desk with her stationery. The box had been lovingly covered with a piece of cream-colored cotton strewn with tiny blue forget-me-nots. She had tied a pale blue ribbon around it and confidently written those words, "Acceptance Letters." I guess it never occurred to her that she might get some rejections.

Mama gathered her notes, got a copy of the *Writer's Market,* and began writing. However, before she had finished even one article, Dad had left us. Mama was suddenly responsible for the complete care of her children. With six of us still at home, she spent long hours teaching school, keep up our home, and guiding us. She always found time to write us an encouraging note to be found in our lunch box or on our dresser—but never enough time to write her stories. Mama always told us, though, "Don't worry about my writing, darlings. God gave me the dream, and he will bring the dream to fulfillment. I don't know when I will have the time to write or what I'll write, but that isn't important. The important thing is that God knows what he is doing, and all we have to do is be open to his promptings and do as he guides us. God will take care of the dream."

Years came and went; I don't recall now when Mama put the box and stationery away, but I do recall that one day they were no longer on the desk. When I questioned Mama, she only said, "Perhaps someday soon God will give me the time to write stories, but for now, honey, I need to write a letter to your brother."

Occasionally, when I'd see her sitting at her desk, I'd think, *Praise the Lord! Now she is writing her stories.* But instead it was always a letter to one of my brothers in the service, a card to a friend, or a cheerful note to Grandpa.

As we children grew up and began to leave home, Mama would comment that she would soon have the time to write; but then something would always come up—Mama's brother was in a serious car accident and she went to be with him; my sister needed help with her baby; Grandpa got sick and came to live with us; a pregnant teenager needed help; a neighbor had no one but Mama to turn to.

In her mind and on scraps of paper, Mama's stories were born, but Mama never had an article published, for mama never had a chance to write.

Now I reached down into the cedar chest and picked up the box. To my surprise, it was very heavy. Its ribbon was worn from tying and untying.

"What could she possibly have kept in here?" I mused aloud. Carefully I opened it. I began to read the "acceptance letters" that lay inside.

"Thank you, Mom, for your daily letters. I could never have made it through boot camp without them."

"Just a note to tell you how much my sister appreciated your support in the many letters you sent her during her years of illness."

"Thank you for writing me during these long months that I've been carrying my baby."

"My year in prison would have been unbearable without your letters of hope."

"I was so lonely being away from home for the first time, but your stories of Jesus have kept me happy and unafraid."

"Thank you for taking the time to send me the pretty note cards. Sometimes an old man like me feels like no one wants to bother with him."

"Your letter came when I was at my lowest point. You dared me to be my best, and I am now one of the top salesmen in my organization."

"Mama, your letters have helped me retain my sanity during this difficult time. Thank you for the constant support, concern, hope, and, most of all, love."

God does fulfill people's dreams. Mama *was* a writer.

Always Mama

Clara Wallace Nail

rocery and errand day again, and I was on my way to pick up Mama. I hoped she'd be ready.

Of late she'd paid scant attention to the clock. It was frustrating to have to wait for her. Half the time she wasn't even dressed when I got to her house. I'd grown impatient with her childlike ways. Not that she'd ever had a good sense of time, but now she had grown worse. She was seventy-nine years old, and somewhere along the way we seemed to have changed roles. I had begun to think of her in almost juvenile terms.

I drove into her yard, and as I opened the car door I heard the sound of a horse's scream. Beyond the house I could see a flurry of activity in the cow pasture, where several handymen were replacing some barbed wire fencing. I headed toward them. And there was Mama—hurrying ahead of me. I called, but she paid no attention. I ran after her, but she didn't slow down.

Now I could see the horse, a bay I didn't recognize, caught in the barbed wire and spooked. His thrashing rear legs kicked at the men. With nostrils flared and hooves pounding, he let out angry squeals. He was a terrified animal, and my elderly mother was headed straight for him. "No, Mama," I thought out loud. "Don't! It's been too long."

In her younger days Mama could handle any horse. My earliest memories are of the smell of leather, the squeak of the saddle, and Mama behind me, supporting me as her horse moved beneath us. Mama's firm hand was on the rein; Mama was in charge.

An old World War I cavalryman who boarded with us in those days said Mama had the light touch. "Only special horse people have the light touch," he told me, "and your mother has it."

Now just as she reached the big stallion, one of the men tried to stop her. "Miss Nell, get back!" he shouted. "He's a mean 'un. Came running across the field at us."

He was yelling loudly, but I didn't intervene. I was already thinking back to a time when I obeyed whatever Mama said. She put out her arm with a flattened hand, a sign for us to be still. To my surprise, I shook my head at the man as if to say, *It's all right; she can handle it.* At the same time, my mouth was dry as a bone, and I said a quick prayer.

Mama spoke soothing words to the horse. "What's the matter, pretty boy? Let's see about you." She made soft chirping sounds, and her movements were calm and slow, so familiar to me. She put her hand on his thigh, the thigh that moments before had strained with taut muscles to strike out. The trembling stopped. She caressed his flank and patted his neck, speaking endearments all the time. His high-pitched squeal turned to strange little whickers that sounded like a sobbing child being comforted.

The fencing was caught around his leg. He would have to be backed out. One of the men made a sudden movement to go to Mama's aid. Again I shook my head. The animal's size didn't matter now. Mama was in control. With soft commands she encouraged him slowly backward.

Then she spoke to us with a sharp order. "Get clean rags, water, and some of that homemade soap." As I turned to obey, she called after me, "And a strip of sheeting."

Already she was stanching the flow of blood with her apron.

After receiving the material, she sponged the wound clean and pulled the long tear together. While I held one end of the sheeting, she bound it round the stallion's leg with just the right pressure. "This will hold until a vet can see him," she explained. The rest of us remained silent, marveling at her efficiency.

In that moment, I saw something else. Mama was in command. And I was proud of her. She was the mother figure again and I the progeny. The proper order had been restored. Oh, I knew I would still have to be sure her bills were paid and see that she kept her doctor appointments. But it seemed God was reminding me that despite her childish ways, Mama was still the parent. No matter what else changed as she grew older, she still deserved my honor and respect.

The calmed horse was led away to the stable until we could find its owner. I noticed Mama's hand trembled a little when she patted him on the rump. She looked down at her bloodstained dress.

"Well, I'm not quite ready," she said. "You'll have to wait while I dress."

I put my arm around her as we started for the house. "It's okay, Mama. I don't mind waiting."

Visiting Mother

Betty L. Mills

or almost seven years I've been visiting my mother in a nursing home. She no longer recognizes me and just rambles on, not making any sense.

Lately I have been visiting her during my lunch hours in order to see her while she is awake. I had often returned to work upset and frustrated.

One day a fellow worker said, "Oh, Betty, you're so lucky!"

"Lucky?" I retorted. "My mother doesn't even know who I am."

"But you know who *she* is," my friend answered. "My mother died when I was twelve, and I'd give anything now if I could kiss her and tell her I love her. You can do that."

I had never thought about it that way, and since that day my attitude toward my visits has changed. Mother, now almost ninety, still rambles on, but while she does, I pat her hands, I kiss her, and I tell her I love her. And sometimes there is joy, when she speaks her few understandable words—"Bless you. Thank you for coming."

Fields of Yellow Daisies

Carol Kuykendall

he summer day dawned bright and clear. A perfect morning to start a family vacation. The car was packed; the house was locked. And everyone was filled with excited anticipation. Everyone, that is, except me.

As we pulled out of the driveway and onto the highway, headed for Montana, I felt the same dull weight of depression I'd carried around for weeks, ever since my mother died.

"Mommy," six-year-old Kendall asked, her face close to mine in the front seat, "are you going to be sad forever?"

"No, dear, of course not," I answered, forcing a smile. And again I vowed not to let my grief ruin the day. Or worse, ruin this vacation for my husband and our three children.

Please, Lord, I silently prayed, *help heal my sorrow. Help me to remember the joys of my mother's life and forget the pain she endured.* I had prayed variations of that prayer for the past six weeks, since the morning I held my mother's hand, easing her from life into death.

Mentally, I knew her death was a blessing. For years, she had suffered from emphysema Since my father's death eight years before, she had lived next door to us, and though she and I had always been close, during those last years we became even closer. In her last months, as she grew weaker, I spent most of my time caring for her. She was tired, in pain, and ready to die. But in my heart, I was not ready to let her go. I suffered watching her suffer.

Briefly, just before the funeral, as family and friends gathered, I felt some solace. We all reminded one another of her happier, healthier days—riding horses on mountain trails, camping out for weeks at a time each summer, her love of laughter, her fierce family loyalty and unconditional love for all of us, even the silly little sayings she used to shape our lives as we were growing up.

"Think of fields of yellow daisies," was one of her favorites, and to me the most irritating. All throughout our childhood, she singsonged that little ditty to us whenever she expected us to rise bravely above our troubles.

Once she was driving us to the doctor's office for one of our regular polio vaccinations. My skin was crawling with the dread of the inevitable sting of the needle in my arm.

"Think of fields of yellow daisies," she cheerfully suggested, when I started complaining. That made me angry. The thought of yellow daisies didn't change how I felt, not one bit. And besides, I had never even *seen* a field of yellow daisies.

I often thought my mother found the strength of God most vividly in nature. She even had all of us children baptized in a mountain meadow one bright summer day when we all were old enough to understand the significance of the ceremony.

After her funeral, family and friends went their separate ways, and the pace of my life slowed. That's when my depression descended, and now I couldn't seem to shake it. I felt like a sad child, orphaned by the loss of her mommy, and in many ways still dependent upon her emotionally.

Lord, I silently repeated, as our car sped along the highway, *I know I have to let go of the memory of her suffering, but I need help. Please give me some assurance that she is with you and free from pain now.*

It was a tall order for a prayer, I know, and pretty nebulous too. *Anyhow, with the Lord,* I said to myself, *all things are possible.* For the next two days we traveled through Colorado, Wyoming, and Montana. Finally we reached our destination, a cabin on the edge of a crystal-clear lake, rimmed by soft, purplish mountains.

"Surely this setting will lift your spirits," my husband, Lynn, said hopefully as we sat by the lake shortly after dawn the first morning.

"Surely it should," I agreed, trying to sound more cheerful than I felt.

"Let's hike up to that waterfall," he suggested, pointing to a cascade of water coming off a cliff at the far end of the lake.

I didn't feel like a hike at all.

"Come on, Mom!" the kids urged.

I knew I had no choice, so we started off around the lake and up the mountainside. As we climbed higher, the sound of water crashing over the rocks grew louder. My head was throbbing and my feet were dragging. The others ran on ahead, and I was the last one in line on the trail.

Slowly I rounded the last bend and came in full view of the thundering falls. But it wasn't the sight of the cascading water that took my breath away. Tucked away to one side of the glistening falls, in the mist of the tumbling water, was a field of bright yellow daisies, the first I had ever seen in my whole life. I was overwhelmed, knowing at once that I had been blessed—not with a coincidence—but with a gift from God.

For a long time, I sat on a rock, drinking in the beauty of the bright yellow sea beneath me. And, just as I am sure God intended, the grief began to ebb away.

And to this day, whenever I think of Mother, it is not pain and suffering and sorrow that I remember; it is the happy memories she gave me, like that precious field of yellow daisies.

II.

God Gave Us Children

A New Mother's Reflections on God's Love

Kathryn Slattery

aty lies napping, cradled in my left arm. Sleeping babies look like plump, furled flower buds, I've often thought. But on this July afternoon, with every heat and humidity record being broken, I feel no rosy raptures of motherhood. Hot, tired, crabby, and frustrated are more like it. For the six weeks of Katy's life, my life has been a monotonous round of changing diapers, waking three times a night for feedings, soothing her cries.

Now she has finally drifted off in the crook of my arm after twenty minutes of fussing. I sit at the dining room table, my free right hand busily scribbling the first of scores of long overdue thank-you notes. An unfamiliar noise causes me to look up. *Cruncha-cruncha-cruncha.* Across the room our cat, Indy, is nibbling at the leaves of our one healthy potted plant.

I want to yell a loud, outraged *Shoo!* I ache to jump up and chase that mischief till she scuttles to a hiding place under the bed. But wake Katy? Impulsively my fingers close around the blue-striped pen in my hand and I fling it toward the cat. It hits the wall above the plant and clatters to the floor. Indy regards me coolly and continues to nibble green leaves.

I sit still and squeeze my eyes shut, ashamed. Warm drops run into the corners of my mouth. I take a shaky breath.

I'm sorry, God. Not very grown-up of me, was it? Sometimes being a mother makes me feel so overwhelmed. Helpless.

I lean back in the chair and look down at Katy. This fragile bud of a human being. My daughter. I remember so clearly the feeling that came over me the night Tom and I brought her home from the hospital. We leaned on the rails of her crib, watching her sleep in her new home for the first time. I looked at that sweet face, the perfectly modeled fingers and toes, and felt millions of tiny dancing bubbles well up inside of me: a different kind of love. Not like my love for Tom. Or for my father or mother or sister. This love was newborn, like my baby. It filled me with a fierce tenderness. I would do anything to protect this tiny creature, so dependent on me for her life.

The memory is good. Like a gentle hand taking mine. And as I look down on Katy now, something dawns on me.

Without you, God, I'm as helpless as Katy. You take care of me, giving me strength to take care of Katy.

It's late in the summer now and the heat is disappearing. I'm in the basement doing laundry. Katy is upstairs asleep in her crib. Suddenly I hear her cry. There is an anguished note in it, as if she feels utterly abandoned. Slamming the dryer door shut, I dash up the stairs and into the nursery and take her in my arms.

"There, there," I croon, holding her close to my breast, the soft curve of her head in the hollow under my chin. "Please don't cry. Mommy's always here—always. I'll never leave you, my Katy."

Standing in her sunlit room, kissing away her tears, I hear a vaguely familiar ring in my words of reassurance to Katy. We settle into the rocking chair, and as we relax in its soothing rhythm, back and forth, back and forth, it comes to me—Jesus' promise to his disciples after the Resurrection. "I am with you always" (Matthew 28:20, NRSV).

Dear God, you always hear me when I cry out. You are always there, aren't you?

Almost a year has passed. Katy is beginning to walk. Sitting cross-legged on the lawn, I watch my intrepid explorer start up the steps leading to the wooden deck at the back of the house. At the base of the steps is a slab of poured concrete. Poised on the first step, Katy turns to face me, her eyes shining with pride in her accomplishment. Her legs, unsteady, begin to wobble. . . .

Even before I move to catch her, I know it is too late. Down she goes, face first, whacking her forehead on the concrete.

"Katy!"

Her brow is scraped and bleeding, already purple with an ugly bruise. She is screaming, and as I pick her up, nightmarish fears crowd my mind: *concussion . . . skull fracture . . . brain damage . . .*

Still holding Katy, I race up the steps and into our bedroom, where the well-worn copy of Dr. Spock's *Baby and Child Care* lies waiting in the bookcase. Katy's cries seem to be subsiding as I scan the book's pages about head injuries. According to Dr. Spock, Katy is showing no symptoms of having suffered anything serious. I sponge her forehead with a cool washcloth and hold her on my lap murmuring words of love. Minutes later she is all smiles, playing with Indy as though nothing had happened.

But I am still shaken.

Oh, God, I feel Katy's pain so deeply. Suddenly I grasp something of the magnitude of your love for us. Your children. I cry when I think that you loved us so much that you let your Son live . . . and suffer . . . and die . . . for us.

A crisp fall morning, a morning when little nuisances

have stolen the time. Within the hour Tom will be home from the office, and we are supposed to be off for our long-awaited weekend in the country. But Katy is still in her nightgown. Seated in her highchair, she has more egg in her hair and on her face than in her tummy, and she is blissfully oblivious to our need to hurry.

Across the room the television is on. A big letter "K" dances across the screen and Katy catches sign of it. She throws her hands skyward—launching a full mug of milk across the dining room.

"Katy—"

I am about to scold, but I catch myself. In recent days I've noticed how sensitive Katy seems to my reprimands, especially when my tone is harsh.

Katy regards me warily.

"Katy," I repeat quietly, bending over to pick up the empty mug. "Do you know what you say when you spill your milk?" Smiling, I touch her tousled head. "You say, 'Oops!' "

A big sunny grin lights Katy's face; I wipe up the floor, feeling so thankful for not giving in to irritation.

Father God, your love is never corrupted by moods or time pressure or any of our human foibles. You love me in my worst moments and, in your perfect love, offer me forgiveness.

I look at the little figure in the highchair. Katy has created a new love in me, mother love. She has given me fresh glimpses of our Creator's love for all his children. A love that is protective, ever present, sacrificing, forgiving.

Thank you, Almighty Father.

Mommy Praying

Linda J. Burba

 could tell from the start that this day would be no exception. Three-year-old Matthew climbed into bed with me, lay there quietly for no more than two minutes, with his ice-cold feet robbing warmth from my legs, and then began squirming.

"Let's wake up, Mom. I want breakfast."

I grunted assent, though my eyelids were still heavy with sleep, and my head burrowed into the pillow a bit deeper. When the whining picked up in intensity, I knew Matt would soon have his twin brother, Michael, and baby Mark aroused. I got out of bed.

So the morning started. After breakfast, I gave Mark his bath while Matt and Mike pulled all their toys out on the living-room floor. Then they ransacked three drawers in their bedroom, fought over who got to wear the new yellow socks, and came out crying because, alas, this was a wash-day and favorite clothes were still in the laundry. I pulled out some alternative shirts and pants and tried to convince the twins that these would do.

Soon Mark began rubbing his eyes and fussing a little. It was time for his morning nap. Another diaper change, and he was down in his crib for the time being.

The twins by now were all dressed—underpants on back-wards on Matt, shirt on backwards on Mike, but nevertheless dressed. We sat on the couch and read a children's story, knelt down to pray before the day's play, and they were off.

This would be one of the two quiet times of the day. I had learned early in my Christian life, long before we had children, that my spiritual well-being is dependent on daily communion with God. But finding a time of quiet was another question. With three small boys, there never seemed enough chance to concentrate on "effective, fervent prayer," eyes closed and shutting out the world. After putting a load of wash in the machine, making beds, and straightening the house a little, there was barely time for the reading part of my devotions. *I'll pray during their afternoon naps,* my mind noted.

I sat down with the Bible at the kitchen table where I could see the front yard. I'd been reading through the psalms, noticing what distinct mood changes David went through. I think David must have understood mothers.

Shortly, Matt came running in. "Mom, Laura and Jennifer say I'm *'icky'*," he complained. "They hate boys." I told him to ignore them. He didn't know what "ignore" meant, but it seemed to satisfy him that he had tattled. He ran back out.

I read a few more verses.

Matt sauntered back. "I need a rag."

"What for?"

"To wash the porch!" (Said in an isn't-it-obvious tone.)

Rather than argue, I got him a rag. I vaguely wondered where he would get the water, but decided I would solve that problem if it arose. Right now I was *trying* to have my devotions.

Mike came to the window, walking stiff-legged as if he'd delayed a certain duty too long. That was not the problem. I soon found out. "Mom, Matt wetted me with the hose." I yelled at Matt to turn off that hose, and I got Mike some dry clothes.

I read a few more verses.

The next interruption in my reading was Mike's, too. "Can I go bare feet like Matthew Wing?"

"Of course," I responded without enthusiasm. "Put your shoes in the house so the puppy won't carry them away."

"Can't I just put them on the picnic table?" *Always an alternative plan!*

"Sure." And I got through a few more verses.

Matt came around. "Mom, can I take off my shoes like Mike?"

"Okay. Put your shoes on the picnic table so Clipper won't carry them off."

"I thought we're s'posed to put our shoes in the house."

"*Either* place is all right today." I was trying to read.

Finally, they went off to play at their friend's house. Mark awakened as I finished the psalm I was reading. Its praise section was uplifting, and for a moment I reflected on the sentiments Paul expresses in another part of the Bible: "In whatsoever state I am, therewith to be content" (Phil. 4:11).

I hummed a tune as I resumed my tasks, remembering the day's beginning when I had knelt beside my bed for a few moments of prayer. I'd looked up and seen Matt's pleased smile as he knelt directly across from me, hands folded, listening. He had said, "I prayed to Jesus, too, Mom. And I thanked him for my mommy praying here right now."

My moments with God's word lift me. The prayers encourage me. And little lives are watching, listening, and learning from my daily example. The spiritual responsibility of that fact humbles and challenges me.

When the boys are grown up, they won't remember the interruptions. But I hope they will remember seeing Mom read her Bible and hearing Mom pray.

First Day of
School

Nancy A. Carlson

 ear Lord,

My little girl starts school tomorrow. She is anxious and excited. I doubt that she'll sleep a wink tonight. Help her, please, to quiet down and try to rest.

Lord bless her tomorrow as she puts on her new dress and shoes. We've walked the route to school many times this summer, so I know she knows the way. She's an independent youngster, Lord, but please let her allow me to walk with her just this once.

Be with her, Lord, as she goes inside the school. Let her not be lonely or afraid in this new and challenging world. Be with her teacher; help my little one to be respectful and appreciative. And, oh Lord, be with me, for a whole new aspect of my education is also beginning. Tomorrow I start learning how to let my daughter go. There is no better way than to entrust her into your care.

Well, Lord, it's quiet in her room now. I think she's fallen asleep . . . thank you. Amen.

I Don't Want to Be a Mother Today

Sue Monk Kidd

 tiny wail pierced the silence of the bedroom. I moved mechanically into the worn-out path from my bed to the nursery like a tired old soldier with battle fatigue. The numbers on the clock glowed green, iridescent and grim. It was 4:02 A.M. . . . Mother's Day.

The little cry flung itself furiously into the darkness. It was not her hungry-cry. That one had shattered the night at 2:50. This was the colic-cry . . . the third one tonight. I lifted my three-month-old daughter from her crib and dropped wearily into the rocking chair, my eyelids sinking closed like iron anchors dropped to sea. She screamed into the crook of my elbow. I rocked back and forth, trying to weave time into something bearable. The creak in the chair groaned heavily. *The sound of motherhood,* I thought glumly. My arm began to throb beneath her as sleep crept slowly into her breathing. I dared not move. Just a few more minutes . . .

"MAMA! I'm thirsty," came a loud invisible voice out of the night. I opened my eyes to an abrupt narrow slit. Three-year-old Bob stood in the doorway like a lost shadow. He stepped closer, clutching a stuffed dinosaur.

"Go to bed, and I'll bring some water in a little while." My whisper had the ragged edge of desperation.

"But I want some water now!" he halfway yelled.

The baby jerked and cranked up her cry.

I could almost hear the last gasp down inside my heart. "Now look what you did! You woke the baby. Now go to bed!" I shouted. He didn't. He stood there and added his wail to the baby's. It was too much. My eyes turned away, falling on the green diaper pail. It was full again. I looked from it to the door. At the end of the dark hall, the den was littered with toys, pacifiers, and broken cookies. And beyond that, short and tall baby bottles lined the kitchen counter like a miniature skyline. My small world.

And suddenly in that middle-of-the-night moment, something happened deep inside me. The flame of joy that burns so mysteriously inside each mother's heart simply went out. I sat in the nursery like a snuffed candle and drew the darkness around me. Actually my despondency had been gathering for weeks. It wasn't the kind of thing I liked to admit, but it was true. Something had gradually gone out of my mothering . . . the sparkle, the eagerness, the delight. It had all been swallowed up by an ocean of frustrations and demands. Oh, I loved my children. But, lately, caring for them had become a burden.

The cries raged. "Lord, I know it's Mother's Day," I whispered, near tears myself. "But I don't want to be a mother today. I'm sick of it."

The terrible honesty of my words startled me. How could I say that! How could I feel this way! I wondered if all mothers sometimes despaired of being mothers. Or was it only me?

My husband waded into the shrieking darkness, rubbing his eyes as if he'd wakened into a real live nightmare. "What's going on?" he said.

"I'm thirsty and she don't love me," cried Bob.

The baby squalled, her red face bobbing against my shoulder like a furious woodpecker.

"Here, give the children to me," he said, bravely. "You go to bed."

"They're all yours," I said, thrusting Ann into his arms.

I fell into bed, despising the way I felt. "Oh, Lord, help me," I prayed as I drifted over the edges of sleep. "Help me find some joy again."

I woke to the inevitable wail. My eyes focused on the window where the first sliver of daylight hemmed the curtain with a silver ribbon. The same sense of despondency filled my chest. I rose, dreading the day. I dreaded preparing the children for church . . . the bathing, feeding, dressing, redressing. Every task was like a heavy gray bead on a chain around my neck.

On the drive home from church, Bob's voice floated over the front seat. "We talked about mothers in Sunday school."

"Oh, really," I muttered.

"My teacher said I made you a mother when I was borned."

"It's born. Not borned," I corrected.

"Tell me the story of when I was borned—I mean born."

I glanced around at him, getting a whiff of the carnations pinned at my shoulder. His face was poked out with curiosity. "Not now," I said, looking away.

By mid-afternoon the sky was charcoal gray. A slow drizzle of rain washed the den windows. In a rare moment of quiet, I stood at the solemn panes, my depression deepening.

"Mama, *now* will you tell me the story of when I was born?" Bob stared at me.

I sighed and dropped onto the sofa. He climbed beside me, waiting.

"It was late one night," I began reluctantly. "Daddy and I had waited and waited for you. We thought you never would get here. But finally you decided to come. Daddy drove me to the hospital." I paused, my heart not in the telling.

"Then I was born?" he urged me on.

"Yes. The first time I saw you, you had all your fingers in your mouth making silly noises."

He giggled. "Like this? "He stuck four fingers in his mouth and snorted.

I managed a smile.

"Did you hold me?"

"Yes, we had a long visit that night," I said. "You were wrapped in a blanket, and your hair was combed up into a curl like the top of an ice cream cone."

I could almost see the hair, the small wrinkled face. It seemed like yesterday.

Outside, lightning splintered the grayness, and inside, Bob's eyes were wide and blue. I looked at the shifting streams on the window and wondered why motherhood could not have remained as fresh and golden as those first moments.

The story seemed ended. But suddenly, a small forgotten piece of it came back to me, almost as if someone had shone a light into a dark place in my memory. "I nearly forgot," I said. "There was a card tucked in your blanket that night. A card from the hospital."

"What did it say?" Bob asked, perched high on the sofa cushion. I squinted my eyes, unable to recall exactly. Suddenly I was searching our shelves, digging out his baby book.

Dust sealed the pages with neglect. Bob hung over my shoulder, his eyes sparkling with mystery as I ruffled through the yellowed memories.

I found the card in the back of the book. Across the front, it was personalized with a slightly faded, slightly smudged inkblot of his hand. Five newly born fingers and one incredibly tiny palm. My eyes drifted over the tender little image down to the inscription beneath it . . . a simple greeting card verse:

"Make the most of every day
For time does not stand still.
One day this hand will wave good-bye
While crossing life's brave hill."

The room grew quiet. Rain trickled on the panes. Bob took the card, his fingertips moved in silent wonder along the edge of the handprint. I watched, my throat feeling tight. How big his hands had become. And so quickly. His fingers were long and skinny next to the little image—his palm a baseball glove in comparison. And suddenly, his hands holding the tiny inkblot became a living picture of time moving, of life flowing swiftly and silently through its passages. It was a picture of how precious and fleeting each moment with my children really was.

As Bob clung to the little card, the words it bore touched me as if they had a secret magic all their own. There was a truth in them of immeasurable value, and I could not resist it. *Make the most of every day. Time does not stand still.*

It seemed strange how a few lines from an old verse had returned just when I needed them. Lines that had somehow made everything clear again and put my problems in their place. *Of course motherhood has frustrations and demands,* I thought. *Every worthwhile thing does. Why not accept them instead of dwell on them? The important thing is to delight in my children now . . . now, before these moments too become yellowed memories.*

With a suddenness that startled us both, I drew Bob to me and hugged him tightly, my heart catching as that fragile flame seemed to ignite me again.

"You're going to pop me, Mama," he said, laughing. But I held on. And with his warm little body curved against mine, I looked down at the card, which had tumbled to the floor, and smiled. For I was quite sure this handprint, with its ancient wisdom for mothers printed beneath, was in truth a Mother's Day card . . . one sent specially by God.

A Mother's Prayer

 ive me patience when little hands
Tug at me with ceaseless small
    demands.
Give me gentle words and smiling
    eyes,
And keep my lips from hasty,
    sharp replies.
Let me not in weariness, confusion,
    or noise
Obscure my vision from life's
    fleeting joys
That when in years to come my
    house is still,
Beautiful memories its rooms
    may fill.

Author Unknown

The Fullness of Life

Lynn Colwell

 rolled over in bed and instinctively reached for the small spiral notebook. Every morning for six years, I'd done the same thing—reached for my marching orders, my neatly printed list of things to do that day. Steve always teased me about my prearranged schedule, but if I didn't organize the night before, how else would I get through the logjam of work each day?

This morning the notation CLEAN HALL CLOSET stood like a glowering general at the top of my list. Dispiritedly, I began picking through mismatched shoes, games with missing pieces, and boxes of unmarked photographs. Then I saw the hammock. It lay in a tangled heap. I recalled how we had laughed, Steve and I, when my brother gave it to us. Except for two very spindly trees, our property was barren then. So we had thanked him and swiftly abandoned the useless gift in the back of the closet. But now, glancing out the window, I saw the two sturdy trees that had grown from those reedy transplants. Then I surprised myself by stepping out into the blinding sunlight. I stood on tiptoe and carefully stretched the hammock between the two strong trunks.

At a glance, one could see this was not an ordinary canvas hammock, but an artfully woven cocoon formed from thousands of red and yellow cords. Within its eleven-foot arc, there was room for a couple of adults or several children to nestle, weightless above the grass.

The baby's agitated cry broke my reverie. Corey was hungry. I was quite adept at nursing while holding her in one arm like a football and using my free arm to dust or vacuum. *But just this once,* I thought guiltily, *we'll rest in the hammock.*

I backed into it and brought in my legs so that Corey and I settled like birds in a swinging nest. The swaying soothed us both, and Corey nursed as I sought the clouds through the leafy canopy. The world was empty of human sound, but I heard a woodpecker rat-a-tat-tatting and the wind rustling the leaves. A hummingbird spied a flower and, swooping down, it fed dantily, its wings a blur. I felt completely at peace. But then, the feeling of guilt: God's world would be here tomorrow, but the baby needed clean diapers today!

At three o'clock I heard the slow footsteps of my six-year-old son. I looked up from folding diapers and noticed his forlorn face.

"What's up, Chris?" I asked.

"Oh, nothing," he replied, unwilling to talk.

"Look," I said, pointing through the window, "a surprise for you."

"Wow! That's neat," he exclaimed. "Can we get in it?"

His small face reflected such happiness that I resisted the urge to say "Not right now," and together we walked outside and slipped into the hammock's embrace. I reached over and put an arm around my son. I hadn't held him that close in a long time, and I was surprised he didn't pull away.

"You know what happened in school today?" Chris asked plaintively. "That big kid Robbie Simmons* has been

*name has been changed

74

picking on me, pushing me down, calling me names. Today in front of all the other guys, he pulled, well, he tried to pull my pants down. Then I . . ." Muffled sobs shook the hammock. I was furious at that bully, but strangely I felt happy too. Lying snug in the hammock, Chris had opened his heart to me. That contained little boy, who rarely spoke his feelings, was trusting me with that fragile part of himself.

That evening Steve dragged in from work looking exhausted. After the children were in bed, I gently led him outside to see the hammock. We couldn't help but lie together and watch the moon rise in the black sky. Soon, swaying in the silent night, old dreams awakened. The pressures of every day had kept our dream-talk dormant. Now we talked away the night and felt closer than we had in a long, long time.

The next morning I awoke to the sound of thunder. Lightning flashed angrily, and rain poured out of a cast-iron sky. I glanced at my bedside table and on it was a note in Steve's handwriting: "Please put the hammock on your list for tonight!"

I laughed to myself, but with the next bolt of lightning, I saw a clear vision of myself suspended above the earth with Corey at my breast, and I could hear myself thinking, *God's world will be here tomorrow, but the baby needs clean diapers today!* True, God's world was here today, but it was stormy and bleak, not a good day for lying in a hammock and relishing the smell and touch of one's young. Yesterday was the day to listen to the unburdening of a small heart and to nurture dreams.

I had learned my lesson. For several moments I followed the raindrops on their winding journey down the windowpane and said a quiet *Thank you* to God for the fullness of life that he offers us—if we are ready to accept it. Then I tore up my list of jobs for the day and called to the children, "Let's run out and taste the rain!"

When the Sunbeams Danced

Frances Adams Schultz

est is essential if you want to recover from tuberculosis," the doctor had emphatically told me, when prescribing a daily two-hour nap.

But rest came uneasily to my unhappy spirit. I was a young mother, my four-month-old son Jack being cared for by a housekeeper, my new home being cleaned each week in a haphazard fashion by a cleaning woman. Only my husband's cheerful acceptance of what was, to me, a dreadful diagnosis, kept me from becoming despondent.

My lovely bedroom was conducive to good health. Windows on the south and west walls made it a sunny place, and in the large square hallway just outside the bedroom door, Jack could play quietly in his waking hours, peeking through the bars of his playpen as he cooed happily.

The sun was shining brightly that afternoon when I awoke from my enforced nap as the draperies were drawn to admit the autumn light. Jack was fed and diapered, and I looked forward to talking to him across the yawning distance that separated us. My arms ached to hold him. My heart yearned to cuddle him, but that had been forbidden. Recuperation at home was granted me only on the condition that the utmost precautions be taken to guard the baby from any possibility of exposure to the disease.

Inside, my heart was crying as I picked up the hand mirror from my bedside table. The sun was reflected in the mirror, and I played with it a moment as the sunbeam danced on the ceiling. Playfully I flashed the reflected sunbeam into my small son's playpen. When he reached out to touch it, I gently moved the mirror and the sunbeam danced out of his hand and onto a small toy that lay just beyond his reach. He chuckled with glee as we played away the afternoon, using a sunbeam as our toy.

From that afternoon until the time I once again was able to hold my son in my arms, we played with God's gift to us—the sunbeams. There were still times when I felt my heart would break with the pain of seeing him grow from a small baby to a toddler, when I could not touch him. But our sunbeam game gave us a golden chain that linked mother and son together.

Bubbles and Rose Petals and the Smoothness of Satin

Nancy L. Riley

can't do it," I said softly, then a little louder, "I just can't do it!"

I slumped against the wall of my bedroom and slid down to the floor. Head in hands, I started to cry and mutter. After a few minutes of self-pity, I looked over at my tiny three-month-old son, lying on the floor on a baby blanket.

Already Seth had endured surgery twice—with another operation scheduled before his first birthday. Added to his struggle to survive was this sad diagnosis—Down syndrome.

Three weeks after his birth, my husband and I had taken him to a rehabilitation center in Fort Collins for an "evaluation." We were told that we were fortunate to be so young and full of energy (we are both in our twenties), and we could be thankful that we had only one child so far. Raising him would be a lot of hard work, the evaluating therapy team warned us.

"'Normal' babies seek out their own stimulation from the environment," the therapist told us. Our baby would be passive and content to lie still in his crib. If we wanted to enhance his development beyond helplessness, we would have to "stimulate" him.

Somehow, I didn't understand the idea of "stimulation." I wanted to protect Seth from life's difficulties. Instead, three times a week, we visited therapists, who manipulated his slender limbs and coaxed his toneless muscles to work. Timidly at first, I attempted to imitate them at home. Gradually it became easier to exercise his legs and play with his soft hands. But something was missing. I didn't seem to be getting anywhere with this conception of "infant stimulation."

Now Seth was watching me watch him as I leaned my head against the wall and asked, "Why should I prod and push you until you cry? Why can't I just sit in a cozy rocking chair and hold you tight?"

He just stared back at me curiously, his arms limp at his sides and his legs sprawled uselessly on the blanket. *What is going on in his mind as he stares at me?* I wondered. And suddenly the thought came that Seth must find me a very depressing mother. All I seemed to do was stare at him and wonder what to do with him next. *Is that all he will remember of his childhood?* I wondered. *Heaven forbid!* I squeezed my eyes shut tight and prayed to God that I'd find a way to help my baby.

Well, what about my own childhood? Maybe that would help. What good things could I remember? Treating myself to some reminiscent daydreaming, I started with the "Princess Purple Comforter" dream.

When I was eight, we moved from a small town in Nebraska to a bustling college town in Colorado. My parents divorced shortly after the move. My sister and I lived with our mother in an apartment building that had a storage attic full of padlocked "cribs" for extra belongings, one for each apartment. One afternoon while my mother was at work, I felt particularly lost and sad, so I took the padlock key off its nail and stole away up three flights of stairs to the attic.

It was quiet and tranquil up there; I still remember the musty smell. By the time I had opened the padlock to our crib, I was sweating from nervousness and the stuffy atmosphere. Would I be discovered as I explored this forgotten treasure chest? There wasn't much treasure to look at, mostly just Christmas decorations in boxes. But then I saw it—a dark purple comforter inviting me to slip my hands between its cool, satin folds.

Before long, I was parading between the cribs with the comforter wrapped around my shoulders, trailing behind on the dusty wooden floor. Such a rich, deep purple! Such smooth fabric! For a few minutes, I was a beautiful princess, advancing stately through statue-filled palace gardens, nodding and smiling serenely at my retainers. . . .

After trying to fold the comforter the way I had found it (it kept sliding off the boxes), I padlocked the crib and scurried down the steps before Mom arrived home. But that was just my first visit. I made many more trips up those steps to luxuriate in the comforter's satiny softness.

Now, as I sat with my infant son looking up at me, I smiled at him, remembering the smooth satin comforter and the luxurious feeling it gave me whenever I wrapped myself in it.

"Your skin is that soft, too, Seth," I told him. *Isn't it funny,* I thought, *how a special memory can make a person feel so much better—just the way recalling a certain Bible verse can bring comfort at difficult times.*

One of the worst times in my life had been when my father died a year before Seth was born. I recalled standing in the cemetery on a cold January afternoon. While the wind whipped my skirt around and turned up my collar, I read the message on a grave marker; "I will not leave you comfortless; I will come to you" (John 14:18). And at that moment the pleasant memories of my father came rushing back and made me feel so good that I found myself smiling.

That did it for me in my dilemma with Seth. I decided to make certain that our son would have plenty of memories of God's Word, and plenty of memories of good things in life to see him through the rough days ahead.

"Let's see now . . . what will your memories be?" I asked him. He only blinked his eyes. I smiled and glanced at a shiny blue bed cover on the floor of my closet. It was a satin comforter. I had forgotten we had one. Without hesitation, I slipped it out and pulled it over to where Seth was lying. Tenderly, I placed him in the center of the folded comforter. His eyes grew very large and he stiffened for a moment. Then he slowly turned his head to the side and moved his arm up and down, sliding it gently against the satin.

"That feels nice, doesn't it?" I said happily, and something came to me: stimulation . . . invigoration . . . awakening of the senses—pleasant sensations! Why, this is easy! Ideas began to surface quickly. I grabbed a pencil to write them down:

- A warm, tranquil bubble bath for Seth—by candlelight— with iridescent bubbles rising to the ceiling.
- Rubbing a frozen block of sweet, tart orange juice against his lips and gums on a summer day.
- Giving him a handful of fresh, smooth rose petals to play with till they become wilted and damp.
- Dangling his little feet in a big bowl of dry kidney beans.

That list has continued to grow, while our son has grown into a happy, sparkling-eyed two-and-a-half-year-old with mischief on his mind. And his mommy—that's me—has learned that when God arrives with the comfort he promises, it may be something as simple as pleasant memories. With his help, we're working to make more of them every day.

Motorized Mother

Patricia Lorenz

'm tired of spending my whole life in that car," I grumbled, scowling as I grabbed the car keys off the kitchen counter. My son Michael had just reminded me that we had to go out to buy his basketball shoes that evening.

"I'm averaging two hundred miles a week just driving you kids to games, lessons, rehearsals, shopping, cheerleading practice, and taking you to friends' houses! Two hundred miles a week and nobody cares!" My voice faded when I realized nobody was listening.

As a single parent, I was the one to do the driving whenever the four kids needed to be driven somewhere around Oak Creek's sprawling twenty-eight square miles.

"Mom, don't forget there's the dance at school tonight," Julie reminded.

Back home from *that* jaunt, I collapsed in front of the TV to read the newspaper, when suddenly six-year-old Andrew was at my side. "Mommy, can we go to the store now?"

"No, dear, not now," I said wearily.

"But your birthday's tomorrow," Andrew whimpered.

Ah, yes, my birthday. I'd forgotten. I'd promised to take him shopping. He'd been saving his nickels and dimes to buy me a present. He'd decided upon earrings and expected me to help pick them out.

"All right, Andrew," I said. "Let me put my shoes back on and get ready. We'll go now." How do you say no to such a big heart implanted in such a little body?

At the store we browsed among the carousels of earrings, giggling at the strange ones, oohing and aahing at the beautiful ones. Andrew pointed to a pair he liked. I told him they were beautiful. (They were also on sale for three dollars, a dollar less than what he had clutched in his cowboy coin purse.)

Knowing he'd made up his mind, I said, "Andrew, decide what you want to do while I go over here and buy socks for Michael." I knew he needed to be alone.

From the next aisle I could hear his pride-filled voice saying, "Yes, please," when the lady asked him if he needed a box for the earrings. "It's my mom's birthday and I'm going to wrap them in red paper with white hearts."

After a stop for an ice-cream cone, we headed home, and Andrew disappeared into his room with the red paper and a roll of tape.

"Get your pajamas on, honey; then come to my room and we'll read your bedtime story in my bed."

When he jumped in the bed, Andrew snuggled close to me.

"Mommy, this is the happiest day of my life!"

"Why is that, honey?"

"It's the first time I've ever been able to do anything for *you!*" Then his arms surrounded me in a spontaneous bear hug.

While Andrew plodded out loud through one of his first-grade readers, I thought about my own acts of giving. I was always *giving* to my four children—especially behind the wheel of that car. Yet somehow I was never really happy about it.

Later I tucked this little boy with the big heart into his bed. "What about prayers, Mom?"

I'd forgotten. "Oh, of course, honey."

I held Andrew's small hands in mine and thanked God for my small son—and for all my children. I asked God to help me be a happier, more cheerful mother.

Later I looked up the verse that had been running through my head, the one about God loving a cheerful giver (II Corinthians 9:7).

Then and there I decided to stop being such a grouch about all the driving. And as I became something I thought I'd never be, a cheerful chauffeur, I found that I was listening to things I'd never quite heard before. On the way to band practice or drum lessons, Michael, age fourteen, thought out loud about whether he should go out for football. He also told me about the girl in his class who had called him the night before, discussed whether he should get a job after school, and talked about what he wanted to do with his life.

When Julie, age fifteen, was in the car with me, she bubbled on and on about the latest antics in her cheerleading squad, about the boy who'd asked her to homecoming, about the student council fund-raiser, and about getting extra help in geometry.

On the way to Jeanne's piano lessons, confirmation classes, and a special event downtown at the Milwaukee High School of the Arts, where she was a senior, we talked about where she wanted to go to college, what was happening in her art classes, and why she felt her social life was at a standstill.

Amazed by what I'd missed as a cranky mom honking and griping her way around Oak Creek, I began looking forward to wheeling around town with my four kids in tow. Given a chance, the kids opened up. We laughed together, debated, questioned, shared our feelings, and grew much closer. I still drive two hundred miles a week, but I look forward to every mile, because driving time has become family time in our car. Prime time. Time for giving, cheerfully.

The Child I Couldn't Have

Rose Sinclair*

hank you for letting me know," I told the nurse on the phone. Then I hung up, fighting back tears.

The tests had just come back from the lab. They confirmed what I had feared all along—that my husband, Jay, and I would never be able to have children. Now, as I walked through our big house, its halls echoing with emptiness, I longed to fill them with the sounds of a child.

And now, too, the guilt that I thought I was rid of came surging back. It stemmed from the fact that when I was nineteen, before I met and married Jay, I became pregnant. I gave the baby up for adoption, for even though giving him up was like giving up a part of myself, I knew I had no way to take care of him all by myself.

For months afterward, I had terrible nightmares. I awoke at night sweating profusely, remembering the squalling of that tiny, wrinkled, red infant just after birth. I heaped the guilt upon myself, not realizing that if I just asked for it, God's love could enfold me.

That evening I gave Jay the sad news when he got home. I told him I was sure that God was punishing me for the mistake I had made as a teenager.

"Don't feel that way, Rose," Jay said, trying to comfort me. "I'm sure he knows what he's doing."

*names have been changed

I buried my face in the warm hollow of Jay's shoulder.

We began to consider adoption, but I viewed it as a very distant hope. I really wasn't seeing God as a working force in my life, despite my professed belief. The truth was, I wouldn't let God be.

"There aren't many infants available," the doctor told us. "Would you consider adopting an older child?"

"I want an infant so badly!" I felt my feverish longing nearly burst through to the surface. *To replace my own little boy,* I thought to myself.

"I know. I understand," the doctor said. "It may take awhile, but we can try to find a baby for you," he assured us, recommending that we contact an adoption agency to begin the process of interviews and forms and home visits as soon as possible—which we did.

Months went by without hearing anything further from the adoption agency after the initial application process and home study. In the meantime I immersed myself in gardening. I spent the warmer spring days preparing the ground for seed and planting. In six weeks' time I was rewarded by a rosy rim of radishes pushing through the dark soil and the tender arched heads of little beanstalks proudly growing in line.

I watched them grow into tall, healthy plants, and I found I had a kind of maternal feeling toward them.

Finally the adoption agency called. "We have a five-year-old boy who is available for adoption."

I was filled with bitterness. "I told you I wanted a baby, not a full-grown child," I said, trying to keep my voice even.

"Yes, I know. But we try to give you the opportunity to consider older children when they become available."

"Thank you." I slammed down the phone and, tears streaming down my cheeks, ran outside.

Stumbling, I ran between the rows of beans and corn in

my garden and finally slumped down in the trench that I had dug for the water to drain from. When my self-pitying tears finally abated, I looked around me at the garden I had "mothered" all spring. There next to me was the first fruit of my labor, a small cluster of green beans hidden in the intertwining leaves of the beanstalk. I longed to be able to nurture a small human being the way I had those beans.

And suddenly, as I sat there, the only answer became as clear as if God were speaking to me. Had I ever asked God to forgive me for what I had done so many years before? Or had I assumed that my sin was too great for him to forgive?

"Oh, God, forgive me," I croaked.

My thoughts tumbled and rolled. A part of me seemed to be lifted out, as if it were a burden I never really knew I was carrying. I felt God's presence caress me as I sat there among the leaves of the beanstalks, in the golden gleam of the corn silks, with the sweet, strong smell of the earth all around me. My son would be five now, I suddenly realized—the same age as the boy whom the agency had called me about. Why hadn't that occurred to me before? Momentarily I shoved the thought aside. *Someone will want him,* I thought, as I headed toward the house. But inside I knew that children over three were often extremely hard to place, and that that little boy needed a home, needed us, *now.*

Moments later, as if in a dream, I found myself dialing Jay's office number.

"Jay? Listen, the people from the adoption agency called today . . ." As I had known, it didn't matter to Jay how old the child was.

As I dialed the agency's number, I could feel more warm tears coursing down my cheeks. "Could you tell me if you've placed that little five-year-old boy yet?" I asked the social worker. "I think we'd like to meet him."

When Jay and I arrived at the adoption agency, I saw the inscription over the doorway once again, and this time I understood its real meaning for me. "Your children are not your own, but they belong to your Father who is in Heaven."

While we waited to meet our future son, those words made me realize that it didn't really matter who was the parent and who was the child, for we are all God's children. I understood it so clearly when we met Brian—a slender, blond little guy with a wide grin that revealed a missing front tooth, a child anxious for love and affection and the security we could give him.

Of course, from that day on, it was not all easy. There were barriers we had to break down in order to get to know one another, to fit into each other's patterns.

But the greatest reward has been that since then, I have felt the comforting presence of God so many times, often in the simple laughter that fills our house now, but mostly in the precious gift of love that Brian has given to us.

My life would surely be different if I hadn't uttered those four simple words, asking for God's forgiveness that day in my vegetable garden. I am so thankful that God filled me with his Spirit—changing me and making me able to be open and loving to the child he had waiting for us.

Who's My Real Mother?

Grace Thompson

he soft yellow of the summer morning sun was slanting through the windows as I straightened the bedroom. It's a task I enjoy, and I was humming softly when I sensed a presence behind me.

It was Lisa, our fifteen-year-old. She had a strange expression on her face.

"Why, Lisa," I said, "you startled me. Is something the matter?"

"Who am I?" she asked.

A cold little shiver went down my spine. "Why, you're Lisa Thompson," I said, making myself smile.

"NO! I mean, who am I, really?" Her face was twisted with a desperation I'd never before seen there.

My husband, Ray, and I had adopted Lisa. When she was four, we had explained her adoption to her. Ever since, she had behaved as if she understood that we loved her deeply and completely. Sometimes I had wished she would be more demonstrative in her love for us, but she had always been a wonderful child, and our little family of three had been my constant joy.

"Who are my parents?" Lisa cried.

"Oh, Lisa, you know you're adopted, but Daddy and I are your . . ."

"You're not my *real* parents, and you aren't my *real*

mother! I want to know who she is!" I squeezed my hands behind my back.

"I don't know, Lisa."

"You do!" she said, her teeth clenched to hold back her tears. "You're keeping me from her!" She stormed from the room as I sank back on the bed, stunned.

A scene of fifteen years before played itself back to me. I was in a doctor's office, and he was counseling me on adopted children. "Some never give their natural parents a second thought," he said. "Some become obsessed by them. It's like appendicitis. Sometimes it's never a factor, but if it is, it's a very big factor, indeed."

Would Lisa become obsessed? I wondered. *Is she already?*

I really didn't know who Lisa's natural mother was. One August night after Ray and I had given up on ever qualifying for an adoption, I had received a call from an obstetrician I knew. He could have a baby for us in three weeks, he said.

Then, on a golden Saturday morning in September, our attorney drove into our yard with a five-pound baby girl, three days old. I slipped my arms around her. It was like embracing God's tenderest little miracle. Surely, I thought, she had come to us through God's providence. I was thirty-six years old, and I had been praying for a "Lisa" since my marriage seventeen years before.

The adoption papers were locked in the safe at Ray's office, but even they were a slender thread, for they bore only the name of Lisa's natural father and a fictitious one for her mother. I had thought that's the way they would always remain—two anonymous names tucked away in a dark corner of a solid safe.

But after our confrontation in the bedroom, I began to live with a gnawing fear that I could lose my precious child.

We never knew what triggered Lisa's sudden obsession with finding her natural mother. All we knew was that she rummaged for her birth certificate and found it in our old mantle clock, then she called the doctor who delivered her. She called the lawyer. She called family friends. Even when she discovered her birth records at the courthouse sealed, she didn't give up.

As time went on, Lisa became more anxious and insecure. Her school work suffered. Her attitude toward Ray and me, but especially me, was guarded, aloof. We arranged regular sessions with a psychiatrist for her, but they didn't seem to help. Then, the summer before her eighteenth birthday, Lisa sank into a frightening depression. "I'm just nobody," she would say. "I'll never be happy till I find out who I am . . . who I really belong to."

Whenever she spoke like this, my heart twisted. *Had I been that bad a mother? If Lisa found her "real" mother, would she try to walk out of our lives forever?* "Some kids become obsessed . . ." the doctor had said.

"Oh, Ray," I would tell my husband in our moments alone. "I don't want to lose her. We've tried so hard to be good to her . . ."

One blistering hot Sunday afternoon I climbed our stairs tiredly and started past Lisa's room. Her door was closed, a sight I'd grown used to. It seemed impregnable . . . to time, to psychiatrists, even to my love. I reached out and touched the door. That locked door was holding us both prisoners—Lisa inside, me outside. "Oh, Lisa," I said under my breath, "Why do you shut yourself off so? You know we love you, want only the best for you . . ."

I backed away from the door and gripped the stair rail behind me. *Love you . . . want only the best for you.* I had just said. *Want only the best . . .* it repeated back to me. Lisa wanted to know her natural parents. That was "best" to her. Could it be that I was causing the prison of the locked door in front of me by refusing to let go, by circling Lisa in self-ish love—a love terrified of losing?

Lisa's problem, then, was as much mine as it was hers. If I really had enough faith—in Lisa, in myself, in God—shouldn't I break open the circle of selfish love that I was trying to surround Lisa with? There in the stillness at the top of the stairs a thought came into my mind. . . . *Do you love Lisa enough to find her natural parents for her?*

I shuddered. If I succeeded, I could lose her. But it was clear to me now. What was best for Lisa lay beyond that closed door. And it was I who held the key. "God, help me." I breathed.

He did. He filled me with resolve. I talked it over with Ray, and we both agreed that Lisa's longing went beyond the advice of a lawyer or a psychiatrist, even a doctor. It was a matter of loving enough to let go.

A few weeks later, eighteen Septembers after that first golden one, Ray and I walked into the office of a private detective. "We'd like you to find our daughter's natural parents," Ray said. We gave him the details.

"I'll start an investigation," the young detective said. "When I find something, I'll give you a call."

As we drove home, a sense of loss was already gnawing inside me.

The call came the week before Thanksgiving.

"I've found them," the detective said. "Can you come to my office?"

Ray and I left immediately. Seated once again by the detective's desk, I braced myself for the news.

"Your daughter's natural parents married ten days after they gave her up for adoption," he said. "But they were divorced a few months ago. You'll find her mother's name, address, and phone number listed here."

I stared at the name, stunned, suddenly wondering if I could go through with this.

Three days later Lisa was waiting ecstatically for a telephone call from her natural mother. I fidgeted in the den, watching the old mantle clock that still held Lisa's birth certificate. Lisa talked for over half an hour, then burst downstairs.

"She's coming," she cried. "She's coming to see me tomorrow!"

I froze. It was happening so fast. "Oh, Lord," I whispered, "don't let me lose her."

I listened numbly to her exuberant plans to meet her mother in front of an ice-cream parlor on our town's mall in less than twenty-four hours. "Afterward, I want to bring her here," said Lisa.

I nodded.

The next morning Lisa rushed off to the mall early, while I sat at our kitchen table in a warm semicircle of bay windows. Lisa's chestnut-colored horse trotted across a field behind our house. I remembered the little girl who had ridden him so skillfully, waving to me at the fence. Now she sat on a bench outside an ice-cream parlor, searching every face for a mother she'd never seen. It seemed incredible that I would soon meet her, too. "Please, Lord, help me," I prayed. "Help me to accept Lisa's natural mother and to understand Lisa's feelings for her."

Suddenly they stood framed together in the doorway— Lisa and her natural mother . . . the same height, the same eyes, the same auburn hair. Their likeness took my breath.

"Hello," I said, walking toward them. As I looked at the young woman's beautiful face, I saw Lisa's own image. And, strangely, I felt my heart go out to her.

The week after Thanksgiving, Lisa met her father and two brothers. Her world grew more complete. Her depression and her haunting search for an identity were over. Lisa was secure. But an aching fear filled the back of my mind: *Now what?*

On December 2, Lisa drove off to spend the day with her natural mother. She had talked of nothing but this second visit for days. As I watched her go, I had an urge to hug her good-bye, but Lisa gave me a breezy wave instead. *When she returned,* I agonized, *would it be to pick up her belongings?* Legally, she was ours, but what good are legalities if the heart yearns for freedom?

The hours of the day stretched interminably. As the afternoon blended into dusk, I found myself slipping to the bay windows in the kitchen, watching for Lisa in our car. I bit my lip. "Oh, Lisa," I asked the darkness, "aren't you coming back?"

Suddenly I heard a car motor. Then footsteps at the door. I tried not to show my relief as Lisa strode into the kitchen. "I'm glad you're home," I said.

Then, a tiny miracle. Lisa came and folded her arms around me. "I'm glad I found my natural parents," she said. "I hope I can always be friends with them. But this is where I belong."

Her embrace lightened and she whispered something I'd scarcely ever heard her say before. "I love you, Mother," she said. "More than ever."

As we clung together, the wonder of that moment came home to me, just as Lisa had. And I recognized it as a truth that God himself had experienced with his only Son: Love that is willing to give up what is precious for the sake of another never really loses. It only opens a window for love to come back . . . more love than ever.

Ange's Boy

Marilyn Helleberg

f Tom had been a few years younger the night he came to us, shivering from the January cold and clinging to his black dog, I could have put my arms around him and said, "Go ahead and cry, honey. Let it all out." It would have been easier that way. But instead, he was fourteen and dry-eyed, and his grief was tightly locked up somewhere inside him; so I petted the dog he held so close and led them both into the warm kitchen.

The mother in me grieved for the part of him that was still a child as I watched my husband, Rex, carry in the few belongings that were all Tom had left of his mother and father. The Christmas-night car accident that had taken the lives of Tom's parents had also left a big hole in my husband's life. Tom's mother was Rex's oldest sister—the one who had taken over the family when their own mother had died. Now it was our turn to take care of Ange's boy.

I had been so sure that this was the right decision, but as I showed Tom the curtained-off room I had fixed for him and went back into the kitchen to make popcorn for the family, the awesome responsibility I had assumed suddenly began to close in on me. I opened the kitchen window a little, even though it was snowing outside. Our small house was already crowded with our own family of five, plus two dogs, and our eight-month-old baby demanded so much of my time. How would I ever work one more person into my crowded household and busy schedule? More important still, how could I ever reach the brutally wounded spirit of this quiet, shy teenager who would be embarrassed by any physical expression of our love?

The children were all clamoring for Tom's attention now, as we sat at the kitchen table eating our popcorn. I think he was glad when I said it was time for all to get to bed. I hoped that Tom wouldn't notice the tension in my voice as I said good night to him.

I noticed first that there was more washing, more ironing, more mess because we were so crowded. And I was spending more time doing the never finished things—grocery shopping, cooking, dishes, chauffeuring.

Tom, meanwhile, was facing his devastating loss with courage. Though he was a guest for the first two weeks, in an atmosphere of strained politeness and overconcern, it wasn't long before he was "flying" the baby around the house and laughing and joking and, yes, fighting with the older children. He seemed to adjust quickly to the new school.

But I knew that there were times when the sealed wound ached within him. When we made a trip to Lincoln and stopped to check the empty house, when one of our children brought out an old family picture in which Ange was holding Tom on her lap, when he was elected to the student council at school and someone said, "Your mother would have been so proud of you." At these times especially, I wanted so desperately to put my arms around Ange's boy and say, "I *understand* how you feel."

But somehow I just couldn't. There seemed to be an impenetrable wall surrounding his hurt; and though I sensed that the boy on the other side of the wall was trying to get through it, too, we simply could not reach each other.

In spite of worries and added work, we managed to get through the winter; and almost before I realized it, spring was here. I was not surprised that Tom seemed depressed and edgy after the trip to visit his parents' graves on Memorial Day. The next day was gray and gloomy, and the children had been bickering all day. So I didn't think much about it when Tom stomped out the door with his dog on a leash, after a fight with our ten-year-old over nothing at all. But our daughter followed him, and in twenty minutes she was back, breathless and on the verge of tears. "Mom! Tom's running away. He's on the fairgrounds road."

I put down the potato I was peeling, phoned Rex, and left the older children to watch the baby. I drove to and through the fairgrounds, then circled block after block, but Tom had disappeared. Tears started burning my eyes. "Oh God, *please* bring him home."

By this time, Rex was also searching in his car, so I started home to check on the children. Tears were stinging my cheeks now as I realized how much I loved this tall, quiet boy. Not because I felt sorry for him. Not because I was *expected* to love him. Not even because he was Ange's boy. I loved him because he was Tom, and because some-where deep inside me, there was a place especially for him—a place no one else could ever fill if I lost him now.

Then all at once I was aware of something strong and solid and organ-toned that had been running all the way through the kinks and tangles of adjustment—something that had helped me cope with the added responsibility—that had made the locked doors a challenge instead of a defeat—that was making our busy lives rich and full instead of merely crowded. It was a *feeling*—warm and buoyant—like the feeling you have when your child tracks mud across your newly scrubbed floor to give you a big hug and kiss, and incongruously, you feel suddenly happy, realizing how lucky you are to have people needing your love. The extra work and responsibility then become a blessing—because there is love.

As I pulled into the driveway, the children came running out to meet me. Tom had come back while we were out searching.

I found him lying on his bed, scratching his dog's ears. As I sat on the edge of the bed with one hand on his shoulder and the other petting his dog, I heard myself say, "I *understand* how you feel, Tom."

The wall had crumbled, and I had at last entered the place where his grief was. Then Ange's boy said, "I'm glad to be home." And I realized, with a sudden stab of joy, that he meant right here, in our house.

A Foster Mom

Karen J. Kanatzar

ne day the phone rings. A newborn boy, victimized by drug abuse, is in need of a home. You pray for wisdom.

You meet the social worker at the hospital to gather up the little bundle, this new member of your family. You give thanks for this opportunity of service.

You carry him out in a small wicker basket, similar to the one that saved Moses' life. You pray for strength to meet the task ahead.

You settle into the old rocker, filled with awe at this tiny, perfectly formed little person. You praise God for his wonderful creation.

You realize your life will never be the same. You've made a commitment to a totally helpless creature. Even though you're old enough to be a grandmother, you're starting over as a mom. You pray for the vigor of youth and the wisdom of experience.

You're up every three hours, around the clock. It isn't easy, but it's so much harder for the little one as he struggles to free his system of drug dependency. You pray for stamina for both of you.

You present the baby before the church family to dedicate him to God's kingdom and pray for healing of all the hurts he has suffered in the womb. You trust God's faithfulness.

You eat cold meals or eat with one hand now because a little person needs to be held. You pray for a svelte figure as a reward. Fortunately, God has a sense of humor.

You allow an additional hour for collecting baby paraphernalia every time you leave the house. You pray for patience.

Household chores go on hold until that blessed nap time. Then you opt for a nap too, instead of cleaning, cooking, and so forth. You pray for grace to endure dust bunnies.

He sleeps four hours at a time, then five. Finally he sleeps through the night; it is a victory for you both. You've become a team. You thank God for his healing touch.

Every place you go—upstairs, downstairs, inside, outside—you have this short hitchhiker hooked to your hip. You pray for muscle tone.

You see his first smile, his first tooth, his first pat-a-cake. You see him develop from a little taker into a giver. You see him becoming independent as he explores his new world via the tummy crawl. You laugh, you cry, you rejoice, and you fall more and more in love each passing day. You give all the love you have. You see him learn to bond, to trust, to love. You see him become a healthy boy—physically, spiritually, emotionally. You praise God for answered prayer!

Then one day, seven months after his arrival, the phone rings. The social worker says the judge has ordered the baby returned to his mom. She's been drug-free for two months. You cry. You remember the promise: "Come to me, all who labor and are heavy laden, and I will give you rest." You go to Christ for comfort.

On his last night at your home you tuck him in his crib, kiss him on the top of his head, and rub his back until he falls asleep. With moist cheeks, you begin collecting all his clothes, toys, and medical papers. You sit down and write his mom a letter, finish his first-year calendar, and then write him a letter, which you can only hope he will find someday when he's old enough to read. You weep, unashamed. You pray for him—oh, how you pray!

On reunification morning you give him his cereal and bottle. You hold him snugly and cry. He lies very still, knowing something is different. You give him his bath and put on a special little outfit. Finally the social worker rings the doorbell. You tuck him into his yellow snowsuit and zip up the zipper. You give him a kiss on his button nose. The social worker slips out the door with your son in her arms. You cry to God in anguish.

The tires of the car crunch the gravel as the social worker drives away. Even though you're experiencing the death of a precious relationship, there is no funeral, no memorial service, no family or friends gathered to comfort. After all, you're only the foster mom.

You take down the baby swing and walker. You wash and put away the last load of baby clothes. You clean up the changing table and close the door to the nursery, because it's too painful to see the empty crib. At last . . . you get angry and cry out to God, "It isn't fair!" You know he understands. After all, the cross wasn't fair. He says, "Be still, and know that I am God."

Finally you acknowledge, once again, that this precious child was only a temporary gift—as are your biological children. God created them. He is their Father, and he loves them more than you will ever be able to. You once again place your life and your little son's life into his care. You silently hear the words, "Well done, good and faithful servant."

You accept grief now as a friendly companion, and you go ahead with your life.

Then one day, the phone rings.

I'll Drive, Mom!

Carol Kuykendall

 i, Mom—I'll drive!" Lindsay greeted me cheerfully that bright spring afternoon as she opened the car door and tossed her school-books on the backseat.

"Hmmm?" I answered, playing dumb and gazing at my almost-sixteen-year-old daughter. She had just received her learner's permit, a piece of paper that gave her permission to change places with me in the car so I could teach her how to drive—on *real* streets, in *real* traffic. Exciting for Lindsay. Heart-stopping for me.

"You sure you want to?" I asked doubtfully, looking around the high school parking lot, which had suddenly come alive with the sounds of exuberant teenagers and screeching tires. I might as well have asked if she was sure she wanted to grow up, or go to the senior prom.

"Oh, Moth-*er*!" she replied in the exasperated voice she used when I asked the absurdly obvious.

I shrugged hesitantly and slid all the way over to the passenger seat. *Why does that seem like such a long slide?* I asked myself as I watched my girl-child climb in and scoot the seat forward until the steering wheel nearly touched her shoulders. She honked the horn and waved to a friend, turned the key in the ignition, and pulled the shift lever into reverse. Suddenly we shot backward and jolted to a stop.

That's when I knew why it was a long slide. I was afraid. Afraid of how car keys suddenly change a child into an adult. Afraid of the responsibility of trying to teach her all she needed to know. And afraid that when it was time for her to drive off by herself, she wouldn't be ready.

"Whoa, sorry about the whiplash there," Lindsay said with a grin.

"Just be careful—and don't forget your seat belt," I said, clicking my own into place. I felt like a test pilot gearing up for a trial run with a rookie. I concentrated on my deep breathing, the kind I practiced for relaxation during labor pains before Lindsay was born.

"Mom, you worry too much," Lindsay told me as she shifted into drive.

She was right, of course. Worrying had always been an important part of my job description as a parent. If she said "headache," I thought CAT scan. If she said "stomach-ache," I feared appendectomy. If I heard a siren and she wasn't home, I wondered if I could get to the emergency room before she did. I prayed and told God I was giving him my fears, but I didn't.

Lindsay eased out of the parking lot and onto the high-way, gathering speed as we went down a small hill.

"Slow down!" I cautioned, sneaking a look at the speedometer.

"Mom, I'm going the speed limit," Lindsay informed me with exaggerated patience.

In the distance I could see a four-way stop. "Be careful!" I warned again, putting my hands on the dashboard to brace for the sudden stop. Instead, we slowed down gently. "The car on your right has the right-of-way," I instructed, "but defensive driving means expecting the unexpected. Always look both ways!"

Lindsay nodded and moved forward smoothly. "See, Mom, I can do it!" she said with a confident smile.

When we finally pulled into our driveway, I felt like the mother in the cartoon taped to our refrigerator door. The smiling teenager is climbing out from behind the wheel of the car. "Thanks for the lesson, Mom!" the caption reads. Meanwhile, the mother is seated on the passenger side with a look of terror frozen on her face and her feet thrust right through the floorboards. I laughed when I cut it out. That was before Lindsay got her permit.

The next few outings, I didn't feel much better. In merging traffic I closed my eyes and prayed. On narrow country roads, I was sure Lindsay was about to sheer off the mailboxes on my side of the road. In free-for-all shopping-center parking lots I reminded her to look both ways.

As Lindsay's birthday approached, I tried to think of an appropriate gift to mark this milestone celebration and decided upon a key chain with her own set of keys to our car. I searched the stores, but all I could find were ones that said, "Let's party!" or "I love weekends."

"We could engrave your own message on one of these," a salesman suggested, showing me several plain ones.

"Perfect!" I decided, choosing a gold heart.

"What do you want to say on it?" he asked.

I paused, thinking of Lindsay alone in the car without my advice.

"Look both ways," I told him.

The morning of Lindsay's birthday, we celebrated with candles in doughnuts and presents at breakfast. "Look both ways!" she repeated when she opened the box containing her own set of car keys."How could I ever forget, Mom? It seems like you've been telling me that all my life."

Later that day, after she passed her driving test and got her official license, obviously her best present of all, she drove me home and then asked if she could take the car over to a friend's house.

This was the moment I'd feared. Her maiden voyage. Alone.

"It's okay, Mom!" she assured me. "I can do it."

I merely nodded, fearful of the sound of my voice.

As I watched her pull out of the driveway I thought of Jochebed, Moses' mother, who placed her little baby in a basket and let him float down the Nile River. She knew the dangers that lurked in those waters. But once out of her grasp and out of her control, she had to stand back and watch him go, trusting he was in God's hands.

I'd done all I could do. Probably I made some mistakes. Probably I left some things out. But now it was time to let go and trust. Besides, I thought with a faint smile, she had her keychain message, "Look both ways."

That's good advice for me too, I thought. Look down at the fear, and then look up to God. Knowing that I'd done the best I could, it was time to trust him.

Becoming Acquainted at Last

Lois Williams Theuring

s I watched my son John push the log farther into the flames, I wondered if I had made a mistake bringing him with me. Stamping the ashes from his sneakers and pulling his jacket collar up around his ears, he stood with his shoulders hunched against the wind and thrust his hands deeper into the pockets of his jeans. This eleven-year-old "middle child" of mine certainly didn't appear to be enjoying himself.

I had planned to spend the weekend in blissful solitude on the mountaintop. Whenever the hustle and clamor of my eleven children threatened to paralyze my mind and plunge me into maternal insanity, I would take off for a weekend of quiet meditation. My husband and children seemed to enjoy these occasional jaunts of mine as much as I did. It gave them an opportunity to "rough it" at home—eating delicious, unbalanced meals, contentedly wallowing in unmade beds, not having to change socks and underwear every day or wash behind ears.

Lately it had seemed that John was becoming lost in the squeeze of family activity. Everyone was excited about his big brother going away to college; little brother was joining the Cub Scouts that John had just become too old for; little sister was charming everyone with her kindergarten art work. John was too young to acquire family fame and too old to be charming and cute. He always seemed to be left standing at the perimeter of activity, just watching.

So I had decided to take him with me on this particular camping trip to the mountains, even though John is not an outdoors type. He's more of the "sit by the fire with a good book" variety. But I hoped it would be a good opportunity for us to just be together—and maybe get to know each other better.

Though it was only 5:30 P.M., it was already pitch dark in the heavily wooded area. Our supper sizzled and sputtered aromatically on the iron grating over the fire. The night air felt crisp and clean on my back while the blast-furnace heat of the fire threatened to roast my front. I backed away a little from the flames, but John huddled closer. He worriedly observed the starless sky and pessimistically forecast rain. Each time he heard an unfamiliar sound he stiffened, ready to bolt, and hoarsely whispered, "What's that?" He peered warily through the formidable blackness, searching for the source of the strange creature sounds that lurked in the mountain forest.

After supper we snuggled deep into our sleeping bags. I lay close to the logs so I could easily feed the fire throughout the night. John lay forlornly staring into the flames, occasionally checking the black sky for falling raindrops. I wondered what thoughts occupied the mind of this son who had managed to seem a stranger to me for eleven years.

Surely we had something in common that we could talk about to help make the long night pass more quickly. I wanted so much to know John—to understand him. I knew that if I began by asking "opener" questions, he would feel put upon to answer, and I didn't want that kind of companionship from him.

So I began reminiscing, just kind of talking out loud to myself, about my own childhood days. John looked at me with interest. And slowly he began nostalgically recalling some of the events of "when I was just a little kid." Gradually the barrier between us dissolved as we shared the good events, the bad events, and the just plain silly ones that had molded us into our present persons.

John scooted his sleeping bag a few inches closer to mine. "There's something I've been wondering about," he said.

I steadied myself for something that might be difficult to answer.

"I was wondering," John continued, "if God made us . . . and he knows all about what we need . . . well . . . why do we pray for stuff?"

I was silent for a few moments, thinking about my answer, for his question was not really what I'd expected at all, no facts of life or other tricky area for a parent. Yet it was certainly an important one, and I sensed that my answer was important to him.

"Well, John," I began, "the way I see it, I always felt like I was belittling God by reminding him of the things that I needed. Some say we ask favors of God as a form of praise—by asking, we admit our total dependence upon him. But each person has his or her own way of worshiping God. No matter what you say or do, if you don't *feel* it— well, it just isn't going to get through.

"Now, I like to look around at all God's magnificent handiwork," I continued. "That really makes me *feel* my dependence upon him—and I like being dependent upon God. When I get up here on the mountaintop, where I can see for miles and miles around, I get all tongue-tied in my mind and all I can think of to say is, 'Wow, God, you're the greatest!' "

John thought about that for a moment, then said, "You know, that's just the way I feel sometimes—only I don't much like to be sitting here in the dark in the middle of all God's handiwork; I'd rather look out the window of a nice warm room and see it.

"But," John went on, "I just don't feel right asking God for things I know he knows I need. Sometimes at church, I even forget to pray, and I just sit there, maybe thinking about how come the birds always know just when to come back in the spring or something silly like that."

"But, John, don't you see?" I said, "That *is* prayer. Wondering is a form of prayer. Some people call it meditation. No matter what it's called, it all comes out to admitting that God is the greatest. Who else *but* God could engineer such a world?"

John was silent a moment. "Well . . . anyway . . . I was just wondering . . ." His voice trailed off as he gave the still-black sky a furtive look. "I guess if it's going to rain, it'll rain and we'll get wet, but if it's not, it won't and we'll stay dry. I think I'll worry about something I've got some control over—like—Mom, how do you get this zipper on my sleeping bag uncaught?"

Together we got control of the zipper. Resettling ourselves in our bags, we lay quietly togeher, staring pensively up into the black void above us. After a little while I saw a tiny point of light break through the black.

"Look, John," I said, excitedly pointing to the little dot. "Isn't that a star over there?"

John squinted against the bright light of our fire and studied the blackness where I had pointed.

"Ye—a—h!" he sighed.

The gently rustling oak leaves that partially obscured our view made the star look like it was being turned on and off.

"It looks like someone up there is winking at us," John observed.

"Sorta does at that," I agreed.

With the good feeling of someone watching over us, we laid down our heads, thoughtfully staring at the winking star till we fell asleep.

The next morning we awoke simultaneously, almost as if

some invisible alarm clock had gone off. It wasn't quite daylight yet, but happily, it was no longer as dark as it had been the night before. John shivered in the morning dampness and surveyed the sky.

"I really can't tell yet if it's going to be a cloudy day or a nice one," he said.

As with one thought, we rolled over onto our bellies, facing east. Propping our chins in our cupped hands, we anxiously awaited the new day for our answer.

Then, almost reverently, John whispered. "Here it comes!"

A thin slice of fluorescent orange appeared over the mountain horizon. We watched it slowly slip from behind the picket fence of pine spires, until it loomed full in the sky like a glowing hot cannon ball, exploding away the fog that filled the gorge below us. For a long time neither of us said a word. John was the first to break the silence. "We just *watched* our morning prayers!" he said joyfully.

After a hearty breakfast, we spent the rest of that day tramping through the mountain forest. As we walked, hand in hand, mother and son, we observed God's handiwork, discovering prayer after prayer.

It was with some reluctance that we drove down the mountain to the bustling highway and headed home that evening. John gave me an embarrassed hug and said, "Mom, I don't really like to sleep outside on the ground, and I don't really like sooty ham and eggs, but ... if you ever come here again ... well ... can I come too? It was really neat being able to talk together without anyone butting in." He paused for a moment, turning around to watch the mountains shrink behind us. "Yeah, it was really neat."

All I could do was nod in agreement. My son and I were becoming acquainted at last.

Single with
Children

Patricia Lorenz

sk any separated, divorced, or widowed person: When you're used to sharing your life with someone, to be suddenly "single" can be the most devastating, loneliest experience in the world. Starting a new relationship is the farthest thing from your mind.

When my husband and I divorced four years ago, I was so busy taking care of our four children and trying to carve out a career that I hardly had time to brush my hair, let alone think about meeting someone to spend time with.

But my children had different ideas. After a year of being my "dates" at movies, they began saying, "Mom, why don't you join that Single Again group at church and meet some men?"

I started praying wildly. *Help me, Lord! I don't know how to meet men or go out on a date! Besides, who wants a forty-year-old woman with four kids and a massive mortgage?*

But after another winter of being alone in the house every weekend while the kids were busy with their school friends, I worked up my nerve and joined the Single Again group at church.

A few weeks later the entire membership went out for a fish fry and dancing afterward. Twenty-one women and one man. And that poor guy danced with every one of us, bless his heart. When the dance was over though, he left alone. Sort of limped out the door, actually.

Lord, fish sticks in the oven at home would have been more fun.

For the next few months I kept my social calendar filled by attending my son's high school basketball games, getting more involved at church, and treating myself to an occasional dinner out with other single women friends.

Then one day it happened. I was invited out to dinner by a man I'd talked to on the phone at the radio station where I work. I was terrified, and my children knew it. "Mom, he's probably cute and maybe even rich! Maybe he'll take you to a really nice restaurant."

Well, he was rich all right. Too rich. And twenty years my senior. He not only took me to a very nice restaurant, but he also mentioned that he owned the place. He had just returned from South America and was anxious to take me to his penthouse to show me his antiques.

I'm sorry about the lie, Lord. I really do like antiques.

At home that night, Jeanne, my oldest, was waiting up for me. "So Mom, tell me all about him! Did you have fun?"

I took a deep breath. "Honey, I'm just going to lay it on the line. He was too old and too rich."

"Mother, with that attitude, you'll never find a man," Jeanne quipped.

She's probably right, Lord, but I'm just getting used to being "head of household," and I'm not sure it's time to complicate it. Besides, I rather like the responsibility. Weren't you proud of me, Lord, when I learned to use an ax to split wood for the wood burner? When I revved up the chain saw to cut the wood down to size, I felt good. And Lord, after a weekend of wood splitting and sawing, I don't have the energy to smile politely, let alone look for a date!

A year later, after putting over 15,000 miles on my little car, running the kids to their activities all over kingdom come, it happened again. My second date.

This gentleman was in advertising and suggested that I might do some copywriting for him. We didn't talk business during dinner; the conversation revolved around his two passions in life: golf and tennis. And for a woman who has never picked up a club or a racket, it was a real "D & B" night—dull and boring. Then when the check came, he pointed out that the meal was tax deductible. I didn't feel much like a "date" after that.

When I reported to my kids, Jeanne replied, "That's what you said about your date last year! You're too picky, Mom. Do you *like* being single?"

So what's wrong with being single, Lord? Who am I anyway? Someone just searching for another half of a couple?

During the next year my social life seemed to get busier—without any more dates, I might add. I joined the religious education committee at church. I wrote for a local Christian singles magazine. Andrew, my youngest, and I made some new friends at a single parents and children's group that met for dinner and discussion every week. On Fridays we watched Michael play basketball and Julie cheerlead.

Although my life was filled with activity, I still wondered, "Who am I?"

The next year my friend Jody called. "You have to meet Ben. He's single, your age, no kids, and wants to meet someone who likes quiet evenings watching TV. He doesn't go out much, but he's very good about fixing things around the house. You might like him."

Like him because he's a handyman?

Ben came over one Saturday afternoon, and I could tell right away he wasn't for me. Rather than waste any more of his time, I told him I had to run some errands. He said, "I'll come with you, and then we'll rent a movie to watch later on."

I sputtered a bit, then muttered, "Well, if that's what you really want to do."

That evening, just as the movie began, my children started coming home—Julie from her baby-sitting job, Andrew from visiting his dad, and Michael from his job at a local pharmacy.

So there we were in the family room. Me in my big green rocker next to the wood burner. Ben on the couch next to my chair. Andrew next to Ben. Julie next to Andrew. Michael on the love seat. A few minutes later Tony and John, Michael's best friends, came over and squeezed in on the couch and love seat.

Well, now, wasn't this cozy? Mom, her date, eight-year-old Andrew, and four teenagers. Michael kept looking at me sort of funny, like, "Where did you find this one, Mom?" I felt like I was on trial. Ben stood up, rubbed his slicked-back hair, and went over to investigate the innards of the wood burner again. He liked that contraption, obviously more than he liked being in a room with jovial teens, a hip-and-trendy second-grader, and a woman who yawned a lot.

O Lord, I know my friends and I have been grumbling for three years about my "meeting a nice man," but I can hardly wait until this one goes home!

Such thoughts kept flitting through my head during the entire nine hours Ben stayed at our house that Saturday. When he finally left at midnight, I had to admit that being with someone for the wrong reasons is a lot worse than *not* being with anyone at all.

All right, Lord, I know. I'm not ready to find a nice man and settle down again. I'm already settled! And I like who I am. I feel as if there's a light that's all mine, burning inside me, reminding me who I really am. Just as Saint Luke said:

"If you are filled with light within, with no dark corners, then your face will be radiant too, as though a floodlight is beamed upon you" (Luke 11:36, *TLB*).

Yes, Lord, I know what that light is. And thanks to that special light that poked its warmth and brightness into the dark, cobwebbed corners of my heart, I know who I am at last—a capable woman, a caring mom and, most especially, your loving Pat.

What Being a Mother Is All About

Patricia Brennan

 appy Mother's Day!" I thought bit-
terly as I pushed open the heavy
oak door. This was one place I had
never thought of being on this day
or any other—the visiting room of
the county jail.

The room was narrow and
shabby, its few old chairs badly scratched. The windows
were so encrusted with dirt and dead flies that very little filtered through them. I felt so out of place; I wanted to shout,
"I don't belong here. I'm a fine person and a good mother.
It's not my fault that my son is in this jail." How could
Michael have been involved in a robbery? How could he
have brought such shame on me?

I took my place at the end of the long check-in line and
looked around. I could imagine from the very posture of the
woman ahead of me that she must have been here many
times. As she turned her face to look at me, her eyes
seemed as lifeless as two black buttons. "Dear God," I
thought, "don't ever let me get like that!"

A young girl nearby was holding an infant, and even the
baby was listless. Only his eyes moved as he stared up at
his mother's oversized earrings. *Why do they all act like
robots?* I thought. It was terrifying. I tried to picture my
lovely home in the suburbs, but it seemed a million miles

away. I wanted to get back there, back to where I felt like a worthwhile person.

Finally I reached the desk and gave my name. The guard there didn't even glance up as he told me to take the elevator to the top of the building. "Look at me!" I wanted to say. "I'm not like these others! My son isn't a criminal, just a boy who got in with the wrong crowd."

That was it, I assured myself as I joined the little cluster of people waiting for the elevator. It was those other boys who got Michael started on drugs, got him into the robbery that had landed him here. At home he'd been taught honesty and decency, respect for others. He had always hated violence.

I stepped into the rusty elevator with the others who'd been waiting and, as it clanked its way upward, my sense of unfairness mounted with it. Life had been hard enough, divorced and raising a son alone—was I expected to supervise every minute of his time as well?

The elevator jerked to a stop and we were deposited into another waiting room, this one with no windows. We all sat down and waited for our names to be called. I was so tense I couldn't breathe; I was close to panic when suddenly I felt a hand on my arm.

I turned. It was the woman I had seen in line ahead of me. She said, "This your first visit?" I nodded because I didn't trust my voice. She smiled and told me this was the first time for her too. The eyes that I thought so emotionless now shone with love as she spoke about her son, also in prison.

"I just can't wait to see him," she said, "and tell him it's okay. The family at home, all of us, we're ready to help any way we can. Isn't that what families are for?" She began to describe her son's good qualities, which in her eyes far outweighed the causes of his current difficulties.

And as she talked, a stunning realization swept over me.

She was concerned for her son, while my concern had all been for myself. My feelings, my pride, my precious reputation. It was Michael who was in jail! He was the one who had committed a crime. He was the one who needed strength to face his punishment. He was the one who needed love and support.

I could feel my self-pity drain away as the woman and I compared notes about our sons and their problems. She went on to say, "It's easy to love our kids when they're winning the prizes, but the time they need our love most is when they've made a mistake."

Before I could answer her, I heard my name being called. I gave her hand a squeeze and headed toward a row of glass booths. Taking a seat, I waited. A high glass wall separated the visitors from the prisoners; we would have to talk through a pair of small telephones. I would not be able to kiss my son or touch him.

Suddenly Michael was there—so thin, so tall, so young. His beautiful hair was gone, shaved. He was wearing a much-too-large brown uniform. For some reason it bothered me that it was not ironed.

He didn't look at me until he sat down and picked up his phone. Then he tried to smile, but his eyes filled with tears. He looked so much the way he did as a little boy—trying to be brave, not wanting me to know how scared he was.

In those few seconds a scene from my son's childhood flashed through my mind. Michael must have been about four or five. He was drawing pictures, as he often did by the hour, at his easel blackboard. That day, however, he was muttering, half out loud, half to himself, "It's upside down, it's upside down." Curious about what he meant, I asked, "What are you drawing, dear?" He looked up at me with his large, solemn eyes. "I don't know," he said. "It's upside down."

Now the thought struck me—as a mother, had I been upside down? Did I have my values in the wrong places?

Had my concern for appearances and what the neighbors would think been greater than my concern for my son? I heard myself singing a too-familar song—"In our family we don't dress like that, or act like that, or speak like that." I remembered Michael's long-haired friends hanging around the yard because I would not invite them inside. By closing the door to his friends, had I also closed the door to him?

I had been so busy looking at the outside that I hadn't taken time to find out what was going on in the hearts and minds of those young people. Maybe if I had, I would have sensed my son's distress before it brought us both to this windowless, drab-walled room.

For one brief moment I thought of that other mother, the one I had just met. *Dear God, let me be as loving, as accepting as she,* I prayed.

Michael and I began to talk. I don't remember what we said, but we were communicating, getting through to each other. Thay day, perhaps for the very first time, I saw my son not as a reflection of my performance, good or bad, but as the unique and fascinating human being he is. Though a glass wall stood between us, I had never felt us so close.

That was five years ago. Today Michael is married and attending college, and the jail experience seems a long way behind us. I look back on it often, though, with gratitude— gratitude for the day when, with help from another mother, I discovered what being a mother is really all about.

The Lunch Box

Marion Bond West

n the early 1960s my husband and I became the parents of two little girls, two years apart. Quiet, obedient, demure children. I quickly assumed the role of a confident, smiling mother, with enormous time, energy, and enthusiasm—even patience.

When the girls approached eight and six, twin sons arrived. Superactive, loud, demanding, headstrong. Julie, my oldest little girl, became my faithful helper, folding mounds of diapers, strolling the babies, helping her sister, Jennifer, get ready for school, reading to all the children while I prepared meals. I could always depend on her, and I did. Perhaps too much.

The carefree days the girls and I had known when we enjoyed long, delightful tea parties under the weeping willow tree vanished abruptly. Supermom disintegrated bit by bit, and a tired, grim woman replaced her. Sometimes I cried silently from sheer weariness. Julie often saw me and tried even harder to help. She never complained.

It was only after Julie was grown and married that I learned of the hurt she'd felt back then. One day she laughingly asked me, "Remember my school lunches you made, Mom? All my friends took their lunches in cute little lunch boxes, and I wanted to be like them. Did you know I was embarrassed to eat with my friends? Those fancy lunch boxes of theirs were always filled with wonderful things their mothers had put in them."

I leaned forward, our faces inches apart, listening intently. Julie somehow seemed to have become a child again and spoke freely. "Jeannie's lunches were always the best. She had little sandwiches cut into halves, triangles, and circles, and packed in small sandwich bags. She had neat little carrot sticks! She always had a folded napkin for whatever holiday was approaching. You should have seen her lunch box near Valentine's Day. Her mother wrote her name on heart-shaped cookies.

"On cold days Claire had hot soup or hot cocoa in a thermos. And their mothers often tucked notes in their lunch boxes . . ."

I listened to Julie, fascinated, as she went on. "Sometimes, Mom, you threw a couple of unwashed, unpeeled carrots in a sack—the largest sack I'd ever seen—and spread peanut butter on two hard pieces of bread, and threw in an old apple and a crumbling cookie. I folded the sack forever, trying to make it small."

"Why didn't you ever tell me?" I asked, a ball of sorrow beginning to form in my stomach.

She laughed a genuine laugh, and appeared grown-up again. "You were so busy. I could see you were trying as hard as you could with the boys, and you just never got caught up. I knew you were always tired. Anyway, Jen and I had cute clothes with matching hair ribbons. You always helped us with posters, and picked us up when we had to stay late at school and couldn't ride the bus. Remember the raincoats you bought us with matching umbrellas?" She tried very hard to make it okay. After all these years she was still committed to helping me.

I couldn't drop the subject. "What did it feel like when the lunch bell rang?"

"Well . . . I always dreaded lunch. I hid my sack under

some stuff in the cloak room and always . . . hoped that maybe . . ." She brightened. "Once, I found a grocery ticket in the bottom of my sack and for a moment . . . I thought you'd written a note."

"I never knew you wanted a lunch box," I spoke in a whisper of regret.

Years passed, and from time to time I thought of the lunch box Julie had yearned for years ago. In my mind, she sat alone in a corner of the lunchroom with a grocery sack almost as large as she, while her friends chatted away eating dainty sandwiches and reading assuring notes from their mamas.

Last September Julie's two little girls were in kindergarten and second grade. She phoned me from five states away to tell me they'd just got on the school bus for the first day of school. "Mama, they picked out their own lunch boxes. Jamie's is pink and Katie's is yellow. I made their lunches last night." Excitement spilled through the telephone, filling my kitchen and my heart. "Triangle sandwiches, Mama, with the edges trimmed. M and M's. Grapes. Cheese. Home-made cookies. A drumstick . . . everything in separate bags."

"Julie, Julie!" I fairly screamed into the phone. "Did you remember the notes?"

"Yes. Oh, yes!" she responded.

One day I was fervently cleaning out the garage. Julie's father had died a few years earlier. I had remarried and moved to my husband's farm a thousand miles away, so all the things in this garage were unfamiliar to me. I reached down to the bottom of a dusy cardboard box and pulled out something. A tin lunch box! On the front was the lovable smiling television tiger who gobbled up a certain brand of cereal and growled a happy "Greeeeat!" The lunch box was old—probably from the 1960s. I sat cross-legged on the garage floor and held it tenderly on my lap, as though it had been dropped right out of heaven, aimed just for me.

Dear Lord, is it possible that you're giving me a second chance?

Go ahead, a silent voice urged. *It's not too late.*

I took the lunch box to the kitchen sink and washed it as carefully as if it were crystal. My imagination stirred and stretched, like a sleeping cat slowly awakening. What does a mother put in a lunch box for a grown-up daughter who lives a thousand miles away? Mounds candy bars, Life Savers, gum, a little box of raisins!

Remembering Julie's passion for old, sentimental things, I included some paper dolls nearly ninety years old—in a Ziploc bag. An antique lace handkerchief, a very old hand-embroidered tea towel. Such a tiny space to pack in so much . . . love. I tucked in a very old, quaint, jeweled hair comb, a small book about friendship published in the early 1900s. In this book, I printed, "Julie, pretend this a washed, peeled carrot, cut up properly."

In a tiny satin container, I enclosed an antique pin a friend had given me years ago. Some small packages of Julie's favorite cosmetics and hair products also went into the lunch box. When it would hold no more, I carefully placed a folded napkin on the top—a napkin with a big brown turkey and golden leaves and the words "Happy Thanksgiving." Of course I'd hidden in the very bottom of the lunch box a note printed in large red letters: I LOVE YOU, JULIE BABE. HAVE A GOOD DAY, MAMA.

Driving to the post office with the carefully wrapped package, I reasoned joyfully (if not logically): Never mind that the lunch box is over twenty years late. Never mind that Julie is almost thirty. At last, she was about to have a lunch box! *Please Lord, don't let it be too late,* I prayed.

Three days later the phone rang. I didn't recognize the voice at first. Someone was squealing, laughing, crying. "Mother, I never realized that I'm still seven years old. It was so . . . emotionally heavy I could barely breathe.

Everything is sitting right out on the kitchen counter. When I opened the lunch box it was just as though I was sitting at the long table and I could even 'smell' school and all my friends were watching me!"

"So the lunch box wasn't too late, after all?" I croaked.

"Too late? Oh, never." Then she paused. "Most of all, though, I loved the note you put at the bottom. Back in the second grade, Mama, maybe I wished for a triangle-shaped sandwich or a peeled carrot stick, and, especially, a note. But I always knew you loved me, Mother."

Love Will Keep Us Close

Frances Liming

y mother used to tell me about the time when I was five years old and overheard a friend tell her, "My, your Frances is getting big. Soon she'll be leaving you and going to school." That night my mother heard me praying, "You can do it, Jesus. I know you can." When my mother questioned me, I explained, "I just asked Jesus to keep me small enough so I'll never have to leave you."

"But Jesus wants you to grow up and go to school," my mother told me. "Love will keep us close, no matter how far apart we are."

Obviously my prayers weren't answered by keeping me physically small. I went to school, married, and had a child of my own. But my prayers were answered in the very close relationship I always had with my mother.

Even so, I never fully understood what she told me until my son Steve volunteered for Army service and left for training camp. At first I missed him dreadfully. Then one day I remembered my mother's "love will keep us close," and I was able to overcome my feelings of aloneness. Though we were separated, love did indeed keep Steve and me close—through mail, telephone, and our concern for each other. As an adult I was able to say, with the same faith as the five-year-old, "You can do it, Jesus."

A Fortune in Memories

Hope B. Friedman

t's only an old beat-up box, but if the house were on fire it's the first thing I'd race for.

As I rummaged through it in search of a clipping recently, I discovered treasure after treasure once again. There, for example, inside a small tin aspirin box, was a mite-sized string of blue and white beads bearing our family name. Slowly I twisted it around a finger, marveling that it had ever encirlced the wrist of the lovely daughter who is now the mother of two children of her own.

I picked up a yellowed envelope and read the now-faded words: "Evan bit into this soap while bathing when he was a year old." The soap slid from the envelope into my hand. On one side were the indentations of two tiny teeth; on the other, four still smaller ones. Today my six-foot scientist son towers above me, yet as long as I have this wisp of soap, he remains my little boy.

Next, a frayed family classic caught my eye. John Mark, our youngest, had labored over it in first grade—a Father's Day card now tied with twine and curling with the years. The words "For Father" that he had wanted on the cover had been too large to get on one line, and somehow the words had come out on three lines as "For Fat hen." What moments of merriment the family had enjoyed for years over that, especially as my husband showed signs of growing portly!

Here was a bundle of letters—notes from missionaries who had made our house their stateside home, thank-yous from lonely people who had shared our holidays with us, people whose names I might have forgotten were it not for this special box.

Next I came to Kent's letter. Kent, our eldest son, did not quite make it to age nine. Bulbar polio struck, and two days later he was no longer with us. Tenderly I opened his only letter, one he had written to his grandmother. Every erasure, every misspelled word, every lack of punctuation brought him back. I brushed away tears as I always do when I read it: "I am being a good boy . . . I am helping mother. . . ."

As I tucked the letter back in the box, I came upon a small, very new envelope—the birth announcement of our fourth and latest grandchild.

And finally there was the clipping I was hunting for. As I began to close the box once more, my eyes fell on the most recent entry of all, the card my husband, Paul, propped against my coffee cup on Mother's Day. Inside it were the words of a lovely poem by Heinrich Heine: "I loved thee once, and I love thee now. . . ."

I love thee . . . *Of course,* I thought, *that's what every item here is saying, each in its own way.* My battered old box is a true treasure chest, for it holds a trove of love's sweet tokens and a fortune in memories.

THE
ETERNAL
CITY

PAULA MORRIS

Point

Library of Congress Cataloging-in-Publication Data

Morris, Paula, author.
   The eternal city / Paula Morris.
      pages cm
   Summary: Laura Martin is on a class trip to Rome when Mercury, a dark-eyed boy with wings on his heels, appears to give her a message, and Laura soon realizes that she is at the center of a brewing battle between the gods and goddesses—and only she and her friends can unravel the mystery behind what is happening.
   ISBN 978-0-545-25133-4 (jacketed hardcover) —
   ISBN 0-545-25133-8 (jacketed hardcover)
   1. Mercury (Roman deity)—Juvenile fiction. 2. Gods, Roman—Juvenile fiction. 3. Goddesses, Roman—Juvenile fiction. 4. School field trips—Juvenile literature. 5. Friendship—Juvenile literature. 6. Rome (Italy)—Juvenile fiction. 7. Detective and mystery stories. [1. Mystery and detective stories. 2. Mercury (Roman deity)—Fiction. 3. Gods, Roman—Fiction. 4. Goddesses, Roman—Fiction. 5. Mythology, Roman—Fiction. 6. School field trips—Fiction. 7. Friendship—Fiction. 8. Rome (Italy)—Fiction. 9. Italy—Fiction.]
   I. Title.
   PZ7.M82845Et 2015
   [Fic]—dc23

                                                                 2014033962

10 9 8 7 6 5 4 3 2 1   15 16 17 18 19

Printed in the U.S.A.   23
First edition, June 2015
Book design by Yaffa Jaskoll

FOR SELMA, WALTER, AND CORNELIUS VOSS

. . . young Romulus
Will take the leadership, build walls of Mars,
And call by his own name his people Romans.
For these I set no limits, world or time,
But make the gift of Empire without end.

Virgil, *The Aeneid*

PROLOGUE

When the volcano first began to rumble, the birds of Rome could sense it.

Seagulls swooped inland from the Mediterranean coast, shrieking their warning. The peacocks strutting around the Villa Borghese zoo pointed their beaks at the cloudless June sky and cawed, loud and insistent. The hooded crows, in their sleek livery of black and gray, rallied on tile rooftops and crumbling walls to conspire and confer.

They all knew that the old gods were angry, that Vulcan, the god of fire, had issued a warning. His brother, Mars, the god of war, had been whispering in his ear, complaining that the gray-eyed goddess Minerva—wise, fearless, strong—was meddling in the human world again. Both Vulcan and Mars were the sons of Juno, the greatest goddess of Rome.

Their mother had never liked Minerva, the favored daughter of the mighty Jupiter, king of all the gods. Minerva was too all-knowing, too powerful, and even now—many, many centuries after her temples and shrines in Rome had been sacked, dismantled, buried, and built over—she saw the ancient city as her citadel, her domain.

The brothers, seething in rage and suspicion, found an ally in Neptune—god of the sea. Mars also called on those foul sisters, the harpies, to enter the city, ready to do his bidding.

But Minerva had allies as well. Her brother, Apollo, and his twin sister, Diana, both experts in archery. The Pleiades— the Seven Sisters—whom modern Romans imagined were nothing more than stars in the sky. And Mercury, the gods' swift-footed messenger, who could travel across worlds and times and boundaries. When Minerva needed him, he was ready.

On the frescoed wall of the Villa Farnesina, the nymph Galatea sensed the reins in her hand tug: The dolphins pulling her scallop-shelled chariot were moving. She felt the splash of a wave against her foot, her red cloak billowing higher as a restless Neptune whipped up the wind. But the three chubby

Cupids circling her head were no longer pointing their bows and arrows at her. They raised their bows toward the sky, poised for a different sort of attack.

With every high-pitched, frantic cry, the city's hooded crows were trying to tell the Romans bustling about that at any moment it would begin, that the city's ancient streets soon would be engulfed, once again, by darkness and war.

But no one understood the old omens anymore. They'd forgotten that Juno ruled the peacocks in the Villa Borghese, that the crows served Apollo, that the vicious harpies, too, could take the form of birds. They'd forgotten that Rome was a playground and a battlefield for the gods.

And when the gods were at war with each other, there was nothing anyone on earth could do to stop them.

CHAPTER ONE

Laura Martin wasn't even meant to be in Rome that June.

She should have been back home in Bloomington, Indiana, not hanging around the lobby of a cheap hostel with eleven other kids from Riverside High. The school's annual Classics Trip had almost been canceled that year due to low enrollment in the class. This irritated Laura. Classics was her favorite subject, and she was planning on studying ancient history in college. Her best friend, Morgan, on this trip as well, always said that Laura only liked old things—vintage clothes, vinyl records that had to be played on a turntable, used books that smelled of dust, black-and-white movies . . .

Thankfully, their teacher, Mrs. Johnson, had petitioned the principal and the Classics Trip was saved. Every student had to pay his or her own way, which was no problem for Morgan's family. Laura had had to babysit hyperactive toddlers, save every penny of birthday money, and work as a camera elf in Santa's Grotto in the mall over Christmas. But it was worth it—she had made it here. Twelve days, three countries—Turkey, Greece, and Italy—and every day more interesting than the next, despite the muggy heat and a succession of crummy hostels.

Rome was the final stop. They'd spent the past two days here, touring the Forum, the Pantheon, and the Colosseum. Now, on their last morning, Mrs. Johnson told the group they could do anything they liked.

"Anything you like *within reason*," she cautioned, her voice hoarse from playing tour guide. "Everyone stay out of trouble. And be back here by six, please, for our special last-night dinner."

She winced and gripped her stomach, leaning against the lobby wall, as if the lurid orange wallpaper would give her support.

"I think we may be killing POTUS," Laura murmured to Morgan, trailing the other kids out the glass doors into the swampy heat.

"And that, after all, is a federal crime," said Morgan, mock-earnest. All three teachers on the trip shared last names with former US presidents—Mrs. Johnson, Mr. Harding, and

Ms. Wilson. But only Mrs. Johnson, Laura and Morgan had decided, was worthy of the title of President of the United States. Sometime during the long, hot overnight boat ride from Greece to Italy, the whole group had started using the nickname.

"Though *we* were the ones who came up with it," Morgan liked to complain, annoyed that most of the other kids on the trip ignored them. This was mainly because she and Morgan were the youngest; they would be starting their junior year in the fall, and everyone else was going into their senior year.

It was obvious to Laura that there were three factions among the seniors: the cool kids, the shoppers, and the geeks. The cool kids were the best-looking, and liked to brag about the sports they excelled at and the colleges they'd be applying to. The shoppers had the most money, or just the most obvious desire to spend it: they preferred haggling for scarves in the Grand Bazaar in Istanbul to exploring the ruins at Pompeii. The geeks were two boys, Dylan and Jack, who wore *Star Wars* T-shirts and complained about stupid things, like the absence of lettuce in Greek salad. When POTUS talked about Virgil— one of the famous poets of Ancient Rome—Dylan asked if she meant the Pokémon character of the same name. Laura didn't know why he was even on this trip.

Ryan Kray and Dan Sinclair were the handsomest of the

cool boys. Dan had messy dark hair and chiseled cheekbones, and seemed incredibly aloof. Ryan was blond and loud, and wore skinny yellow jeans because he thought they looked "European." On one bus ride in Greece, Ryan had tried to get Laura's attention: The sun was in his eyes, and he wanted her to close the pleated window curtain next to her seat. "Hey, Mutant Girl!" he'd shouted.

Laura had dark hair and olive skin, and really, she thought, her eyes should have just been a nice, ordinary brown. Instead they were gray, and sometimes seemed a grayish shade of blue, or sometimes even a dull green. That's why Ryan called her Mutant Girl. At least, she *thought* that was why. She wished he'd bothered to learn her actual name.

"He's a guy who wears banana pants," Morgan had pointed out, trying to cheer her up. "Who cares what he thinks?"

Now, as she and Morgan headed down the narrow alley behind their hostel, Laura decided to stop caring about *any* of the other kids. It was her last day in *Rome*. Beautiful, ancient Rome. Laura had been dreaming about this city since she was a little girl, when her grandfather would tell her stories from the end of World War II. He had been stationed here as a young soldier, just eighteen years old, and he said even with the rubble and the rats, it was his favorite city in the world. Laura saw why; Rome felt like a mythical place, not at all part of any real world familiar to her—the world of strip malls, highways, and drive-throughs back home.

Now everything she'd studied and read about in Classics class this year was alive around her, in all its fragmented and decaying beauty. It was all so *old*, Laura kept thinking, though not daring to say it out loud. Before they'd left Indiana, POTUS had issued them with a What Not to Do list, and anyone transgressing had to pay a two-euro fine toward the official "Teachers' Gelato Fund."

Prohibited behavior included saying "Everything is so *old*" or "This is awesome," as well as persistent dawdling, wearing earbuds during tours of ancient sites, or complaining if there wasn't air-conditioning. There were so many possible transgressions that the teachers were pretty much able to buy themselves ice cream three times a day.

Laura's own What Not to Do list would be slightly different, she decided. Ryan wouldn't be allowed to call her Mutant Girl. Students couldn't sit in their usual cliques every single night at dinner. Of course, various items of clothing would be banned: *Star Wars* T-shirts, banana pants, and the Ugg Fluffie sandals that the shopping girls insisted on wearing, even though they kept complaining about aching legs. Most important, Ms. Wilson—aka Woody, after her namesake Woodrow Wilson—

couldn't sing the theme music from that old movie *Three Coins in the Fountain* ever again.

"Follow me!" Woody called now, leading them along another narrow street. She was the school's art history teacher, and kind of chaotic, in Laura's opinion. When they hit a main road, Woody—blinded by the brightness of the sun—almost stepped into the path of a speeding Vespa.

"Why is Woody with us?" Morgan whispered. "Isn't it supposed to be our free time?" She pulled her shoulder-length blond hair into a high ponytail, to avoid what she called the "neck sweats" when the heat of the day got too intense.

Laura wished she'd gotten her long hair trimmed before they left Bloomington. During this trip, Morgan had insisted on trying out various "Greek goddess" styles on Laura's hair, and all that braiding and twisting just made it wavy and crazy.

"Woody's obsessed with the Trevi Fountain," Laura explained, brushing a stray dark curl out of her face. "She wants to throw a coin in to make sure she'll return to Rome one day."

"She could just buy a plane ticket, like a normal person." Morgan made a face, and Laura grinned.

Although they were all given to eye rolling behind Woody's back, most of the students were following her lead today and heading for the Trevi Fountain. Maybe, Laura thought, they were so used to doing everything together that going off alone seemed radical and strange. Just two of the shopper girls had broken ranks by going to the busy Via del Corso, and Ryan Banana Pants had stayed back at the hostel, complaining that he felt sick and achy.

Laura and Morgan walked together, Laura snapping photos and Morgan posing. Their roommates, Nicole and Courtney (enthusiastic members of the "shopper" camp), were doing their best to incur fines for persistent dawdling, stopping to gush over fake Prada and Gucci bags spread out on blankets in the street.

The rest of the seniors walked in their usual clusters, engrossed in their usual private conversations. Occasionally Laura thought she saw Dan look back at her, as though he was about to ask her something. But maybe this was just wishful thinking. He probably thought of her as "Mutant Girl" as well.

Walking up ahead alongside Woody was a strange girl named Maia, who'd joined them the day they arrived in Rome. She had sleek, short black hair and a catlike face that would have been pretty if she didn't spend so much time frowning.

Apparently Maia was going to be a new student—a senior— at Riverside High School in the fall. Her parents—professors of some kind, in Italy for an academic conference—had managed to talk the principal into letting Maia crash the end of the Classics Trip.

Laura had tried talking to her a few times, but "Mystery Maia," as the other kids called her, wasn't exactly forthcoming. There were rumors that her parents were either exiled nuclear physicists or spies. Laura didn't know about that, but she did know that Maia had a long, multisyllabic Russian last name, that she was born in Vladivostok, that both her parents— Russian father, Korean-Russian mother—were starting jobs at the Indiana University, and that Maia tended to talk like a professor herself.

"The movie didn't make up the tradition of throwing coins into a fountain, you know, Ms. Wilson," Maia was saying, marching down the street alongside Woody. "The ancient Romans threw coins into rivers and lakes, as an offering to the gods, to request a safe return from a journey."

"We'll be throwing our own coins in soon." Woody sounded almost breathless with excitement. "Should we sing the song?"

Maia ignored her. "And the Trevi Fountain was built on the site of an underground Roman aqueduct," she continued. "Well, the end of one, where it opened into a public square."

Laura knew this: The aqueduct was built by Agrippa to supply water to his baths near the Pantheon. She wished those baths were still there. But like so much of ancient Rome, they had been stripped or built over, until only pieces were left.

"Someone make her stop," Morgan whispered to Laura, fussing with her ponytail.

"Woody or Maia?"

"Both. This is supposed to be our day off. One last chance to have fun without having to *learn* anything, or get asked the difference between . . . I don't know. Trajan and Trojans."

"Trajan's an emperor," said Maia, shooting an *are you stupid?* look back at Morgan. Laura hoped she hadn't overheard *all* their conversation. "And Trojans were the inhabitants of ancient Troy."

"Oh yeah! Silly me," said Morgan. She raised her eyebrows at Laura as soon as Maia's sleek dark head was turned.

"Be nice!" Laura whispered.

"You know that stuff, too," Morgan hissed. "But you don't blab on and on about it, do you?"

"I could recite the names of emperors for you again," Laura teased. Morgan had told her once that it was the best-known cure for insomnia, Laura's chronological list of Roman emperors.

"You can really do that?" said a boy's voice to her left, and Laura realized it was Dan. She felt her cheeks burning.

"Don't encourage her," Morgan groaned. She didn't seem intimidated by Dan at all, maybe because she claimed he wasn't that cute. "It's the world's most boring party trick."

The walk signal flashed at them, and everyone set off across the street. Dan strode ahead with some of the others from his group, not waiting for Laura to reply. It was just as well, Laura thought. She didn't have anything particularly interesting or witty to say. Better to lose herself in the sights of the city.

Rome looked like a stage set, with its pale buildings, shuttered windows, and huge wooden doors with handles shaped like lions or snakes. When she looked up toward the bluest of skies, she saw lush roof terraces lined with vine-covered trellises. Every narrow street seemed to lead to a cobbled piazza or to a serene stone fountain carved with dolphins or nymphs.

And now, quite suddenly, they were approaching the most amazing fountain of them all. The famous Trevi Fountain, white and enormous, its tableau of muscular men and giant horses wedged against the wall of a palazzo like a multistory altar. Its gushing spouts drowned out the chatter of the huge crowd of people around it, everyone taking photos and tossing coins into the frothy pale water.

Laura had seen pictures of it before, but it was much larger and more impressive than she'd expected. More beautiful, too, as though it was carved out of the purest vanilla ice cream, with such lifelike detail—seaweed, grapes, and reeds—petrified in bleached marble.

"Man, this is awesome," said Jack, plucking at the neck of his T-shirt. Luckily, Woody was too distracted to fine him for using a banned word. She was already charging down the crowded stairs, making for the rounded rim of the fountain. It was entirely lined with people sitting with their backs to the water, throwing coins in over their shoulders.

"Carved by Pietro Bracci!" Woody shouted, waving a spindly arm in the air. "Such strong lines! Such movement!"

"Hey, Neptune looks like he's dancing," said Dylan, nudging Jack, and Maia shot him a bemused look.

"That's not Neptune," Maia said. "It's Oceanus, the son of Gaia and Uranus. But the men holding the horses back— they have fishtails, see? So they're representations of Triton, Neptune's son."

"Class dismissed," said Dylan, smirking, and Laura felt sorry for Maia. However much Laura and Morgan might feel like outsiders, Maia really was: Even the geek boys thought she was weird. Part of it was her insistence on supplying information all the time; another part was her abrupt manner. Laura's mother talked about people who "didn't suffer fools gladly," and Laura had never understood what she meant. Listening to

Maia, though, she was starting to get the idea. Laura heard people burbling nonsense and she just ignored it. Maia never could.

"That's right, that's right." Woody fumbled in her purse for a coin. "The mighty Triton! Notice that one horse is calm and the other is restless."

"What does that mean?" asked Nicole, chomping on gum. POTUS would have made her throw it away, but Woody never noticed anything.

"Well, it's a question of balance and energy, isn't it?" gushed Woody in her overdramatic teaching voice. "It gives dynamism to the composition . . ."

Laura stopped listening, squinting at the statuesque female figures in their carved draperies, stationed on either side of Oceanus. She checked her guidebook. The woman on the left was Abundance, struggling with her cornucopia. The one on the right was Health, which Laura decided was a very dull name for a woman brandishing a spear and keeping a wary eye on a writhing snake.

The sun was so bright that Laura's head started aching. She fumbled in her bag for her sunglasses. The heat and the light were playing tricks on her, she decided: For a moment, the snake seemed to be moving, slithering up the shapely arm of Health. Laura shook her head, the way a dog shakes after running out of the sea. Sculptures couldn't move.

Woody had managed to squeeze into a place on the fountain's edge, eyes shut, a coin glinting in her hand.

"Oh, may as well," said Morgan with a resigned sigh. She pushed through the thick crowd until she was sitting on the edge as well, back to the water, preparing to throw her coin. Most of the students were doing the same thing, Laura noticed—apart from Maia, who never seemed to join in. Maia was frowning, hands shading her eyes, at the Triton brandishing a conch shell.

"Laura, come make your wish!" Morgan called, and Laura waved at her, smiling. It was true that she'd love to return to to Rome one day. Ideally without three teachers and eleven other kids.

An insect brushed against her wrist, and Laura instinctively flicked her hand to wave it away. Without meaning to, she smacked the person standing next to her.

"I'm so sor . . ." she began, forgetting to say *scusi* or *permesso* or whatever it was they'd been told to say in Italy. Then she realized, with a start, that it wasn't an insect skittering across her skin; it was another person's hand. The person standing right next to her, whose fingers were closing around Laura's bracelet, tugging at it so hard that the chain dug into her skin.

Someone was trying to steal the most precious thing Laura owned.

"No," she said, her trembling voice low: She was too astonished to shout. With her other hand she grabbed at her own wrist to try to wrench it away from the mugger, clamping her fingers over the bracelet.

Everything was blurred and hurried: Laura was pulling hard, and elbowing whoever it was in the side. She wanted to scream, but she couldn't; her heart was beating too fast, and all her energy was focused on pulling her arm free.

All of a sudden Maia was there, still frowning, and she shoved the mugger in the chest. With one final almighty effort Laura pulled her arm free, the bracelet's chain broken but still sticking to her clammy arm. And just like that, the mugger melted into the crowd so quickly that all Laura got was the briefest glimpse. It was a woman, she registered. Dark hair, dark eyes, pale skin. A mean expression, as though Laura was the one stealing something.

"Thanks," Laura managed to wheeze, looking up from the broken bracelet dangling off her wrist. But Maia had already walked away, down the steps toward the fountain, as though fighting off a mugger was the kind of thing she did every day.

CHAPTER TWO

Laura realized she was shaking. They'd been warned about pickpockets; POTUS had told them to carry their bags strapped across chests, not letting them dangle from shoulders. But Laura had never imagined someone would try to steal the bracelet off her wrist.

Now, for the first time since they'd arrived in Rome, the sky seemed to be darkening. Gray clouds blocked the intense blue, and Laura was relieved: It was too hot, too sunny. She slipped the broken bracelet off and carefully stowed it in the zipped front pocket of her bag. The chain was silver, and could be mended, she guessed. Luckily, the stone looked undamaged.

That was the most important part, the part that had

sentimental value. Her grandfather, who died when Laura was seven, had left it to her. Laura remembered him showing it to her once, when she was a very small girl, and she had told him she thought it was beautiful.

It *was* beautiful: a grayish-blue stone the size and shape of an almond. A star sapphire, her grandfather said. Though it looked more like a polished pebble, Laura thought, shot through with its own tiny constellation. Her grandfather had picked it up somewhere overseas during the war.

Her mom had it made into a bracelet when Laura turned fifteen, a year ago, and since then she'd worn it every day. It reminded her of everything she'd loved so much about her grandfather—his kindness, his strength, his stories, his smile. But with every passing year, Laura felt as though she could remember less and less about him, and about the time they spent together. She wasn't even sure what she really remembered and what she'd heard from other people. It made her sad to think someone that special to her could just disappear from her memory. That was why the bracelet was so meaningful. No way was some random thief going to steal it.

Dylan clambered up the broad steps toward her, looking sweaty in his *Star Wars* T-shirt. Laura didn't know how he could bear wearing black clothes in this heat.

"Someone just tried to mug me," she told him.

"I think someone's mugged my head," he said, and Laura noticed how strained and pale his face appeared. He lowered himself to the ground and stuck his head between his knees. "I feel like throwing up."

"Are you okay?" Laura was concerned by his pallor. "Should I get Woody?"

"I should just go back to the hostel," Dylan muttered. "Where's Jack?"

"I can't believe all you guys are getting sick on the last day," Laura said, thinking of Banana Pants back at the hostel.

"Girls, too," Dylan mumbled, and Laura looked down at the fountain's edge. Woody was standing up, frantically fanning Nicole's face. Courtney sat slumped on the ground, her eyes closed. Morgan was kneeling down, patting Courtney's head as though she were a puppy.

"It can't be food poisoning, can it?" Laura asked. "We all ate exactly the same thing for every meal yesterday. Maybe you have sunstroke."

"Not very sunny now." Dylan raised his head, grimacing up at the gray sky. A rumble of thunder sounded in the distance, and everyone around the fountain seemed to exclaim in unison, excited at the prospect of rain after so much heat. Squawking seagulls zoomed overhead, circling the small piazza.

There was something eerie about their cries, Laura thought, suppressing a shudder. She hoped that she wasn't getting sick with this strange illness as well: It would make the long flight home even worse. Woody was shepherding kids up the broad steps, and some of them looked barely able to stand up. Raindrops pattered down and thunder growled again, sounding closer this time. A storm was coming.

One seagull dipped so low that its wing brushed Laura's hair: It shrieked, loud and menacing, right in her ear. She flinched, ducking to get away, but it circled back, ready to dive-bomb her again. Laura scrambled up the steps: She needed to get out of here before she got drenched or robbed or smacked in the head by these manic birds. Morgan was beckoning to her, and Laura shouldered her bag, ready to follow.

She took one last look at the cool blue water of the fountain and stopped. Her eyes were playing tricks on her again. Laura could have sworn that she could see one of the horses moving—the rearing horse, the one on the left. It threw its giant head back even farther and churned the air with its front hooves. The carved Triton gripping its mane was half pulled out of the water.

Laura closed her eyes and opened them again: Could no one else see this? Was she hallucinating?

"It's raining," said a voice behind her: Mysterious Maia. "We should go."

"Do you see anything . . . anything *moving?*" Laura asked her. The rain was growing heavier and the crowd had begun to scatter. "In the fountain?"

"I saw that seagull launch itself at your head," replied Maia, giving Laura one of her quizzical looks. "The Roman augurs would say that was a bad omen."

"Whatever," said Laura. She wasn't in the mood for bad omens. She needed to get to Morgan, get back to the hostel, and lie down for a while—until she stopped seeing stone snakes and horses moving.

"When in Rome!" Maia called after her, and it sounded more like a warning than a joke.

Everything in the hostel was orange. The sinks in the bathroom were orange. The sheets on the bunk beds were orange. The desk in the lobby was orange Formica, and the officious guy who worked there had such a fluorescent fake tan that they'd dubbed him Agent Orange.

Back in their shared room on the third floor, Morgan closed the garish orange curtains to block out the sun. The rain had stopped as suddenly as it began. Courtney and Nicole were both lying on their beds, already half asleep. Actually, Courtney was lying on Morgan's bed, because she was too weak to make it up the ladder to her own upper berth. Laura couldn't believe how pale Nicole looked right now.

"I feel all shivery," she'd whispered to Laura before she closed her eyes. "I ache everywhere."

Woody appeared in the doorway, brandishing bottles of water from the vending machine in the lobby. Laura took two and placed them within reach of her two sick roommates.

"That's six of you who aren't feeling well," Woody reported, "including poor Mrs. Johnson. And a teacher from one of the European groups said most of her students are sick as well. In fact, *she* was feeling ill herself. It's like some kind of flu, except at the wrong time of year. Very odd. But maybe everyone will feel better by tomorrow. I hope so. Otherwise the trip home will be *very* unpleasant."

"Should we stay here this afternoon? You know, to . . . take care of them?" Morgan sounded as reluctant as she looked. She'd already changed into a white muslin sundress and was itching, Laura knew, to go out again. Laura was still in her slightly damp T-shirt and shorts, but figured she could change later.

"No," Woody said, her mouth drooping. "Mr. Harding and I have agreed that we'll take turns at keeping an eye on things here. You two go off and have a good time."

"Well, at least we're rid of everyone for a few hours," Morgan murmured to Laura as they set off down the hallway. "Should we check out the graves?"

Laura had really wanted to explore the ruins of Nero's Golden House, but it wasn't open to the public at the moment. So she didn't mind indulging Morgan, who was desperate to see the graves of the poets Keats and Shelley in the old Protestant cemetery. It wasn't part of their official Classics Trip itinerary and today, as Morgan had reminded Laura maybe ten times, was their only chance.

"Mmm," said Laura, wondering if she should have left her broken bracelet in the room rather than carry it around in her backpack. Maybe with Nicole and Courtney staying in the room, the bracelet would have been safe. But she'd rather have it with her, in case she could get the chain mended somewhere.

"Let's make sure Jack and Maia don't see us and try to tag along." Morgan clattered down the narrow staircase. "They probably wouldn't be interested, anyway. Or else Maia would know everything about it, and bore us to death."

"I guess," said Laura, though she felt bad, scampering off

like this. Sometimes it was nice just to be around other people, especially in a strange city, even if they weren't exactly your BFFs.

As it turned out, there was no chance of escaping unnoticed. In the lobby, Jack was slumped like a rag doll in one of the orange plastic chairs, pulling on the cords of his Purdue hoodie. Maia sat huddled on the floor, writing in her diary. She was frowning with concentration.

"She's probably writing: *Day Three, still no friends*," Morgan whispered, nudging Laura. Laura nudged her back even harder.

"You guys, we're going to get the Metro out to the Protestant Cemetery," Laura announced. She ignored Morgan's fingers pinching into her arm. "You can come if you'd like . . ."

"Sure," Jack said. "May as well. Nothing else to do."

"Campo Cestio?" asked Maia, slamming her diary shut. That girl really was like a cat, Laura decided: self-contained, hard to read, almost insolent. She scrambled to her feet, dusting off her shorts. "That's its correct name, you know. And with four of us, I think it'll be cheaper to catch a cab."

Morgan sighed theatrically.

"*Just* as I predicted," she hissed at Laura, and pushed open the foggy glass door. "Thanks for not listening to me."

"I never listen to you," Laura teased, hoping Morgan would cheer up.

Outside, the afternoon air was humid, still heavy with rain. She refused to let anyone spoil her last day in Rome—not sulky Morgan or listless Jack or weird Maia, not even marauding seagulls or brazen muggers or looming storms. This was the most amazing city she'd ever seen in her life, awash in history and stories and secrets. Who knew what they'd uncover this afternoon?

The cemetery entrance was an archway with ornate iron gates and a sign announcing Campo Cestio's opening hours.

" 'The Old Cemetery for Non Catholic Foreigners,' " Jack read aloud. "That's us!"

"Speak for yourself," Morgan said. She strode through the gates and up the gravel path as though she knew exactly where she was going.

"And you—I guess you're, what? Russian Orthodox?" Jack asked Maia. She stared at him as though he were speaking a foreign language.

"How is that relevant?" Maia sounded more puzzled than affronted.

"Just trying to, you know, make conversation," said Jack, pouting.

"Maybe we should all split up and wander around by ourselves, okay?" Laura suggested. "Meet back here in forty minutes?"

Before the others had a chance to reply, Laura bounded away, feeling only a little bad about leaving Jack with Maia, or Maia with Jack—she wasn't sure who was worse off. But this was too peaceful a place for squabbles. Laura hadn't spent much time in cemeteries, apart from the military cemetery back home where her grandfather was buried. That was a vast expanse and super-orderly, all the gravestones white and identical, with signs telling people not to leave fresh flowers or wreaths because they encouraged the roaming deer.

This cemetery was quite different. With its trim green hedges, soaring trees, and drooping wisteria, it looked more like a well-tended small park. Narrow paths rose up toward the high back wall. The elaborate tombs and creamy gravestones were topped with carved urns or angels.

Laura crunched her way up the most central path in Morgan's wake, inhaling the sweet after-rain smell of the greenery. Raindrops still glistened on leaves and on the vibrant pink petals of the hydrangea bushes. Laura walked past a grave that was just a pedestal balancing a draped headless torso, and the name carved into the base simply read BELINDA.

An elegant stone angel bent over another tomb, her face covered. Her heavy wings and draped robes—even the sandals on her feet—looked so real that Laura couldn't resist reaching out to stroke the stone folds.

"Over here!" shouted Morgan, waving, and Laura pulled back her hand.

"Okay," Laura called back. She made her way down the steep gravel path, unnerved by the incessant cawing of a crow flying overhead. They were called hooded crows here, Laura had learned, because they looked as though they were wearing a little gray cape over their black feathers.

The sky was dark now, and she hoped the rain would hold off. The crow above Laura's head cawed again and dipped lower, as though he was following her. A seagull had swooped in as well, circling the crow, its echoing cry loud in her ears. The birds of Rome all seemed so frantic today, Laura thought, and aggressive. Maybe they were freaked out by the intense weather.

She hurried down the path and turned past a tombstone she hadn't noticed before, topped with a jet-black marble figure of a boy with wings curling around his shoulders. The look on his face was bored, and he held a large dart in his right hand, pointed at nothing in particular. Cupid, Laura thought: the god of love. He looked more like a sulky teenager playing some lame game in his parents' basement.

Both birds dove and wheeled, getting closer and closer to the ground—and to Laura. The crow held something in its beak, but she couldn't make out what, exactly, even when the crow dropped it. As the tiny piece of debris fell, the seagull flew toward it, shrieking, and the crow gave chase, pecking at the gull's tail. Were these birds actually *fighting*?

The black marble figure of Cupid raised his hand in one swift, elegant movement and threw the dart into the sky. Laura couldn't believe her eyes. Her heart thumped with something between shock and exhilaration, watching the dart soar higher and higher into the air. It wasn't possible for something carved to move; it wasn't possible for this stone dart to be launched. But there it was, speeding into the sky.

The dart, black as the gathering clouds, hit the seagull in its snowy breast. Laura gasped, clutching at a straggly bush to steady herself. The seagull was falling, dropping at great speed. The crow cawed—almost in triumph, Laura thought, if that were possible.

The crow flew toward the cemetery's walls just as the dead gull thudded onto the damp turf at Laura's feet. The dart was still buried in the soft feathers of its breast.

Laura grabbed a limp branch and crushed it in her shaking hand. This couldn't be happening. Grave ornaments didn't launch missiles into the air—not in any normal place, anyway. Where was Morgan? Where was anyone else, to look up at that dark, seething sky right now and tell her that she wasn't going crazy?

The dart slid from the dead bird's prone form and flew, like a boomerang, back into Cupid's hand. And then, before Laura could move, the bird's corpse vanished, dissolving like a vapor, a mist. In an instant there was nothing left of it apart from a spot of red blood on the green grass. The sky turned black and Laura thought she could smell fire.

Something soft as a feather brushed Laura's face—one brush, then another. She looked up, afraid that the stone Cupid was busy shooting more birds. But all she could see above her now was a billowing charcoal cloud, with ash falling like gray snow from the sky.

CHAPTER THREE

Il volcano!"

"Eruzione! Eruzione!"

Laura ran toward the shouting voices near the cemetery's main building, where every visitor or cemetery
worker—invisible until now amid the lush foliage and steep
paths—seemed to be congregating, babbling and exclaiming.
Jack's face emerged out of the gloomy haze, his eyes wild with
excitement.

"It's a volcano," he told her. "A volcano has erupted and this
is like, like . . ."

"An ash cloud." Laura recognized Maia's voice, as assured
and calm as ever. "The volcano's to the south, in the Colli
Albani. It hasn't erupted like this for thousands of years."

"How do you know all this already?" Laura swung around to face her. Maia might have sounded as matter-of-fact as normal, but the falling ash made her look very strange, as though she'd been crawling through spiderwebs in an attic.

Maia shrugged. Laura would have been annoyed by her smug expression if she weren't still struggling to grasp what was happening.

The crowd assembling near the gates looked and sounded increasingly hysterical. One man was crossing himself; two Asian girls huddled under an umbrella, scarves drawn over their mouths. A woman in black was weeping, jabbing at the numbers on her cell phone. Someone in a military-style uniform stood at the gates, his gestures frantic, shouting at them.

"We have to get back to the hostel," Maia said, frowning at the crowd. "Where's Morgan?"

Laura had no idea. It was hard to see clearly or even walk through the ash; it was like wading in a sea of gray down. Last time she'd seen Morgan, her friend was off in search of Keats's grave. It could only have been minutes ago—five, ten?—but it felt like an eternity. Laura had seen the Cupid shoot the arrow, had seen the gull fall, had seen the bird disappear completely from view. How was any of this possible?

"There!" shouted Jack. He marched toward a ghostly figure staggering toward them, her fair hair and white dress gray with ash, and grabbed her by the arm.

"I feel terrible," Morgan gasped, leaning on Jack for support.

"It's just ash," Jack said. He batted some away from his mouth and grinned, like a kid playing near a Halloween bonfire.

"No, I mean . . ." Morgan bent over, gripping her knees. "I was feeling sick before . . . before *this*. My head is swimming. I didn't even make it to the grave when . . . *this* started happening."

"Volcanic eruption!" Jack sounded delighted. Morgan groaned. "Hey—maybe we're all going to die, like in Pompeii."

"We're not going to die," Laura snapped, though she wasn't sure. How close was this volcano, anyway? Would the ash cloud be followed by torrents of boiling lava? The Seven Hills of Rome had been formed by volcanic eruptions, but that was millions of years ago.

"Can we get a cab?" bleated Morgan.

"Here!" Maia was calling them from the sidewalk just outside the gates. She'd managed to find a taxi, of course, even in the chaos of the ash rain. Maia, thought Laura, helping a rag-doll-like Morgan stagger toward the waiting car, always seemed to know exactly what to do.

Back at the hostel all the lights were on, though it was still early in the afternoon. Agent Orange on the desk was jabbering away in Italian on the phone, smacking one hand on the counter to make some agitated point. High on the wall, the TV showed pictures of a smoldering mountain and a vast traffic jam on the highway, with close-ups of swirling ash. Leslie and Jane, the two girls who'd gone shopping earlier, were slumped in plastic chairs, looking dazed and ashy.

"What *is* this stuff?" Leslie moaned, trying to brush ash out of her long hair.

"A volcano erupted, and there's an ash cloud," Maia told her. "It won't kill you."

"But the volcano might," added Jack, sounding gleeful. The girls looked like they were about to burst into tears.

"I feel so . . . bad," Jane groaned, and Laura jabbed Maia in the arm.

"You should help them," Laura hissed.

"Why?" Maia looked bemused.

"Help them get upstairs. They must be sick, like Morgan. You guys help them, and I'll get Morgan up to our room."

It wasn't easy pushing and tugging a dizzy, breathless Morgan up so many flights of stairs. Laura was desperate to tell her about what she'd seen—Cupid's dart, the dead bird disappearing—but Morgan looked more ready to faint than to listen to such a far-fetched story. Maybe it had all been a hallucination, Laura thought, a symptom of this illness felling everyone around her. But she didn't feel foggy. What she'd seen was crystal clear in her memory, even the soft thump when the bird hit the ground, and the glistening patch of blood it left on the ground.

"I think I'm going to be sick," groaned Morgan. Laura steered her in the direction of the shared bathroom at the end of the hall and then went in search of help. Nicole and Courtney were both fast asleep on the lower bunks of their shared room, and there was no way Laura could push Morgan up the bunk-bed ladder without someone else giving her a hand.

She tapped on door after door, peeking in to see who was around. Most of the sick girls probably had no idea about the ash cloud, because they were lying in bed with the curtains drawn, or they were fast asleep. There was no one at all in the female teachers' room. Laura tore up the stairs to the fourth floor, where the boys were staying, but most of them seemed to be in much the same state, zonked out.

Only Dan Sinclair was awake. He was sitting on the floor

of his room, legs stretched out, flicking flecks of ash off his jeans.

"Yes?" he said when Laura peered in. The room smelled of gym socks. It reminded her of her brothers' bedroom, where things seemed to be fermenting. The other boys in the room were silent lumps in the bunk beds. She wasn't sure whether to go in or not.

"You don't have to hide out in the hallway, you know," he said, and Laura felt herself blush. She hated the way whenever there was an awkward social situation, her face went red.

"Are you okay?" she asked. It felt strange speaking to Dan, let alone asking a personal question. They never talked in school. At least, unlike Banana Pants Ryan, he didn't call her "Mutant Girl." He didn't call her anything at all.

"I never get sick." Dan sounded slightly offended. "I'm just here because, you know, there's an *ash storm* outside."

It was hardly a storm, Laura thought, but she wasn't brave enough to squabble with Dan, who was good at everything and clearly knew it. She felt embarrassed, and wanted to close the door and back away. But that wouldn't help her get Morgan up a bunk-bed ladder.

"Would you mind helping me—um, downstairs?" she asked after what felt like an endless pause. "Everyone else is, you know, sick."

"Sure," said Dan, jumping to his feet and dusting himself off. He sounded kind of embarrassed as well, though Laura wasn't sure why.

By now the girls' floor looked like some kind of zombie hospital, with the strong—Laura, Dan, Maia, Jack—helping the weak up and down the hallway, leading them to and from the bathroom or to any available bed.

"Why aren't *you* sick?" Maia asked Jack, in what Laura was beginning to recognize as her signature blunt/rude manner. "All the other boys are."

"I'm very healthy," he told her, grinning. He was short and a little chubby, and did have a robust look about him. "Never missed a day of school, unfortunately."

"Dan's not sick, either," Laura pointed out, but Maia didn't seem surprised.

"We might need him," she said.

"What?" Laura asked, confused, but Maia looked away, saying nothing. Mrs. Johnson—POTUS—had reappeared, clearly sick herself but doing her best to direct traffic. Maia and Laura had to move to a room two floors up, she said, and would be sharing with a girl from one of the European school groups. Jack and Dan had to move to the sixth floor, in the hostel's old attic.

"I don't think we need to move," Dan argued. Laura remembered something that Morgan had said early in the trip, that just because Dan was the smartest kid in his grade, he sometimes acted like he was equal to all the teachers, even POTUS. "We can squeeze in wherever down here. It's only for one night."

"I don't want you getting sick as well," POTUS said, steadying herself against the grubby wall. Her face looked gray, even though she hadn't been outside for an ash dusting. "And it's going to be more than one night, I'm afraid."

"What do you mean?" Laura asked. She was eager to get home and see her family. Rome wasn't quite as enticing now with all this sudden, creepy strangeness—the extreme weather, the erupting volcano, birds getting shot out of the sky by stone Cupids. She fingered her wrist, startled at first that the bracelet was gone, before she remembered it was tucked safely away in her bag.

She thought back to the thief and to the moving statues at the Trevi Fountain this morning. It all felt like a strange dream, disturbing because it was so vivid. Laura wished she could talk it through with someone, to try to make sense of what she thought she'd seen.

"The ash cloud," said Maia flatly, by way of explanation. She handed her backpack—as neat and compact as its owner— to Jack as though he were a doorman at a fancy hotel.

"Maia's right," said POTUS. She looked half asleep on her feet. "The ash cloud means that all planes are grounded. Not just in Rome but in most of southern Europe, and the air travel ban may spread if the cloud grows. We can't leave."

"Cool." Jack beamed, and hoisted Maia's backpack onto his shoulder.

POTUS sighed. "I called the principal, and he's letting all your families know about the delay. Though they've probably all seen it on the news. Well, at least now we have a chance to recover from whatever this is." She gave a feeble wave toward the dim rooms on the hall.

"I have a track meet on Saturday," said Dan, frowning.

"Too bad," Maia told him. She wasn't in awe of anyone, Laura observed—not the teachers, and certainly not other students. Dan looked at Maia for a moment, as though he'd never seen her before in his life, and turned back to POTUS.

"So, get settled in your new rooms," she said, ignoring his indignant expression, "and Ms. Wilson will try to get you some pizza or something for dinner tonight. I think it's best if you all stay inside until we know it's safe out there."

This wasn't at all the big final night they'd had planned, with a nice dinner at a nearby fancy restaurant that apparently served homemade pasta and a world-famous fried artichoke dish.

Instead here she was, climbing the stairs with strange Maia to find a strange room where some strange European girl might be lurking.

Room 32 had shabby curtains and garish smiley-face stickers plastered down one of the bedposts. Sitting cross-legged on one of the top bunks, reading a book, was a girl with fair spiky hair, wearing tortoiseshell-framed glasses and a striped sailor top. She looked at Laura and Maia and closed her book with a snap.

"Hi," Laura said, forcing a smile. She spotted her suitcase dumped—by Jack, the world's most enthusiastic porter—on one of the lower bunk beds, and dropped her backpack next to it. Maia was still standing in the doorway, gazing up at the new girl in her usual brazen way.

"You call yourself—what?" Maia asked. Laura's face prickled with embarrassment: Didn't Maia know you were supposed to introduce yourself before demanding someone else's name? Also, Maia was clearly fluent in English; why did her phrasing sound so foreign?

"Sofie," said the girl, unsmiling. She pronounced it *Zo-fee-ah*. "It's a German name. I'm from Hamburg, in Germany."

"We're from the US," Laura said quickly, before Maia could say anything else rude and/or strange. "Bloomington, Indiana. I mean, we go to school there."

Laura knew that Maia wasn't really from Indiana—she was originally from Russia, or maybe the Planet Zog, for all Laura knew—but for the purposes of this extremely awkward meet-your-roomies moment, she was from Bloomington.

"Indiana?" Sofie sounded amused.

"Yes. And I'm Laura," Laura continued, trying to ignore the other girl's sarcastic tone. Her neck was stiff from looking up. "And this is Maia."

Maia walked to the window and stared out at the gloomy alley. She was terrible at conversation, Laura thought.

"Are you the only one not sick?" Laura asked Sofie. "From your school, I mean?"

"I am not here with my *school*," Sofie told her, looking affronted by the very idea. She unfolded her long legs and stretched them out, like a ballet dancer limbering up. "We are on holiday now. I am traveling in Italy with some friends."

"*That's* why you're here," said Maia, as though she'd just solved a mystery. "Who are your friends?"

"Germans." Sofie sounded bored. She slipped the book she'd been reading under her pillow, as though she didn't want them to see it. "You don't know them. And now they are all sick, of course."

"There's just us and two boys—two who are not sick."

Laura was speaking the most stilted English, and she wasn't sure why. Sofie made her feel flustered.

"Boys?" Suddenly, Sofie looked interested.

"Dan and Jack." Something pinged inside Laura, like homesickness: She wished the boys were here right now. Jack was goofy and immature a lot of the time, but at least he was cheerful. And Dan might think himself better than practically everyone else, but it might be helpful to have someone confident to do all the talking and introductions. Maia was no help at all. Now that she'd finished examining the view, she was peeling the sheets off her bed and feeling along the length of the thin mattress.

"What are you doing?" Laura asked her.

"Checking for bedbugs. Even good hotels get them, you know."

"And this is not a good hotel," said Sofie.

Laura wondered if she should check her own bed, but she didn't want to slavishly copy Maia. What she really wanted to do was pick up her bags and run, back to her old room, where the other girls were more or less normal.

"So you have two boys," mused Sofie. "Interesting. They are not sick at all?"

"Not yet," said Maia.

"And there is the Danish boy," Sofie said. The tiniest of smiles flickered across her face. Maia stopped shaking her sheets and frowned. "He is on a school trip like you. He is very tall. A Viking."

From the smile on Sofie's face, Laura guessed that "Viking" must be a code word for cute.

"Do you know his name?" Laura asked. Sofie gave a one-shouldered shrug and said nothing. Silence settled in the room like a heavy blanket.

"Our teacher is bringing us pizza later," Laura said at last, because she couldn't think of anything else to drum up some intelligent conversation. Maia was now absorbed in remaking her bed, stirring up dust when she shook out the comforter. "I'm sure you can have some, too."

Sofie sniffed, and dug around under her pillow for the book. Obviously she found Laura's conversation dull. If Laura was honest, she found it pretty dull herself. It was so hard talking to unfriendly people. She couldn't wait for the stupid cloud to drift away so she could go home to her family, who liked to laugh and talk and play board games. If her dad were here, he'd be leaning way too far out the window, taking way too many photos; her younger brothers would be leaning out as well, trying to catch ash on their tongues. Her mother would be coming up with stupid newspaper headlines, like "Ash the World Turns" or "Eruption Destruction: Vacation Disruption."

After obsessively checking every neat pile of folded clothes in her backpack, Maia settled onto her bed and started scratching away in her diary, her dark head bowed low. Sofie kept reading. Laura walked over to her new bunk and tried to distract herself by reorganizing the things she'd thrown, in haste, into her suitcase. She turned her back on Maia and Sofie, in case they felt like making snarky comments about her messy packing: She really wasn't in the mood.

Her backpack, Laura realized, had deposited an ashy residue on the new comforter. She unzipped the bag's pocket to fish out her broken bracelet. The chain looked so fragile, rudely snapped by that horrible person who tried to mug her. Looking at it made her feel tearful, even though she knew she could get it fixed at home.

She rubbed a finger over the gray-blue stone, suspended in its silver setting. It felt reassuringly smooth, exotic and familiar at the same time. Long ago she'd decided that this gray-blue color was the exact shade of her grandfather's eyes. That was probably untrue, Laura knew, but she liked thinking of it that way, as a link to the past, and to some of the happiest times in her childhood. She looked like him, people said.

Laura tried to dust the ash off her comforter and realized that she had stupidly been walking around with the main compartment of her backpack open a fraction, offering just enough of a gap for ash to infiltrate.

"Annoying!" she murmured, but Maia and Sofie didn't say anything in response. Everything in her bag—phone, camera, notebook, guidebook, lip gloss, hand sanitizer, and a red pashmina shawl belonging to her mother, used as a cover-up when the group toured a church—was smutty with ash. Laura laid them all on the floor and carried her backpack over to the window, to empty out the rest of the ash into the alleyway.

She cracked open the window just wide enough to squeeze the bag through. The air smelled of distant fire, with a hint of smoke. The alley below lay empty and quiet. Before Laura tipped her bag upside down, she remembered her pen—the purple one presented to her at the hostel in Athens by the cute guy who worked evenings on the desk. Not something, she decided, to just throw away into the street in Rome.

She tugged the bag back inside and felt around for the pen: There it was, lurking in the ashy debris at the bottom of the bag. And something else was rolling around with it—a piece of gum? No. A pebble, maybe?

Laura fumbled around until she grabbed it. Maybe the stone was something spewed hundreds of miles by the volcano, a molten chunk that one of her brothers might like as a souvenir.

Laura pulled the stone from her bag and gasped so loudly that Maia asked her what was wrong. But she couldn't reply, couldn't say a single word.

The stone in her hand was a smooth gray pebble, the size and shape of an almond, shot through with a constellation of gold. A star sapphire, the exact replica of the one in her snapped bracelet, lying there on her dusty bunk bed.

CHAPTER FOUR

Well," said Woody the next morning, handing out pieces of fruit and squashed energy bars. "The breakfast room is closed, and nobody seems to know *anything*. So this is breakfast, I'm afraid. Okay?"

Their teacher was trying to sound bright and breezy, Laura thought, but she wasn't doing a great job of pretending. Laura accepted a bruised banana from her. Woody was rattled, obviously—they all were.

They now meant Laura, Maia, Dan, and Jack, as well as the two new European kids. They all stood clustered together in the hostel lobby, Dan standing apart from the group with his hands in his pockets, as though he was better than everyone else.

Laura wished that Morgan was here rather than dozing away in bed on the quarantined floor. Laura was desperate to tell her about the mysterious appearance of a twin star sapphire in her bag—how did it get there? what did it mean?—but Laura wasn't allowed to visit her. Woody had escorted them down the stairs that morning to make sure they didn't take any detours into the Forbidden Zone.

Sofie, her blond hair even spikier today, and wearing jeans so tight Laura wondered how she would be able to sit down, was gazing in open admiration at the Danish boy she'd mentioned last night.

"Hi," he said, smiling at Laura. "I'm Kasper. I'm from Copenhagen. The only one left standing from my school, it seems."

Laura couldn't help wishing they had some Vikings at Riverside High. No wonder Sofie got a secret smile on her face just mentioning him. Kasper was so tall he made Dan look average height. His hair was thick and golden, and his eyes were the kind of intense blue that would send most of the girls in Laura's class into a prolonged giggling fit. He was wearing a checked shirt with rolled-up sleeves, and the kind of baggy, zippy trousers that snowboarders wore. Around his neck dangled a black piece of leather with some kind of orange stone or piece of glass hanging from it.

"Any more—food?" Woody asked the group, sounding desperate. She tried to shove a limp-looking energy bar in Jack's direction.

"I have a nut allergy," he told her.

Sofie clucked her tongue. "Americans are allergic to everything," she muttered.

"I have a nut allergy also," said Kasper, toasting Jack with his own unopened bar. "So maybe I am an honorary American."

Laura was meanly pleased to see Sofie squirm. If she was trying to impress Kasper, it wasn't working.

"Have this orange," Woody insisted, pulling more fruit from her canvas carryall. "We're very pleased to have you as an honorary American! Both of you, in fact. We're a little group today. Just us. I'm Ms. Wilson. Or Fräulein Wilson. Or—ah, whatever 'Ms.' is in Danish. Though the students call me Woody, I believe. Ha!"

Woody—clearly a nervous wreck—grinned in a worrying, maniacal way, and Laura desperately wanted this standing-around-in-the-lobby part to be over. She wasn't even sure why Sofie was here: She wasn't on a school trip and didn't need to be supervised. Maybe she just wanted to hang out with Kasper, and this was the only way.

"What are we going to do today?" Laura asked finally. "Is it . . . is it safe to go outside?"

"Oh!" Woody looked confused. "I think so. The cloud is still up there, of course, but that stuff falling down . . ."

"Ash," Maia told her.

"Yes, yes, the ash. It's gone. I mean, it's up in the sky." Woody gave a vague wave of one hand. "So we can do something. What would you all like to do?"

"Can we go off by ourselves?" That was Dan, of course.

Woody shook her head so hard that her earrings jangled. "I promised Mrs. Johnson that we'd stick together."

"What were we *supposed* to be doing today?" Jack asked. "I lost my itinerary thing."

"Flying home," Dan said. "Remember?"

"My class was going to the Pantheon today," Kasper said. He pulled a folded piece of paper from his pocket and handed it to her.

"Yes, I see." Woody squinted at the page. "It's in some other language. Danish, of course! But yes, I see it. Pantheon. If only Mrs. Johnson were here."

"Does she speak Danish?" Maia asked.

"No. I mean, maybe. What I meant was, she knows everything about the Pantheon."

"We went there two days ago," Maia explained to Sofie, who looked unimpressed.

"Maybe we could go again, this afternoon," said Woody, wriggling her toes. Laura had noticed that she always did this when she was excited or nervous. "But this morning I thought we might go to see something very special."

"The church with all the torture pictures in it?" asked Jack, bouncing on the spot. He'd been talking about this place ever since they'd arrived in Rome. It was some church up the hill behind the Colosseum, and each of its frescoes depicted one saint or another being tortured or put to death in a terrible way.

"One of my favorite movies," said a breathless Woody, ignoring Jack altogether, "is *Roman Holiday*. Have any of you seen it?"

Laura nodded. She hated to have something in common with Woody, but *Roman Holiday* was one of her favorites as well—a black-and-white romantic movie with Audrey Hepburn, about a princess on vacation in Rome. She'd watched it with her mom years ago.

Nobody else seemed to have heard of the movie.

"Are we going to watch it?" Jack asked forlornly.

"No, no!" Woody laughed, her toes squirming away in her grubby silver Birkenstocks. "I thought we'd go to see *la Bocca della Verità*—the Mouth of Truth. They go see it in the film. It's an ancient Roman face: a bearded man. We put our hands in his mouth, and if we're liars he'll bite our hands off!"

"You do know that it was a sewer cover, right?" Maia asked Woody, but the teacher was already scrutinizing her map, and announcing that it would only take them half an hour to walk there. When she pushed open the glass door, the smell of smoke wafted in from the alley.

"Great," muttered Dan, falling into step next to Laura. "First we trudge through the streets choking on volcanic ash, then we get to stick our hands down a sewer. We'll all be hospitalized by this afternoon."

Laura didn't reply. She had other things to obsess over right now. By the end of today, would her bag be jingling with miraculously multiplying star sapphires? Would she see more birds fall out of the sky, killed by stone arrows launched by statues? Really, sticking her hand into a mouth carved in a sewer cover—something thousands of tourists did every year—was the least of her worries today.

"As for *him*," Dan said in a low voice, jerking his head in Kasper's direction, "he's going to be trouble. He's no friendly ghost, if you know what I'm saying."

Laura had no idea what Dan was saying. Kasper seemed much friendlier than Sofie, and much more sensible than Woody. She checked that every zip on her backpack was firmly closed, and then followed the others out into the warm, smoky street.

There was only a short line of people waiting outside the church where the Mouth of Truth was displayed. Probably because anyone sensible, Sofie announced, was either driving as fast as they could away from Rome or hiding inside their hotel room, waiting for the volcano to blow.

"We're fine here, really," Kasper said, resting a reassuring hand on Sofie's shoulder. She gave a pleased smirk. Laura wished that Morgan were here: She couldn't exactly nudge Maia to point out something like that. Maia was busy, anyway, scribbling in her notebook, frowning with concentration. "There's no way debris from the eruption could extend this far."

Dan nudged Laura.

"Like *he* knows," he whispered to her. "Like I'm going to listen to some Danish guy lecture us about . . . you know, science."

"Um, there are lots of famous Danish scientists," said Laura. "Niels Bohr, for example. He won the Nobel Prize."

Dan gave her a long look. She bent her head, willing herself not to blush, and hoped that Kasper was right.

The streets of Rome were still pretty busy, after all; people still seemed to be going to work or going shopping. The early summer heat was just as stifling as it had been for the past few days. But the billowing gray cloud up in the sky looked ominous, the streets were sandy with ash, and the city smelled as though a forest fire were burning just beyond the hills. Every TV screen they spotted above the counters in cafés or in shop windows was tuned to twenty-four-hour coverage of the simmering volcano and its mighty ash cloud.

Here in the portico of the church, some people in the line wore hospital masks. An overreaction, Laura thought, especially since they were all protected by the vaulted ceiling, the stone a soft pink in today's hazy light. Birds—crows, pigeons, seagulls—swooped and cawed outside, kept at a distance by the railings guarding the portico and its treasures from the busy street.

Against the wall stood a big stone disk, like a Stone Age wheel, mounted on the sliced-off stub of a column. Even here at the end of the line, Laura could glimpse the huge face carved into the stone. This was the Mouth of Truth. Laura didn't need Maia to tell her it was a sewer cover: She knew that already. But she'd also read that Roman sewer covers like this often depicted the face of a woman, a river goddess. This face was a man's, and it looked like the face of a giant, ready to bite.

They edged closer, waiting their turn with all the other tourists eager to pose for a photo sticking their hands in the giant's mouth. Laura glimpsed its eyes, deep holes bored into the stone. Ridges around the face revealed themselves as wild hair and a beard. *Very sinister*, Laura thought, shivering despite the warmth of the day. There was nothing but darkness visible in its eye sockets, flared nostrils, and gaping mouth.

When their group reached the head of the line, Laura wondered if she should even bother getting her picture taken. It seemed kind of ridiculous, sticking a hand inside a stone mouth. Jack pretended that his hand had been grabbed, writhing and mugging in pretend pain. Woody shrieked with happy approval. Someone was entering into the spirit of things, Laura supposed.

Sofie held her hand on the mouth's lip with a weak, bored smile on her face.

"After you," said Dan mock-gallantly, waving Laura on. When she pulled her camera out of her backpack and handed it to him, he looked surprised. "Why not just use your phone?"

If Laura's father were here, he would have launched into his usual diatribe about picture quality: "Remember, your phone is not a real camera!" he'd shouted to Laura at the airport as she disappeared through passport control—but she wasn't going to explain all that to Dan now.

"Just take a picture, okay?" she asked him, and slung her pack over one shoulder. Woody stage-managed her position, insisting she stand behind the short velvet rope.

There was a loud squawk and a whoosh of feathers: A hooded crow was battering at the railings outside, as though it was being attacked. Laura thought of the crow yesterday, at the cemetery, fighting with the seagull. Had she *really* seen the gull being shot from the sky? Maybe she just had too active an imagination—useful when she was looking at ruins, less useful when she thought she saw things that were scientific impossibilities.

Laura rested her hand inside the stone mouth and managed something that probably looked like a grimace.

"You know, you look much prettier when you smile," Dan said, and though his voice was teasing, Laura felt her cheeks flush. *Ignore him.*

"Turn to the left," Woody ordered. "No, I mean right!"

Laura twisted as instructed, her hand sliding farther along the cool stone of the mouth, and tried to ignore the bird's wings beating against the railings; its squawk sounded like a scream.

Then something grabbed her. For a second Laura thought it was one of the boys, playing a joke, but she could see both Dan and Jack, safely on the other side of the velvet rope, and

Kasper as well, looming above them. Her whole group was there, talking or looking away. But something or someone had clutched her fingers and was dragging them into the Mouth of Truth.

Laura couldn't help it: she screamed, and her whole body jerked toward the stone face. It was almost as though she were being suctioned by a vacuum cleaner, or sucked up by a tornado. She pulled away as hard as she could, bashing her wrist against the stone lip, but she couldn't break free from this enormous, angry force trying to gobble up her hand.

"Very good," Woody was saying, clapping with pleasure. Laura screamed again, with frustration and pain. Why was everyone just standing there? Dan had crouched to take a picture of her, and other people in the line, people she didn't know, were pressing forward as well, cameras and phones in the air. They all thought she was acting.

"Help me!" she managed to cry, wincing when her hand was tugged even deeper inside the chasm. Her arm flailed, skin bashing against stone. Why was no one helping her? Why was this happening? An intense pain shot up her arm, and she heard herself growling like an animal caught in a trap, desperate to pull herself free.

Then someone's arms were around her, wrenching her away from the Mouth of Truth. Whoever it was pulled so hard that Laura's hand slipped free of the stone mouth and its terrible vortex, and they both staggered, knocking over the velvet rope. Laura collapsed to the ground, her knees too shaky to keep her up.

Maia stepped away, picking up the bag Laura had dropped. So it was Maia, of all people, who'd come to her rescue.

"Laura, I think you overdid it a little," Woody chided.

"I wasn't acting!" Laura protested, blinking back tears. She sat up, cradling her bruised red wrist, trying not to hyperventilate. "Something grabbed me. I swear!"

Everyone stood looking down at her. They all thought she was crazy, Laura could see. Only Maia looked worried.

"Didn't you hear her screaming?" Maia demanded, staring at Sofie. Laura couldn't see the German girl's face.

"We thought she was just messing around," said Jack. He seemed embarrassed by Laura's tears, though he wasn't half as embarrassed as Laura herself.

For a moment the only sound was Dan picking up the security rope and setting it in place again, and the whispers of other people waiting in line. Laura's wrist was throbbing and she felt like surrendering to her tears and out-and-out weeping. Instead she dusted herself off with her good hand and clambered to her feet, wishing that everyone would stop staring.

"Well," said Sofie, glaring in Woody's direction. "It was not such a good idea to come here, was it? We should have gone to the Pantheon, as Kasper wanted."

She beamed at Kasper, and Laura couldn't help notice Dan rolling his eyes.

CHAPTER FIVE

They stopped for lunch at a restaurant on Piazza della Madonna dei Monti, a small cobbled square with a fountain. They sat outside, under giant canvas umbrellas, half-hidden by a trellis. On another day, Laura would have stopped to take pictures of the lion heads on the fountain or the little balcony above the restaurant, with its faded wooden shutters and pots bright with flowers. But after the attack by the Mouth of Truth, she was eager to hide herself away in this cloistered café.

While Woody—with help from Sofie, who seemed to speak passable Italian—ordered mozzarella and tomato salads and pizzas to share, Laura sat silently, nursing her sore wrist. The others, she noticed, chatted among themselves, and seemed to be leaving her alone. Maybe they were being tactful, seeing that she was still very shaken and upset. Or maybe they just thought she was an idiot. Laura wasn't the kind of person who liked drawing attention to herself, in either good or bad ways, and this was definitely a bad way.

The day felt swampy with heat, and the bare skin of Laura's legs stuck to her chair. She could see a few people lolling on the fountain's broad steps, and the usual pigeons pecking about. A sleek gray cat prowled just a few feet away, padding back and forth across the cobbles. Whenever a seagull tottered too close or a sparrow flew over in search of crumbs, the cat lunged, scattering the birds.

"Looks like we've got a security guard," Dan said to Jack. He must have been watching the cat as well. It was strange, Laura thought, that a feral cat would be lurking just there. It wasn't chasing the birds, exactly; it was just keeping them away. It had to be a coincidence, surely, that it was patrolling so close to Laura: She could have reached a hand through the glossy leaves twisting up the trellis and stroked its sleek back.

Maybe Dan was right: It was guarding them. But guarding them from what? Seagulls and sparrows? She was being paranoid, Laura told herself. But what about the crow at the Mouth of Truth, who'd been beating against the railings, feathers flying, as though . . . as though it was trying to warn her? And wasn't that exactly the same kind of gray-and-black crow she'd seen circling in the sky at the Protestant Cemetery, attacking the seagull?

Another seagull swooped low across the cobbles, its wings almost brushing the ground. The gray cat arched its back and hissed, its body rigid with tension until the seagull flew away. When Laura picked up her water glass, she realized that her hand—her *good* hand—was shaking. Whatever was going on in Rome right now, she didn't understand it, and she didn't like it.

She wished, for what felt like the hundredth time, that they'd been scheduled to fly out just one day earlier. They'd have missed the eruption and its ash cloud, and she would be safely home by now, downloading photos onto the family computer, handing around little presents, and eating her mom's guacamole. Instead she was stuck in a place where creatures—and statues, and even ancient sewer covers—behaved in random, violent ways.

After lunch they drifted through a maze of narrow streets, shadowy under the ash-heavy sky. Laura walked by herself, not even stopping to take pictures. Sofie was talking and flirting with Kasper, and Jack and Dan were deep in conversation about some action movie. Kasper was steering them in the direction of the Pantheon, followed by Maia. Woody, half in a daze, was the slowest walker of all.

Maybe Woody was disoriented by the way the city looked now: washed out, as though they were walking into a black-and-white film. The familiar, warm shades of Roman buildings—earth colors like gold and orange and brown—were chalky and pale with dust; the water in every fountain they passed looked a brackish gray. Rome was still beautiful—even Laura, in her fretful state, could see that—but there was something chilly, even forbidding, about it.

In the piazza outside the Pantheon, their group clustered around the fountain and gazed at the columns of the great temple. Laura's school had already visited, but the sight was no less awe-inspiring this time around. Today, of course, the dome was dusty with ash, but the piazza was still crowded with tourists taking pictures, diners crowded around little tables, tour guides holding up sticks topped with fluorescent pennants, "gladiators" charging for photographs, a guy juggling tennis balls, and the usual wandering vendors selling novelty toys or wilted red roses.

The dolphin faces in the fountain grimaced through bared teeth or spewed seaweed-colored water into the big basin. Laura bent over the fountain's lip to wash her hands; they were dirty with semolina and pizza grease, and dusty with ash residue. Her sore wrist was definitely bruised, the red marks darkening, but the cool water against her skin seemed to help.

Next to her, Maia leaned over the water, looking with curiosity at Laura's injured wrist.

"That was weird," she said, addressing the dull coins scattered over the bottom rather than Laura.

"What was?"

"You know. That thing at the Mouth of Truth."

"I wasn't pretending," Laura said quickly, feeling her face redden. "Something really *was* pulling at me, I swear."

"I didn't think you were pretending," said Maia, as though such an idea had never crossed her mind.

"Thanks." Laura willed herself not to cry again. She should be grateful that Maia was so literal, she thought. Maia, who seemed to have no clue about being subtle and polite, had heard Laura scream, taken her at her word, and yanked her free.

She wondered if it was okay to confide in Maia about some of the strange things going on. In the absence of Morgan, Maia was the closest thing to a friend she had. And she did *know* things, Laura supposed. Perhaps Mysterious Maia would have some idea about the mysterious stone in Laura's bag.

She looked up to make sure everyone else in their group was out of earshot. Kasper and Sofie were loping toward the Pantheon itself. Jack had wandered off somewhere, probably to buy a snack or a cold drink; he was constantly hungry or thirsty.

Dan stood surveying the busy piazza as though he were the emperor of Rome, and Woody sat slumped on the fountain's low step, fanning herself with her hat.

"Okay," Laura said, "what happened at the Mouth of Truth wasn't the first weird thing that's happened to me. I mean—here."

She shook water off her hands and pulled her backpack onto the fountain's lip. The new stone was hidden in an inside pocket, along with its twin in the broken bracelet.

"I found this in my bag yesterday," Laura told Maia, cradling the star sapphire in her damp palm. "It's exactly the same as the one in my bracelet—see?"

Maia peered at it, gingerly turning the stone over and bending so close that Laura could feel the tickle of her breath.

"It's not exactly the same," Maia pointed out. "It's more green than the one you have."

"Maybe it's still dusty," Laura said. "Here."

She dipped the small stone into the cool water of the fountain, rubbing it between her thumb and forefinger to brush away any ash residue. When she lifted it out of the water, Laura held the stone aloft, hoping that it might glint the way her bracelet usually did. But there wasn't enough sun to catch its feathered golden lines.

Whoosh!

A seagull swooped down out of nowhere, its black bead of an eye terrifyingly close. Laura could almost feel it more than see it—the jolt of its beak against her hand, the prick of its talons, a spray of water in her face, the suck of air that took her breath away. Afterward Laura couldn't believe that she hadn't even cried out. It all happened so quickly. The bird swooped and pecked at her hand; the star sapphire slipped from her grip and plopped into the water.

Laura stood dazed, but Maia plunged her hand down before the seagull could circle.

"Got it," she said, and dropped the stone into Laura's unzipped bag. "I guess that bird thought you were trying to feed it."

"I guess," said Laura, rubbing her pecked hand. Now she had two injured hands, she thought. What next? A broken ankle?

Woody had hauled herself up.

"Gosh," she said, one hand gripping the fountain's rounded stone rim. "I really don't feel very well. I hope I'm not coming down with this flu."

"Maybe you should go back to the hostel," suggested Maia. "We'll be fine."

She threw a wary glance in Laura's direction, as though she was warning Laura to keep quiet about the new star sapphire

and the swooping gull. Laura had no intention of saying anything to Woody, and didn't care whether she stuck around or
staggered off back to the hostel in her silver Birkenstocks.
Their teacher had been no use at all back at the Mouth of Truth,
when Laura was getting eaten alive by some monstrous, invisible force, and she'd been no use here at the fountain, when
Laura was getting attacked by a bird. In fact, she hadn't seen a
thing.

"I'll make sure we get back to the hostel by six," Dan told
Woody in his most officious voice. He caught Laura's eye and
winked. Maybe he wasn't so stuck up after all.

Spray from the fountain splashed at Laura's face, but when
she moved away it didn't stop: rain was falling, fat drops splattering the piazza.

"Well," said Woody, squinting up at the charcoal clouds, "I
do really feel bad. If you're sure you'll be all right . . ."

She lifted her voluminous bag above her head as a makeshift
umbrella and began shuffling away, her sandals slapping against
the wet ground.

"Shelter from the storm?" Dan asked Maia and Laura, gesturing at the Pantheon. Everyone in the vicinity who wasn't
cowering under a café table umbrella or a shop awning seemed
to be heading in that direction, the giant open portico already
crowded with tourist groups.

A seagull—*the* seagull?—cawed overhead, and Laura clasped her bag to her chest. At least inside the Pantheon she'd be safe from the claws and beaks of screeching birds.

Mrs. Johnson had told them on their first visit that nowadays, the Pantheon was a place of Christian worship, so they should be respectful and keep their voices down. But apparently nobody else's teacher or tour guide had told them this. Inside, the Pantheon echoed with chatter in a dozen or more different languages. Every few minutes a droning prerecorded announcement, in Italian and then in English, asked everyone to be quiet, but it didn't interrupt the buzz of talk for more than a few seconds.

The Pantheon still looked kind of pagan to Laura's eyes, despite the church altar and the ornate tombs around its perimeter. There was something about the soaring domed ceiling that made it easy to imagine ancient Romans looking up to the sky through the always-open hole in the Pantheon's roof, the oculus.

The other day when Laura was here, the oculus was a wide blue eye, light pouring through and hitting the colored marble floor in a dazzling sunny oval. Today the oculus was weeping a funnel of silver rain. Attendants were busy roping off a large circle of floor so people wouldn't slip on a slab of wet marble. The falling rain looked otherworldly, a strange waterfall drumming onto the floor from on high, its noise a deep, sibilant note in the swirling babble of talk.

Laura wriggled through the crowd to get a closer view until she felt the black velvet rope, damp against her bare knees. For a moment she closed her eyes, trying to pretend she was alone here—something she'd done at various ruins on this trip.

With her eyes closed, Laura could blank out everyone taking cell phone pictures or passing around chewing gum or posing in sweaty, exhausted groups for photographs. She could imagine she really was back in the ancient world, surrounded by cool marble and the wispy smoke of offertory candles, in the powerful presence of enigmatic ancient gods. The roof here was built of ancient concrete, which the Romans mixed with ash, she remembered. These days everyone ran from ash; the Romans had put it to good use.

When Laura opened her eyes, she felt a little dizzy. It was hard to focus with nothing but the gray swell of rain in front of her. She looked up, blinking toward the dim light of the opening.

Something seemed to be taking shape—something descending from the oculus like a body sinking underwater. It *was* a body, she saw. The shape was a person, formed from black and gray pieces beginning to make sense as dark hair, a long-sleeved gray T-shirt, long legs in black pants . . .

It was a boy, about her age, dropping from the sky.

The boy touched the ground, still deep within the funnel of falling rain. Then he stepped out of the water and over the low-slung rope, so close that Laura could have touched him. His gray-and-black clothes made him look like a hooded crow, she thought, and when he glanced at her, his eyes were as black and darting as a bird's.

He didn't smile, this pale-faced, handsome boy, but there was something calm and knowing in his gaze. Laura felt her jaw drop, but he didn't look surprised at all. Even stranger, he didn't look wet. His clothes were as dry as hers—drier, probably, as hers were still damp from the rain in the piazza.

"Don't be afraid," he said to her in a low voice. He spoke English, but his accent didn't sound Italian, or American, or anything in particular. "I am here now, to give you this message. You are watched over. You will be protected."

Laura gazed into the boy's eyes, transfixed, unable to summon up a single word. He looked back at her, intense and serious, then strode away, heading for the huge main door of the Pantheon.

Laura looked wildly from side to side: Really, had *nobody* else standing around this upside-down fountain seen him?

But everyone around her was still pointing, talking, taking pictures, texting, just as they had been before she'd closed her eyes.

She backed away from the rope and forged an awkward path through the crowd, hurrying to follow the boy. Someone bumped into her and Laura stumbled. She didn't dare stick a hand out to break her fall; she'd done enough damage to her hands today. So she half slithered onto one knee, wincing as bone made contact with marble.

And from here, low on the ground, the crowd surging around her, Laura noticed something about the boy marching away. There on the back of his feet were tiny wings, black feathers on his heels. Something Laura had seen in books, and in paintings, and on statues. Never, ever in person.

Mercury, she tried to say, but nothing came out of her mouth but a bleat.

CHAPTER SIX

Unseen hands were lifting Laura up from the Pantheon's floor. She'd felt so surrounded by strangers there that she'd forgotten the rest of her group were all wandering around inside. The people helping her up, she realized, were Sofie and Kasper.

"Are you all right?" Sofie asked, her face tight with impatience. "You are always in trouble! Are you feeling sick now?"

Laura shook her head. She didn't think she was coming down with the flu. Maybe if she hadn't found the second star sapphire in her bag—and shown it to Maia—she might have thought all this business with birds and boys who fell from the sky was in her own head, possibly feverish hallucinations. But the star sapphire was real, so real that a marauding seagull pecked it from her hand. Also real: the bruises on her wrist from the Mouth of Truth.

And the boy with wings on his heels. He had been real, too. She knew it.

Kasper stood like a genial blond giant, holding Laura's bag with one hand and supporting her elbow with the other. He didn't look impatient at all.

"I saw something . . . weird," she managed to stammer. "And I guess I slipped. But I'm okay, really."

Dan appeared. "What's up?" he demanded, frowning in Kasper's direction, as though their new Danish friend had pushed Laura over.

"Nothing is broken," Kasper said to Laura. He turned her wrist over and gently rubbed it. His hand was very soft, she thought.

"Dude, I think you're hurting her," said Dan.

"It's fine, really," Laura said. It felt ticklish rather than soothing, but she didn't want to hurt Kasper's feelings. Plus the grim look on Sofie's face was priceless.

"Really." Dan shook his head. "You know, I was all over First Aid in Eagle Scouts, so I'm pretty sure this isn't standard medical procedure."

"Maybe we can go to a café and ask for some ice?" Kasper suggested. "It's not raining too much now."

"Maybe Laura can go back to the hostel," said Sofie. "She is hurt everywhere we go."

"We'll *all* go back," Maia said, popping up from nowhere.

"I'm all right." Laura tried not to sound snippy. "The floor must have been wet."

Kasper was still holding her wrist, and the whole situation was beginning to feel very awkward. Scowling Sofie, smiling Kasper, and embarrassed Laura, she thought. And somewhere out there, in the middle of Rome, a boy who may or may not have been the god Mercury. He'd had the winged feet, right? Laura shook her head.

"Where's Jack?" Dan demanded. "Look, I think it's better if we all stick together."

"And you saw a strange thing, you said?" Kasper prompted Laura.

"Oh—kind of weird, I guess," Laura said. Jack walked up then, smiling as though this was all a great joke. She hoped he wasn't going to blab this around school: Laura getting attacked by the Mouth of Truth, Laura collapsing in the Pantheon, Laura being a drama queen.

How odd it was, to think that just a few days ago she was listening to Morgan complain that the older kids on the trip didn't even know their names.

"Laura falls over again," Sofie said to Maia, as though they were some kind of dysfunctional team of detectives, sharing notes. "She is hurt in the hand and the leg."

"I didn't fall over *again*," said Laura, feeling her face sizzle, resisting the urge to rub her sore knee. "This is the first time I've fallen over today."

"Yes, that's right." Kasper nodded sagely. He turned to Sofie. "This morning the Mouth of Truth bit her, but she didn't fall over."

"And that bird attacked you out by the fountain," Jack added. She hadn't even realized he'd seen that, Laura thought, almost choking in a rising tide of indignation.

"You know, I think I *will* go back to the hostel," said Laura. She must not, could not, start crying. Everything seemed to be conspiring against her—the drenching rain, the people she was stuck with, birds and statues—and she wanted nothing more than to be away from it all. Preferably on the screened-in porch at home, lying on the old camp bed, reading a book.

That's where she wanted to be right now: home, where there wasn't any ash falling from the sky. The thought of returning to that shrill orange room in the hostel was dispiriting, but at least she could sob into her pillow without anyone else knowing about it.

"Not by yourself," Dan said. "I thought we'd all go get some gelato."

"I'll walk with her," offered Jack. He zipped up his sweatshirt and pulled on the hood.

"And I will walk with her also," said Sofie, with a melodramatic sigh. "To make sure she does not fall over. Again."

Laura didn't acknowledge Jack and Sofie as the three of them walked out onto the piazza. She was still fuming about what had happened inside. Everyone was ganging up on her and bossing her around and making her feel like an idiot. Make that *more* of an idiot. Maybe when they got back to the hostel she'd defy the quarantine and go seek out Morgan. She'd tell her everything, right up to what the winged-heeled boy had told her. *Don't be afraid. You are watched over. You will be protected.*

Morgan would believe her. She wouldn't make her feel bad or crazy. She would help Laura work out what Mercury, or whoever it was, meant by his "message."

Jack walked alongside her, his Converse sneakers slapping through puddles, hands deep in his pockets. Sofie fell behind, as though she didn't want to be seen with them.

"You don't have to walk me back, you know," Laura said to Jack, sounding meaner than she'd intended. Jack shrugged. A seagull flew, screeching, high above the narrow cobbled street, and Laura flinched. Maybe it wasn't such a bad thing to be walking with someone after all.

None of this was Jack's fault anyway, Laura thought. He was just a boy bouncing through the day like a puppy, one minute all manic energy, the next lackadaisical and floppy. She was sure he'd much rather be going for gelato with the others.

Her right hand stung where the seagull had pecked it and Laura rubbed at the red smear of angry skin. Back at the hostel she had some antiseptic cream, something her mother had insisted on her packing—luckily, as it turned out.

"Is that where the bird got you?" Jack asked, as though being pecked by a seagull was a completely normal thing. "I was over by the other side of the fountain, so I couldn't see everything. I was fishing some coins out of the water to give to the juggler."

"So, what did you see, exactly?" Laura asked as they crossed a street. She glanced over her shoulder. Sofie was still behind them, texting on her phone.

"You were holding up something and then the seagull zoomed down to grab it," Jack explained. "I wish I'd taken a movie of it. It looked awesome, like a circus trick."

"It wasn't a trick." Laura rubbed at the mark on her hand again.

"Was it food? The thing you were holding up."

"No," said Laura. "It was a stone. It's called a star sapphire, like the one in my bracelet. Except it's not that one—it's . . . it's . . ."

She stopped walking so abruptly that the family behind them almost ran her over with their stroller, exclaiming in Italian and frowning at her as they passed.

"What?" Jack called. Laura moved out of the street, to stand by a grand double doorway, its green paint peeling, with a brass lion's head as a door knocker. Jack joined her on the stone step. Sofie sashayed toward them, frowning.

"Look, I'll show you," said Laura. She unzipped her bag and fumbled around for the loose stone. It was dry now, every golden vein perfectly clear. Maia was right: It had a greener tinge than the one in her bracelet, which was a soft gray-blue color.

Jack held the stone gingerly between his thumb and forefinger, peering at it with one eye closed like an expert jeweler.

"Where'd you get it?" he asked.

"I have no idea," Laura told him, looking up at the narrow band of dark sky visible between the town houses lining the street. Perhaps she was paranoid, but she could hear more seagulls now, loud and menacing, squawking to one another across the rooftops. "I found it in my bag last night. I don't know how it got there."

"You must put it away," Sofie told her. "Maybe someone steals it if you wave it around."

"I don't care," said Laura. "It's not mine anyway, is it?"

"Maybe it's bringing you bad luck." Jack handed the stone back to her. "I mean, first you have that thing happen at the Mouth of Truth. Then a bird totally attacks you when you take it out of your bag. Then you fall down inside the Pantheon. Maybe you should get rid of it."

That was the most sensible thing Jack had said this whole trip. Why *was* she carrying the new stone around? Just because it was a match for the one on her bracelet? She didn't even know how it had found its way into her bag in the first place. If the seagulls wanted it so badly, let the seagulls have it.

"Should I go back to the Pantheon and throw it in the fountain?" she asked. It was just as well that Morgan wasn't here, she thought: she would go nuts if she heard Laura asking Jack, of all people, for advice.

"No," Sofie said firmly. "We must go to the hostel now."

"And you didn't find it at the Pantheon, did you?" asked Jack, and Laura shook her head. "So why not just drop it any-where? Look."

79

He pointed at the iron grating of a drain, set into the sloping gutter just inches from their feet.

Laura squeezed the stone in her fist. True, strange things had happened before she found the stone in her bag, but none of them had involved physical harm until today. Jack leaned over the grate, gazing in; Laura followed his lead.

"This is a stupid idea," Sofie was saying, but Laura ignored her. The world below the grate was as dark as the sky, and she could hear water gushing. Once she dropped the stone through the iron bars, the water would carry it away into the sewers, never to be seen again. Not even the seagulls would be able to grab it down there.

She crouched low over the grate and opened her fist. The stone dropped, bouncing on the grate and skittering into the fast-moving water below. Gone forever, she thought, taking its mystery and bad luck with it.

That night, Laura woke up more than once, wriggling in the confines of her bunk bed. The mattress was thin, the pillow was a floppy square, and she couldn't find a comfortable way to sleep. Her knee ached from smacking against the floor of the Pantheon. Her left wrist was still throbbing, and dousing the peck mark on her right hand with antiseptic lotion earlier hadn't taken away the pain.

Sofie and Maia were fast asleep, and the only sound Laura could hear, aside from their breathing, was the occasional patter of rain against the window.

The third time she woke it was almost six in the morning, according to her phone—which she held under the covers so the light didn't wake the others, wishing that it was useful for more than just checking the time. But every text she tried to send home just sat on her screen with a red exclamation mark, refusing to be sent.

No sun peeped through the crack between the orange curtains. It was going to be another day of ash-cloud gray.

Laura thought back to the night before, when the group had all congregated in the hostel's overlit lobby.

"Tomorrow we must do what my friend Jack wants," Kasper had declared, sprawled in one of the lobby's squeaking plastic chairs. "We must go the church with all the pictures of torture."

Sofie and Maia had been sitting in the corner, having some kind of whispered squabble. Dan and Jack were watching the lobby TV: The news was about the ash cloud, of course. Sofie had dragged her chair away from Maia, and sat pouting until she was distracted by Kasper taking off his sweatshirt and pulling up his T-shirt in the process, revealing a taut stretch of tanned skin.

Laura folded her pancake pillow in half and rammed it under her neck. She had to try to get some more sleep. No one else would be awake for hours, especially as they'd all stayed up late playing cards. Even Maia had joined in, after Kasper talked her into it, though she claimed to have never played a single card game in her entire life, and insisted on calling the Joker the "Wizard."

Something was tapping at the window. More rain, Laura thought, snuggling down under her comforter. Maybe even hail this time, because the sound was much sharper: *tap, tap, tap* against the glass. It wasn't hail, she decided, and it didn't really sound like the dull plop of water dripping onto the windowsill. Even when she pulled the comforter over her head, Laura could still hear it, annoying and persistent. *Tap, tap, tap. Tap, tap, tap.* She was never going to get back to sleep, not with this endless tapping.

Laura eased out of bed and crept to the window across the cold linoleum floor. Opening one of the curtains without making a noise wouldn't be easy—they tended to screech and stick on their plastic rails—so Laura lifted one and ducked her head beneath.

She was face-to-face with a hooded crow, perched outside on the windowsill and tapping the glass with its beak. Tapping what now seemed like a message, a strange Morse code. Laura gasped, transfixed by the tiny black eyes searing straight into her. Then the crow took off, a blur of gray and black rising into the dull sky.

Laura clutched at the wall with shaking hands, trying to steady her breathing. The crow was gone, but something else lay on the ledge where it had perched.

It was the star sapphire, the one she'd dropped into the drain. The one she thought she'd never see again after it was sucked into the city's murky bowels. Laura's whole body felt shivery with the shock of recognition, and with an ice-cold fear.

She stepped away from the window, the curtains falling back into place. She climbed into bed, pulled the comforter over her head, and buried her face in the pillow. There was no way she was opening that window, no way she was retrieving that star sapphire from the ledge. Maybe this whole thing was a dream—a nightmare—and when she woke, the sun would be shining, and the stone would be gone.

CHAPTER SEVEN

Only half of Laura's wish came true. When she woke again, Sofie calling to her that the shower down the hallway was free, the curtains were open. The sun was still obscured by the ash cloud, but the star sapphire was nowhere to be seen.

It *had* been a dream, Laura told herself, so relieved that she felt like laughing out loud.

The shower was as lukewarm as usual, but Laura didn't mind. Even her various injuries seemed better today. Maybe Jack was right: The strange stone had brought her bad luck. Well, she was rid of it now. Hopefully it had sunk to the bottom of the sewer's murky depths, and she would stop having nightmares about it reappearing on the window ledge, accompanied by an insistent, beady-eyed crow.

Back in her room, Maia was standing by the window combing her wet hair, dressed in crisp blue shorts and a clean white T-shirt. Laura didn't know how Maia kept coming up with clean clothes. There wasn't a clean or non-creased thing left in Laura's bag. She'd expected to be home by now, dumping everything into the big washing machine in the basement, not recycling the same denim shorts and ratty gray T-shirt or surreptitiously washing underwear in the hostel bathroom.

Laura's stomach twisted with homesickness, thinking of the cool, musty basement at home, the wicker basket balanced on the washing machine's lid. Back in Bloomington, she'd been longing for adventure, for exotic and distant sights. Everything back in their leafy suburb seemed so ordinary, so overfamiliar. Now she'd be quite happy to return to the most mundane parts of her daily life, especially if they came with clean clothes and a room to herself.

"So," said Maia, as though they'd been having a conversation, "there's a problem with the Internet now, not just cell phones. Our parents know we're okay, but we can't send any messages to them today."

"How do you know all this?" Laura asked.

"The woman at the desk told me. Mrs. Johnson was down there at some point. She left some money for us to buy lunch with. A doctor came yesterday, but everyone else is still sick."

"Why aren't *we* sick?" Laura asked, but Maia didn't reply; she just packed her comb away. "And how can the ash cloud possibly cause a problem with the Internet?"

"I don't know." Maia looked uninterested. "There are pastries and coffee in the lobby this morning, by the way. The new woman organized it."

"What happened to Agent Orange?"

"He left the city," Maia said.

"Overnight? But he was there when we went to bed!"

"That's what the woman at the desk told me."

Laura was curious to meet this new font of wisdom sitting in the hostel's lobby, the provider of actual food and actual information—unlike her orange-skinned predecessor.

The new receptionist was young, smiling and pretty, with long wavy dark hair, dressed in a white sundress that looked immaculately clean. When Laura clattered down the stairs into the lobby, the woman was drawing a walking route onto Dan's street map and pointing out the best way to get to the church.

"I was just about to grab you something to eat," Dan said over his shoulder to Laura, leaning one elbow on the reception desk. He'd turned up the collar of his blue polo shirt, which looked ridiculous, in Laura's opinion, but maybe he thought it would impress the receptionist. The counter was high enough to hide the shirt's tomato sauce stain from yesterday's lunch.

"There is no need," Kasper called. He stood by a folding table set up against one wall, holding a paper plate aloft. "I have food here."

Dan narrowed his eyes and glared down at the map, as though Kasper hadn't even spoken.

"Here," Kasper said, handing Laura two small croissants doused in powdered sugar. He flashed her his dazzling smile. He was wearing a faded gray T-shirt with the word NORSE printed on it in giant white letters, and bright-green shorts. His legs were incredibly long and tanned, silky with golden hair. In addition to his necklace, he now wore three bracelets, woven from multicolored threads, strung around his wrist.

"I like those," she told him, and he said he'd gotten them in Peru, when his family went there on a trek. Poor Dan, Laura thought; there was no way he could appear as effortlessly cool and cosmopolitan as Kasper. In his polo shirt and khaki shorts, Dan looked more like a golf caddy.

"Is Peru where you got your pendant as well?" she asked him.

"This?" Kasper fingered it. "No. This is amber. My father gave it to me. He found it when he was a child—in a bog, I think you would call it. Near the place his grandparents lived in Norway, where he went every summer. See, it's in the shape of an animal. It may be quite old. I don't know much about it."

Laura leaned forward to look more closely. Kasper was right: It did look like an animal, with short legs and an elongated head. The amber was scratched, as though someone had etched in a pattern.

"What are they saying now?" Jack called. The others were gathered around the TV, munching their pastries and trying to decipher the Italian news coverage of the volcanic eruption. They'd learned yesterday that Kasper and Sofie both understood a little Italian.

"I think," said Kasper, squinting at the TV, "it says that we will not die. But nobody can fly anywhere in southern Europe and northern Africa. And maybe it spreads farther north now. Also, strange things are happening. Maybe small earthquakes?"

"Yes," Sofie agreed. "Earthquakes, which means the Metro does not run. And there is something about the cloud now—it is very low."

"What about the Internet and cell phones not working?" Laura asked Kasper.

He shook his head. "Nobody says anything about that. Maybe it is just this hostel." His look said that anything was possible in a dump like this.

"We can look for an Internet café when we're out," Laura suggested. She was hoping to email her parents to check in.

"Church first!" protested Jack through a mouthful of food, and Kasper laughed, clapping Jack on the shoulder.

Laura sighed. She wished she could tell someone about seeing maybe-Mercury yesterday. But she didn't think any of them would believe her. She wasn't even sure if she believed herself anymore. Hopefully nothing quite so bizarre would happen today.

The sky was low, its obscuring cloud darker and angrier than the day before. The smell of smoke in the air was intense. A grittiness settled on Laura's skin and in her throat. She wondered if this was what it felt like in the Sahara desert: hot and windy, with sand stinging your eyes.

The walk to "Jack's church" was long and sticky, and the streets seemed much quieter than the day before—less traffic, fewer people, and more shops with their railings resolutely closed. Police sirens screeched in the distance. On one street Laura saw an old woman pull her laundry in—it had been flapping on a pole high in the air—and bang the wooden shutters closed.

Everywhere she looked, in fact, it seemed shutters were clattering and windows were slamming; people were carrying in signs and even potted plants. When Laura and the others passed a small supermarket, a man was staggering through the sliding doors, knees buckled with the weight of two plastic-wrapped crates of bottled water. In the same street, an aproned woman posted a sign in a bakery's window—*Tutto esaurito*—and hurried to close the door. *Everything sold out*, Laura realized: That's what the sign meant.

"Do people know something we don't?" she asked Dan, wondering if they should be buying supplies of bread and water, and hunkering down in the hostel.

"Not sure," he said in a low voice. "It feels weird today. Maybe because the cloud is so low . . ."

A seagull strutted a little way ahead; two more pecked at a split bag of trash. The sharp sound of their caws so unnerved Laura that she instinctively stepped closer to Dan, almost colliding with him.

"It's okay," he said, placing a steadying hand on her back. Laura was mortified: He thought she was snuggling up to him like a scared child! And even worse—maybe she was. "We'll be fine inside the church."

"What if it's closed?" Laura asked. They'd passed three churches already—this was Rome, after all, where there seemed to be an ornate church on every street—and they'd all appeared closed, heavy doors bolted.

"Serena called to check, and they're staying open just for us," said Dan.

"Who's Serena?"

"The new girl at the hostel."

"But I thought the phone there wasn't working." Laura was puzzled. "Or the Internet. And cell phones aren't working anywhere, are they?"

Dan shrugged.

"She told me she'd called them and everything was fine. We just have to knock on the door, and someone will be there to let us in."

"Wow," said Laura, not sure whether to believe him. Serena may have managed to conjure up some breakfast for them, but could she make a closed church open?

"I guess she knows the priest or something," Dan said, but Laura was distracted. A hooded crow was swooping from one side of the street to the other, lacing its way up the Via Cavour ahead of them. For the first time today, Laura felt shivery, cold in her flimsy T-shirt and shorts. The crow tapping on her window last night—that was just a dream, she told herself.

But the seagull Laura had seen shot from the sky: that wasn't a dream. The wing-heeled boy she saw swirling down the Pantheon's funnel of rain: that wasn't a dream. But was it *real*, exactly? Ever since the morning she'd seen—or thought she'd seen—the stone snake at the Trevi Fountain writhing, the city had become a surreal place for Laura, a disturbing, disorienting wonderland.

"He really thinks he's all that," Dan was saying, and Laura didn't understand: Had he seen the Mercury boy as well? It took her a moment to realize that he was nodding in Kasper's direction, the expression on his face almost comically sour. Kasper was walking ahead, with Sofie and Jack, and they were laughing at something he'd just said.

"He's really getting on my nerves," Dan muttered. "Can't he, like, get a train back to Denmark? I mean, I swear to you he's at least twenty years old. No way is he still in high school."

"Maybe he's just tall," said Laura, because she couldn't think of anything else to say. If this were really a dream, surely Dan wouldn't be complaining about Kasper? She wouldn't be able to feel ash flakes brushing her face, or taste them when she spoke.

They turned up Caelian Hill, following the road that led up from the vast stone skeleton of the Colosseum into a quiet neighborhood of big houses and gardens. Laura's footsteps felt heavy, as though she were slogging through water.

The church that Jack was obsessed with was called Santo Stefano Rotondo, and as soon as they reached it, Laura understood the *Rotondo* part. Within the jumble of apricot-colored shapes that made up the church lay the oldest part of the building, round like a temple. The church was surrounded by towering pines and what might usually be a pretty garden. Today the flower beds were cobwebbed with ash, litter blowing around like tumbleweeds. Nobody else was in sight.

Laura passed a tree and did a double take. A long line of hooded crows were perched on a low-lying branch, squawking in agitation. She stood watching them, her bag clutched to her heart, expecting them to fly away at any moment. But the birds just fidgeted and kept squawking, as though they were quarreling.

"Come on," said Kasper, putting an arm around her shoulder, steering her toward the entrance.

Dan knocked on the heavy doors, which were locked: Jack had tried them, anxious to get in. They stood around waiting, nobody speaking. Maia leaned against a low wall to study her guidebook, while Sofie shook the ashy residue out of her hair. Kasper scuffed around in the gravel as though he were tapping around an imaginary soccer ball. The look on his face suggested he didn't think they had much chance of admission.

Laura didn't feel very positive about it, either. Even the mighty Colosseum was closed today. Here on this quiet hill, Rome looked and felt like a ghost town.

The silence was broken by the sound of a bolt clanking, and one of the big doors shuddered open. A dark-haired man in overalls—not a priest, but some kind of caretaker, Laura thought—blocked the doorway, frowning at them.

"Buon giorno," said Dan in slow, overloud Italian. *"Sono studenti . . ."*

"Sí, sí," said the man, beckoning them in with an impatient flick of the hand, as though he didn't need to hear anymore. He held the door open for them as they all filed in, and then closed it again, presumably to deter any other unwanted visitors.

The caretaker scuttled away like an insect, leaving them alone in the empty, silent church.

"See?" Jack said proudly. "I told you it would be awesome."

Really, Laura thought, it was unlike any of the other churches they'd visited. The space felt like a temple, with giant ivory columns around a circular altar.

There were no stained-glass windows, or statues looming over votive candles, or painted ceilings showing cherubs cavorting. The windows were tiny, like portholes; and the floors and walls were the same chalky bone color as the columns. It was such a calm place, silent apart from their footsteps echoing on the marble floor.

The only decoration was around the lower wall: faded

frescoes painted in the sixteenth century, according to Maia. The frescoes, Laura knew, were what Jack had wanted to see. Each panel depicted a scene of torture—some early Christian martyr meeting a horrible fate. Jack had warned them, his voice crackling with glee, that the frescoes would be gory, but Laura hadn't realized quite how brutal they'd be. She'd seen paintings of saints meeting their deaths before—Saint Catherine against a wheel, or Saint Sebastian pierced with arrows— but these were always so stylized that the saint in question looked serene and otherworldly, rather than suffering agonizing pain.

These frescoes—"thirty-four," Maia reported, turning the page in her book—were another thing altogether. One panel showed remarkably calm Christians lining up on the left to get their hands sliced off, and on the right to have their tongues torn out. In one fresco, a person was gored by a bull; others waited to get torn to pieces in the ring by a lion. A woman was boiled alive in a cauldron, only her head visible above the seething water. In one panel, a whole ship of martyrs was set alight, and others lay strewn bleeding in the foreground, crushed to death by huge boulders. Others were flung from windows or were in the process of being buried alive.

Laura wandered past scene after nasty scene of torture, flinching at each new atrocity. Maia and the boys were on the far side of the church, Jack taking pictures while Maia and Dan and Kasper leaned over a hole in the ground that revealed, according to the snatches of their jabber that Laura could make out, chunks of the church's fifth-century floor.

Something about the goriness of the scenes encircling them made Laura reluctant to stand alone. She walked up to Sofie, who was examining another fresco closely, her nose practically pressed to the plaster. In the picture, a man in a golden tunic ran a sword through a woman's neck, while she stood clasping her hands together in prayer. Bodies hung in various tortured states from trees in the background, and another woman sat half buried in a pit of quicksand, snakes slithering all around her.

"Which saints are these?" Laura asked Sofie, peering at the Latin plaque. Before she could try to make sense of it, Laura was distracted by one of the snakes on the wall.

It was moving.

Really and truly, she told herself, it was moving: She could see it rolling out of the water and onto the faded painted grass near the bottom of the picture. Laura blinked and stared, and blinked again. All the fresco's snakes were moving now, slithering onto rocks and over painted grass—straight toward Sofie's face.

CHAPTER EIGHT

Laura reached for Sofie and grabbed her by the elbow. The other girl gasped, maybe because Laura had grabbed her so roughly, but—more likely—because the man in the golden tunic had dropped his sword.

He stared straight at them, his face still a red-cheeked, emotionless blank. Sofie's gasp meant she must be able to see it, too, and in that instant Laura felt a rush of relief and exhilaration: This was really happening! It wasn't just her imagination!

Sofie let out a strangled scream and jerked toward the fresco; Laura couldn't keep a grip on her elbow. The man in the tunic—this painted man, this unreal thing—had placed his hands around Sofie's neck.

He was pulling her headfirst into the fresco.

Laura could see a two-part Sofie now—her torso and legs and feet still in the church, and her head and shoulders in the grip of the painted man, already part of the fresco's grisly scene. Sofie's face was twisted sideways; she looked absolutely terrified. But her screams must have been swallowed by the fresco, because she wasn't making a sound.

Laura threw her bag on the floor and grabbed Sofie's waist. She wrapped her arms as tightly as she could around the girl's narrow frame and pulled. But her first tug seemed to make no impact at all. Just like yesterday at the Mouth of Truth, the unknown force sucking Sofie into the wall was too powerful. Laura dropped down onto her haunches and tugged again, bracing herself for Sofie's weight when she toppled free of the fresco.

But Sofie didn't topple. The man in the fresco was too strong. All Laura could see of him now was one brutish leg, calf muscle bulging, snakes crawling over his sandals. Their tongues flickered at Sofie's pale arms.

"Help!" Laura heard herself squeak. She tugged again, groaning with the exertion, but Sofie seemed to be slipping farther into the picture, the painted snakes leaping to greet her.

Someone was next to Laura now; another pair of arms wrapped themselves around Sofie. Laura glanced up and saw Maia's prim dark head, bent over Sofie's back.

"One, two, three," Maia chanted. "Pull!"

They pulled together, grunting with the effort of it, and for a moment Laura thought they'd succeeded: Sofie took a small step back. But the man in the fresco wasn't beaten yet. Sofie lurched forward again, and Laura felt her grip slipping.

"I can't hold her," she said through gritted teeth.

"Hey!" Maia shouted. "Help us!"

Thank goodness for Maia, Laura thought, readjusting her sweaty grip and hanging on grimly. Yesterday she was the one who saved Laura, and today she was springing to the rescue again. Where were all those stupid boys when they needed them?

Laura rested her head on Sofie's lower back, which was warm with perspiration. She yanked again as hard as she could, but all her efforts seemed pathetic; even with Maia's help, Sofie still seemed stuck fast to the wall, jerking out of their grasp. Laura lost her footing and almost fell, her legs aching from crouching.

The only thing Laura could hear clearly was the thud of

her own heart, but she sensed the pounding of footsteps and felt a change in the air, a whir of another person moving close by. A glimpse of bright green, inches away from her face: Kasper.

In that instant there was a hard thwack and a high-pitched squeal; Sofie staggered backward, with Maia and Laura still attached. Laura fell to the floor, the marble cool and hard beneath her back, Sofie sprawled across her legs. Maia sat slumped nearby, her shoulders rising and falling as she tried to catch her breath.

High above them, Kasper towered like some kind of Norse god, grimacing and rubbing the knuckles of his right hand.

"You punched it?" Laura asked him. He nodded, but he looked bemused, as though what had happened made no sense at all. Which, of course, it didn't.

When she got her breath back, Laura propped herself up on her elbows and stared up at the fresco. The man in the golden tunic was back in position, his sword poised at the neck of the saint, but the snakes were still slithering their way back into the pond. Then they froze—just painted things again, not real creatures.

Dan and Jack raced over, and Dan hauled Laura to her feet.

"You okay?" he asked her, and she nodded. He shot a disbe-lieving look at Kasper. "Did you seriously punch the wall?"

"I was punching the man," Kasper said in an even tone, as though it was an everyday occurrence for him to punch people and save the day, even if that person was a painted figure in a Renaissance fresco. He'd stopped rubbing his knuckles now, and everyone could see his raw red skin.

"The man?" Jack asked.

"The one who grabbed Sofie," Kasper replied.

Dan let out a huff. "Why do you girls keep making up crazy stuff?"

Laura felt a surge of anger that took over the usual shyness she felt around Dan. "We're not *making anything up*," she hissed. She knew what she'd seen; she glanced at Sofie, Maia, and Kasper. They knew, too. Sofie was sniffing loudly and rubbing her neck with trembling hands. She looked pale and shaken when Kasper helped her to her feet.

"Trust me," Dan muttered to Laura. "She saw your stunt yesterday at the Mouth of Truth and decided to copy it."

Laura glared at Dan.

"Please shut up," she said. A day ago, she'd never have guessed she could snap like that at Dan Sinclair. But a lot had changed. Dan looked offended and backed away. *Whatever,* Laura thought.

"Did you see the snakes moving?" she asked Maia. "In the fresco, I mean?"

"No," Maia replied. "I couldn't see anything but Sofie's back."

"I don't understand." Jack was talking, pacing up and down in front of the now-still fresco. "What happened, exactly?"

Sofie turned her face to answer him, her eyes blazing. "I was looking at that," she explained, jabbing an accusing finger at the fresco. "Then something grabbed me, around the neck."

She stroked her throat, and Laura could quite clearly see the red marks, large and angry. The man in the tunic had tried to throttle her. Not even skeptical Dan could doubt the evidence.

"Something *where*?" Dan asked.

"Not something," Sofie corrected herself. "Someone. That man!"

"The caretaker guy? He came up behind you?"

"No," Sofie snapped. "The man in the picture!"

Jack and Dan exchanged a look.

"She's not lying," Laura barked at them. "She was being . . . she was being dragged into the picture!"

"It certainly looked that way," Maia said, who seemed completely unflustered by everything going on. "He grabbed her and was pulling her in. And it was taking us a while to try pulling her out."

Maia was acting as though they had everything under control, but Laura didn't think that was true at all.

"And then, luckily, *Kasper* arrived," Laura said, knowing how much any talk of Kasper's intervention would irritate Dan. "And he actually *did* something."

"He punched the wall," Dan said dryly.

"But not the caretaker dude?" Jack was persisting with this theory.

"That man . . . there." Kasper pointed at the fresco, but in a halfhearted way. He didn't look very sure about what he'd done, or to whom. "I think, anyway."

"So you're saying this guy, who's made out of paint and plaster and other inanimate . . . I don't know, *stuff*," said Dan, hands on hips, "attacked Sofie? And then you punched him and he let her go."

"That's exactly what happened," said Laura, enraged by Dan's attitude. "Are you calling us *all* liars?"

"I'm not saying you're lying. Seeing things, maybe."

"Laura saw snakes moving," Maia added, unhelpfully. "In the fresco."

"Snakes moving? In the fresco?" Dan smirked again. "Maybe she's inhaled too much ash."

"How dare you?" Laura felt the burn of her cheeks. It was

bad enough that all these odd and violent things were happening, but it was even worse to feel disbelieved. Again, Dan fell silent. Laura got the sense that maybe he was starting to feel bad. Well, good.

"What was it like?" Kasper asked Sofie. "Inside the wall?"

Sofie took a deep breath before answering. "The wall was not there," she said, clearly struggling to steady her voice. She seemed mad rather than scared. "I could not feel it. There was just pulling at my head, and then pulling at my legs."

"Like I said—that was us," Maia told the boys. "Laura and me. We were trying to pull you back."

"Thank you," Sofie said quietly, looking down at the floor. "In front of me there was just . . ."

"Air?" suggested Kasper, and Sofie nodded.

"Genau," she said. Laura had heard her say that word a few times, and she wasn't sure what it meant—something like "for real" or "sure," she thought.

"When I punched the man," Kasper said, and Laura couldn't resist looking pointedly at Dan to see the sour expression on his face, "it felt like a man for just one moment. And then it felt like the wall!"

He laughed, and Sofie smiled at him. As though he'd done all the work of saving her, Laura thought, annoyed.

"But think about it," Dan said, trying to be in charge again. "Yesterday something tries to suck Laura's hand into the Mouth of Truth. I mean, at the time, we all thought she was messing around, right?"

Nobody said anything, and Laura was grateful. She could feel her face getting red again.

"Then today, something tries to grab Sofie. In both cases, it's like some inanimate object—a piece of stone yesterday, and today a wall. Why is this happening? It can't have anything to do with the ash cloud."

"And Laura got rid of the bad-luck charm," said Jack.

Everyone turned to look at him.

"What are you talking about?" Dan asked.

"You know. Laura had this charm, and we thought it might be bringing her bad luck. It just appeared in her bag—you tell them!" He gestured at Laura.

"He means the star sapphire," Maia said, her voice and expression neutral.

"It was a sapphire?" Kasper asked.

"It's just a stone," said Laura, embarrassed by the attention. "Nothing super-valuable. I have one in my bracelet I can show you. Anyway, this other stone appeared in my bag, and I don't know how it got there."

As soon as she said this, a memory flickered: the Protestant Cemetery, the crow circling in the sky. Something in the crow's beak falling, falling, falling . . . Could it have been the stone, falling into Laura's bag?

"So I told Laura," Jack continued, impatient with her abrupt silence, "that she should just get rid of it. And we did, walking back from the Pantheon. Dropped it into a drain. Washed it away."

"I told them no, but they would not listen," said Sofie.

"A sapphire?" Kasper asked again.

Laura unzipped her bag and felt in the inner pocket for her broken bracelet.

"Here," she said, holding it up to him. "This is what it looks like. Though the other stone was more green than this one."

Kasper dangled the bracelet's broken chain, and the star sapphire swung in the air. In the dim light of the church it looked gray and dull, like a pebble picked up at the beach and never quite as shiny or precious once you got it home.

"I remember you wearing that," Dan said to Laura, his voice low. "You wear it every day. When did it break?"

"The other day . . ." Laura began, but stopped midsentence. Maia was muttering something to Sofie, and Sofie scrabbled around in her own bag, a small messenger-style bag she always wore across her body. She held something up, pinched between her thumb and forefinger, for them all to see.

It was the other star sapphire, the one with the grayish-green tinge, the one that Laura and Jack had dropped down the drain yesterday, never expecting to see it again.

CHAPTER NINE

Sofie had found the star sapphire early that morning, she told them, on the windowsill of their room in the hostel. She'd opened the window and picked it up, she said, because it was pretty.

Laura's heart was pounding. It hadn't been a dream after all; last night there really *had* been a hooded crow out there on the ledge, tapping on the window, leaving her a gift she didn't want. Jack was right to call it a bad-luck charm. Look what had just happened to Sofie!

"That's the same one," Maia declared, though she didn't bother to go over to get a closer look, as the others were doing. Laura pulled her bracelet out and lay it on the ground, next to Sofie's stone.

"They are like a pair of eyes," Kasper observed. "The color a little different, maybe, but still a pair."

"We threw it down a drain!" Jack was still protesting. "I saw it fall into the water!"

"And now it is back," said Kasper, staring down at the two stones. "When Laura has it, the Mouth of Truth grabs her. When Sofie has it, the painted wall grabs her. And if we throw it away, it comes back?"

This was more of a question than a statement. He looked at Laura, as though she could give him an answer.

"It seems that way," she said.

"Or," said Dan, "we could just leave it here and go. If any of us see it again, we ignore it. If it turns up on our windowsill, we ignore it. If it turns up in someone's bag, we throw it away. Agreed?"

Maia shook her head.

"I don't think it's as simple as that," she told Dan, and Laura's stomach sank.

Kasper handed her bracelet back and she clutched it, comforted by the ridges of the chain digging into her clammy palms.

"We're not in our usual world here," Maia said slowly, and Jack laughed.

"You can say that again," he said.

"Yeah, we're in Rome," Dan said, impatient. "So?"

"It's an ancient place," said Maia, not reacting to his tone. "Ancient forces are at work. Ancient powers. Something that can make a stone mouth bite, or a painted man attack."

Or a statue shoot a bird, Laura thought. *Or a boy in gray and black, the color of the Roman crows, step from the rain with feathers sprouting from his heels . . .*

"This all sounds like superstition to me," Dan said, wafting a dismissive hand in Maia's direction.

"You're the one who said we should throw away the bad-luck stone," Kasper pointed out. "Isn't that superstition as well?"

"Genau," said Laura under her breath, and Sofie smiled at her.

"But maybe Dan is right," said Kasper. "Perhaps we should throw away *both* stones. The one that Sofie found and the one that Laura has on the broken chain."

Laura felt a pang of horror. "No!" she cried, startling everyone—including herself—with the vehemence of her reaction. "My grandfather gave me that! I've had it for years, and I'm not just throwing it away."

"Do you know where he got it?" Maia asked, her voice almost sharp.

"No," Laura admitted. "It was during World War II, when he was a teenager. He was in lots of different places. My mother thought that maybe he got it in North Africa. But he was also stationed in Rome, and my grandmother thinks he might have found it here."

"I have an idea," said Kasper. He took a step closer to Laura and she instinctively backed away; she didn't want him grabbing the bracelet and throwing it away. "Let's go and find a place to use a computer. We can email our families, and Laura can maybe get some more information, and we can read news in our own languages, and . . ."

"Yes," said Dan. It was the first time Laura had heard him agree with anything Kasper had suggested.

"What if we're locked in?" Jack asked, and panic rippled through their little group; Laura stuffed the bracelet into her bag, and they all hurried toward the double doors, as if running there could change anything.

Kasper reached the door first, and twisted the handle. The heavy bolt was open—they could see that—but the door didn't move.

"No!" said Sofie. "We must get out!"

Kasper jiggled the handle again and shoved the door with his shoulder.

"Let me," said Dan, pushing his way into position. Kasper stood back, with just the hint of a sidelong glance in Dan's direction. Dan ignored the door that Kasper had tried, and twisted the other door's handle. With a wheezy creak, it pushed open.

"We came in on the right," Dan said, his voice neutral but his face twitching with a smile. Laura fought the urge to roll her eyes.

"Thank you, at last," said Sofie, the first through the open door. When Kasper waved her ahead, Laura stepped past Dan, pointedly not thanking him: All he'd done was open a door, and she was still annoyed about his reaction to everything that had happened.

It was a relief to be outside, though, in what passed for fresh air on a day like this, in the ashy haze, the humidity settling around her bare legs like a heavy skirt.

Crows still lined the low-hanging branch of the tree outside. *Lying in wait*, Laura thought, glancing away. Was one of these birds her nighttime messenger, dropping the star sapphire on the windowsill and tapping incessantly until she got out of bed?

Laura turned her back on the hooded crows. She could hear the crunch of the gravel under her shoes, the sound of a distant car alarm, the faint hum of traffic. She heard the birds taking off in a flurry, their hysterical squawking overhead now. *Leave us alone!* she wanted to scream at them.

"Come on, Laura!" Kasper called. She hurried to join the others, who were already setting off down the hill.

"No child left behind," said Dan sarcastically. She brushed past him, scampering to catch up with Maia. If Dan couldn't be civil, she was going to keep as far away from him as possible. Like the crows soaring overhead, he was just another thing to be ignored.

They trudged in what felt like circles in the streets near the Colosseum and Forum, sweaty and ashy, with no Internet café in sight. Kasper insisted they make their way to one he half remembered, on a busy road near—or so he thought—Piazza Navona. No buses appeared to be running anymore, and when Dan tried to flag a taxi at the wildly chaotic traffic circle that was the Piazza Venezia, every cab zoomed past, either full or apparently uninterested in picking up a gaggle of disheveled teenagers.

"Everyone's getting out of Dodge," Jack observed, sounding less enthused with every pointless half hour spent wandering. "Maybe we should just go back to the hostel."

A squabble followed about who wanted to go back and who

wanted to keep looking, and who was in charge. Kasper finally held up a hand.

"We are all tired, I think," he said. "But in another ten minutes we will be there, I promise you. Then we can all send an email home, to our families. We can tell them we're okay."

Kasper was right, Laura thought, when—almost exactly ten minutes later—Jack spotted an OPEN sign and shouted back to let them all know.

The place Kasper remembered wasn't a café: It was a just a place to access the Internet, a small street-level office with big glass windows, white walls, and fluorescent lights. Laura could see five computer terminals—no, six—and she practically ran to the counter to hand over money. The guy sitting there, flicking through a magazine, seemed half asleep and almost annoyed to see customers. He muttered something in Italian and waved in the direction of the window.

"He is about to close," Sofie translated, "because of . . ."

She waved a hand at the window as well, and they all knew what she meant: the volcano, the ash cloud, everything. Laura tensed when the guy starting speaking again, burbling and pointing, tapping at the laminated price list hanging on the wall.

"We can have five minutes only," said Sofie. "And only four computers are working."

"I don't need to check email," Maia said. "My parents are in Russia. They never get in touch with me when they go away."

"I thought they were in Italy at a conference?" Laura asked.

"Yes," Maia said quickly. "They were, in the north. But by now they're back in Russia."

"And won't they be worried?" Laura asked her, thinking about her own parents. Her father would be glued to twenty-four-hour news right now, she knew, obsessing over every detail of the eruption.

"No." Maia sounded unconcerned.

"I'll use someone's computer whenever they're finished," said Kasper, his blue eyes intent on Laura. "Really—you all go, quickly. Maia and I will pay the man."

Not even Dan stopped to argue this one. Laura flung herself into the nearest seat, drumming her fingers on the desk while she waited for the right screen to open.

Beyond the smudged windows, ash swirled like dirty snow, covering the road with dusty flakes. People rushed by, brandishing umbrellas or holding their bags above their heads. Why was the guy at the desk taking so long?

The electronic stopwatch clicked into life on her screen. Laura couldn't find Skype, but her email loaded right away, thank goodness.

Mom and Dad, she typed. *Just letting you know that I'm fine here in Rome—lots of kids are sick with the flu, but I'm not. Ash is falling like snow. Weird. But we're safe. Waiting to hear when we can fly home. Can't get online at hostel, FYI. Love, Laura*

She sent it right away, in case the desk jockey decided to throw them out early, then raced through the emails her parents had sent her over the past few days—they were worried, they were concerned, they'd tried calling the American embassy, the school knew nothing, all flights were canceled, the airline was being vague, the hostel wasn't answering its phone . . . and so on.

Laura started typing a new email.

Mom, she wrote. *Everything still fine! Don't worry. I know this is a weird question right now, but do you know if Grandpa found my star sapphire here in Rome? I may be able to check email again tomorrow. XO L.*

Laura pressed SEND, and glanced around. Dan was typing a million miles a minute. Sofie was finished and was waving Kasper over, so he could send an email on her computer.

"Maia!" Laura called, leaning back in her chair. "Do you want to use this one to email your parents? I've sent two to mine."

Maia, standing at the counter interrogating—in what language, Laura wasn't sure—the guy sitting there, shook her head. So she wasn't lying: Maia really was blasé about getting in touch with her family. She *was* weird—or maybe her whole family was like this.

A new email pinged into Laura's in-box. Her mother! She probably had her laptop perched on the kitchen counter, anxiously checking for news.

Honey—so happy and relieved to hear from you. We are terribly worried. The boys told Dad he should fly to Paris, rent a car, and drive down to rescue you! They've offered all their camp money to help pay!!! But apparently it's chaos everywhere in Europe right now. I hope this only goes on a couple more days. We miss you so much.

Not sure about your bracelet—yes, Grandpa was stationed in Rome. He told a story once about driving around in a jeep near a fountain with bees, but—

The window disappeared, swallowing her mom's email, and Laura's screen turned black.

CHAPTER TEN

No!" Laura howled, swiveling to plead with the guy behind the counter. He was standing up now, dropping euro coins into plastic bags and ignoring everyone's protests and pleas. "Can I just have a few minutes more? I was halfway through reading an email from my mom."

The guy barked something in Italian at Kasper, who shot them all an apologetic glance, shaking his head.

"We could come back tomorrow morning," Jack suggested, but Kasper shook his head at this as well and explained: The man behind the counter was closing up shop for the foreseeable future; he was leaving Rome right away, and suggested that they do the same thing.

"Any luck?" Maia's unsmiling face loomed over Laura's computer terminal.

"No—well, maybe," Laura told her. "My mother doesn't know for sure but she remembers my grandfather talking about driving in a jeep past a fountain with bees on it or in it or buzzing nearby—I'm not sure."

"We saw that last week, I think." Kasper walked over and sat on the desk next to Laura, his handsome face tense with concentration. "My school group, I mean."

"Is your school group like some Viking raiding party?" Dan called over, but Laura ignored him and Kasper seemed unfazed.

"Go on," she told Kasper.

"Our first day in Rome," he said slowly, "when we went to the Palazzo Barberini. Bees were the symbol of that family. So the fountain near their house was carved . . ."

"With bees?" Laura felt a thrill of excitement. She leafed through her guidebook while the guy behind the counter shouted at them in Italian. He wanted them out, Laura knew, but too bad. At least inside here they weren't getting faces full of ash.

"Barberini, Barberini—here it is," she said. "The Fontana delle Api. Fountain of the Bees. Late seventeenth century, at the end of Via Veneto."

"Let's go!" shouted Jack, who'd regained his high spirits. Maia frowned at him.

"Why?" she asked. "It's not relevant, necessarily."

Everyone looked at her.

"I mean," she continued, gazing around them like a teacher surveying a particularly stupid class, "all its existence confirms is that Laura's grandfather was in Rome at some point during the war and happened to see the Fountain of the Bees while he was driving around. It doesn't mean that he got the star sapphire there."

"No," Laura said, deflated. Maia was right.

"The bee fountain sounds pretty cool," mumbled Jack, his face red.

"There's nothing to link the star sapphires with the bee fountain at all, is there?" Maia looked at Kasper. He shrugged.

"It was just a small fountain," he said. "With a big shell, and little bees."

"Do you remember seeing anything like my star sapphire?" Laura asked him. "Maybe some kind of decoration around the edge of the fountain?"

"Let me see the stones again," Kasper said.

Laura hauled her bag onto her knees and felt around for the two stones—one, the original, with its broken chain dangling, as well as the interloper, as she thought of it: the sewer sapphire, the windowsill sapphire. She placed the two stones on the table, one at a time, and Kasper scrutinized them, one hand stroking his chin in an almost comical way, like some wise old philosopher. The stones were the exact same shape and size, both shot through with a feathery golden constellation. But Laura's stone was definitely a bluish-gray, and the other stone was a little more green. The difference was very subtle; you had to stare at them really hard to see the difference.

"They kind of do look like eyes," Dan observed. "Like Laura's eyes."

Laura felt herself become self-conscious. What did Dan mean by that?

"I think so," Kasper agreed. "See? At first when I met you, I thought you have gray eyes, but when I looked again, I see that the left one is a little blue and the right one is a little green. Like these stones."

Now Laura felt even more self-conscious, shifting in her chair.

" 'Mutant Girl,' " said Jack, fake-punching Laura's arm. "Right? That's why we all called you that."

"I didn't know you *all* called me that," Laura said, irritation and embarrassment coursing through her.

"Not all of us," Dan said quickly—too quickly, Laura thought, revealing his guilt. "Just . . . some stupid people." He looked at Laura intently before dropping his eyes.

"Can we stay focused here, please?" Maia tapped the table with a fingernail. "Kasper, do you remember seeing either of these stones at the Fountain of the Bees?"

"No," he said, sounding certain. "And anyway, the fountain is only a few hundred years old, not from ancient times. Didn't you say, Maia, that this . . . this strangeness may have something to do with Rome being an ancient city?"

Laura thought of the Mercury boy she'd seen at the Pantheon. Could it really be *Mercury*? How was something like that possible?

Nobody even believed in those old gods anymore. Long ago, they'd meant something, Laura knew; there had been gods in Rome for everything, like doors and dogs and rainbows. But they were just figures of legend and myth, storybook archetypes like witches and goblins in fairy tales.

If Laura told anyone now about what she thought she'd seen in the Pantheon, they'd laugh at her.

"It's just a thought," Maia admitted. "I can't . . . I can't say for certain."

They all fell silent. If Maia didn't have any ideas, Laura thought, then they really *were* stuck.

"Ragazzi!" The counter guy was shouting now, gesticulating at them and the door. *"Andatevene, subito!"*

"He wants us to go," Sofie explained, though it didn't need explaining.

"Come on," Laura said, and everyone scraped back their chairs and picked up their bags. They were all reluctant to leave, she sensed, as unsure as she was what they were going to do next. Find this fountain of bees, that may or may not be a clue to what was going on? Go back to the orange hostel? Wander the streets, bracing themselves for another weird encounter with an aggressive fresco?

Laura scooped up the two star sapphires, jangling them in her hand like marbles. Outside, something like thunder rumbled, except it sounded low in the ground rather than high in the sky.

"No!" Sofie gasped, and Laura grabbed the back of her chair with her free hand. It felt as though a train were passing underneath the floor of the shop, rattling through a submerged tunnel. *But the subway isn't running*, Laura thought, just as the chair under her hand began rolling away.

They all looked at one another—wild, questioning looks—while the banks of fluorescent lights started swinging. The guy from behind the counter, exclaiming in staccato Italian, ran to the door, stumbling when a chair toppled into his path. He wrenched open the door and ran into the street.

"Earthquake!" Kasper said, and hurled himself at Jack, who looked as though he might be about to follow the Italian guy out the door. "Get down!"

The desks were moving, shaking back and forth. Laura threw her bag onto the floor and dropped to her knees. Everything was shaking and rattling. Heart racing, Laura crawled under her desk, grimacing with the pain in one knee from her fall in the Pantheon.

All she remembered from some long-ago earthquake drill at school was to get down, take cover. But why was Dan still standing there, frozen to the spot?

She reached out a hand and pulled his leg, tugging him down. When he dropped to his knees, Laura pulled at him again, almost dragging him under the desk.

"You don't need to save me, okay?" he hissed.

"Well, don't stand around like an idiot," she hissed back, and they both recoiled as something heavy crashed onto the ground nearby and splintered—a computer, maybe, or one of the swinging light fixtures. The floor was still wobbling; Laura clung to a desk leg. She could taste plaster dust and hear nothing but a low growl, interrupted by crashes and something like glass breaking. She and Dan were huddled close together, their heads almost touching; his breath was soft and cool against her face. Laura had to resist the urge to cling to him.

"Laura," Dan whispered, bracing himself against another of the desk's legs. "Put the stones away."

"What?"

"The stones. Put them in your bag."

"Hold the desk leg—this one!" Laura waited while Dan leaned across her. The chair she'd been sitting on to send emails smacked onto the ground. Blindly she groped for her backpack and opened the zipper with her free hand.

As soon as the stones slithered out of her hand and dropped into her bag, the room stopped shaking. Laura realized she was out of breath and that her hands were trembling. Dan was still gripping the desk's legs, intent on keeping it upright, one of his elbows wedged in her rib cage. Outside sirens pealed and car alarms were going off, the sounds discordant and incessant. Even from her restricted view, Laura could see ash dusting the floor. *A window must be open*, she thought, and then: *A window must be broken.*

"Everyone okay?" That was Kasper's voice, and Laura was relieved to hear the chorus of *yeses*. Gingerly Dan released his grip on the desk legs and shimmied out from under the desk.

"Be careful," he told Laura over his shoulder. "There's glass everywhere."

When she emerged, banging her head on the desk on her way out, the room made no sense anymore. It was a mess of dust and puffs of whirling ash, gloomier than before because the lights had gone out. Two of the windows were broken and all but one of the computers had toppled over.

The others were clambering to their feet, pointlessly dusting themselves off as more flecks of ash swirled in through the broken windows. They all looked at one another, their faces something between shocked and relieved, Laura thought. But they weren't all okay, not really. Kasper's arm was cut and bleeding, and Jack was holding his leg.

"Something fell on it," Jack explained, wincing.

"Hostel," said Maia, and nobody argued. They all picked their way toward the door, Dan clearing a path by pushing chairs out of the way. When Laura passed by Kasper, she noticed the blood on his arm again.

"Are you okay?" she asked. He shrugged, as though it was no big deal. But his cut looked bad to Laura, so she pulled her pashmina out of her bag, taking care not to dislodge the star sapphires, and wrapped it around Kasper's wound.

"It needs to be tighter," said Maia, climbing over the debris like a confident mountain goat while Dan stomped and stumbled his way around. When he started sliding on broken glass, Laura took his arm, steadying him. His hand grasped for hers, and they walked to the door together just like that, hand in hand, until it felt awkward and Laura pulled free.

Maia had finished rewrapping Kasper's arm, but there wasn't much they could do for Jack, who was limping badly, grimacing every time he took a step.

Sofie's hair was speckled with pieces of plaster that stood up like white-chocolate shards decorating the top of a cake. She stood by the door—plate glass intact, the *Aperto* sign still turned to the street—and rattled the handle. Like the church door, it seemed to be stuck fast; unlike the church door, there was no other door to try instead.

"We could always climb out the window back there," Kasper pointed out, but nobody seemed too enthusiastic. The glass still in the frame was sharp and jagged, and Jack would have had a hard time making it over with his bad leg. Maia suggested they use a chair to break through the door's glass; Dan argued that they might have more success knocking out the glass in one of the already-broken windows. Sofie started rattling the door handle again, pushing with her shoulder.

"Let me try," Laura said softly, though she suspected it was pointless. She wriggled the handle and tried pushing the door, then pulling, but the door wouldn't budge at all. Kasper was clambering his way to the back of the room, surveying the other possibilities of escape, everyone else calling out opinions and warnings and advice.

"Be careful," she called to Kasper; he was surveying the shards of glass still in place in the window. "Let someone else help."

"I'm already cut," he said, waving his bandaged arm.

"Always the hero," Dan muttered. Laura was about to mutter something back but then she felt something give: The handle she was gripping was moving! At last the door was giving way, opening fluidly!

Someone outside was opening it, letting them out. It must be the counter guy who'd run into the street—stupidly, in Laura's opinion—just as the earthquake began; he was returning to throw them out once and for all.

"Hey!" she shouted, to get everyone's attention. A gust of ash blew into her face, stinging her eyes, and she stepped back to brush her face clear. Sofie, with a squeal of relief, wriggled past her through the open door, followed by the limping Jack and then Maia.

"Come on!" Dan said, gesturing to her to step outside, but she shook her head. The ash flakes felt like a cobweb stuck to her eyelashes, and she wanted them gone before she faced whatever ash-strewn landscape waited for them out on the street.

"After you," said Kasper when he finally reached the

threshold, and Laura blinked one last time before stepping outside.

The busy street they'd walked down looked almost unrecognizable, asphalt split and gaping, paving stones jutting up, cars abandoned at strange angles. The stoplights were dead. Store awnings had collapsed; windows were broken.

A hydrant, jerked free from its moorings, spewed water. The front of one store, all brick, lay crumbled on the street like mashed-up cake. People were climbing through the wreckage, their faces blank with shock, so drenched in ash and dust that they looked like ghosts.

"We have to stay close together, okay?" Laura heard Dan saying, and for the first time she realized how much danger they'd been in, and how lucky they all were to be standing in the street, shaken but more or less intact.

She didn't move for a minute, unsure whether the ground beneath her feet would start roiling and moiling again. A hand touched hers, cold and soft—*Kasper*, she thought, reassuring her, encouraging her on. Dan was right: They had to stick together, and somehow find their way back to the hostel.

But the face she looked into wasn't Kasper's. And the guy who'd held the door open for them wasn't the guy who'd cut off their computers and shouted at them to leave. The guy holding the door open was about Laura's age, with sleek dark hair and eyes black as charcoal, boring into hers.

It was the boy from the Pantheon, the one who'd swirled down from the sky. The Mercury boy. Laura instinctively glanced down at his heels, but his legs were half submerged in the street rubble. Still, she knew it was him.

He brought his face close to hers, as close as Dan's had been inside the Internet place, but he didn't smell like Dan—like sweat and soap and muskiness. Mercury smelled the way the air smelled just after rain, fresh and clean.

"Laura," he whispered, in that accent she couldn't place. She stared into his dark eyes, unable to speak. *He knew her name?* "You have the great goddess Minerva's protection. She has sent us here to watch over you."

"What do you mean, *us*?" Laura managed to say, trying to make sense of his words. *Minerva? Goddess?* What was happening?

His eyes bored deeper into hers. Laura felt as though she could barely breathe. He didn't reply to her question; he just looked at her intently.

"You have her eyes," he said at last.

"Whose eyes?" Laura didn't understand.

"The eyes of Minerva, stolen from her sacred temple and placed in a house of pleasure by an emperor, an emperor the gods punished for that crime," he explained. "For many years the eyes lay buried in the ground, until your grandfather found one and gave it to you. We have been waiting for you to come to Rome to claim the other."

Laura felt her heart lurch. "But—but," she spluttered. "I didn't come here to claim it. I didn't know anything about it."

Mercury bobbed his head; his movements were jerky, like a bird's.

"You are a girl of virtue and intelligence. When Minerva saw you here, she was satisfied. She has no desire to punish you. It is her wish that you have both eyes, and take them with you, away from Rome. Other gods disagree, and they now prepare for battle. But remember that you are protected, and be sure that we will watch over you always."

He jerked his head again and drew his hand away.

"But I don't . . ." Laura began. She didn't know what to think or what to say. This guy—this Mercury!—knew her name. He knew about her grandfather. He was talking about Minerva, and other gods and . . . a battle? And what did that mean, *We will watch over you always*?

It was all way, way too much.

He stepped back—one, two, three paces. Then he was gone, as utterly invisible as, moments ago, he'd been real and

131

present and *there*, holding the door open, touching her hand, talking to her.

A lone crow flapped its wings and climbed into the sky, cawing its plaintive cry. Laura stood still, transfixed as the bird circled and swooped and then disappeared into the hazy cloud of ash.

CHAPTER ELEVEN

Laura's mind was whirling as they all walked down the avenue. They clambered over rubble and skirted broken glass, clustered together like lost children in a dark forest. Kasper and Dan each held one of Jack's arms so he could limp along. Sofie and Maia walked on either side of Laura. A policeman in a white hat and ash-smutted gloves stood on an upturned chunk of asphalt, waving creeping cars off the main road and down a side street.

Everywhere people were pouring out of shops and restaurants and offices, coughing and dusty, some of them bleeding or limping. The air was thick with smoke; maybe some drifting from the volcano or some from a building on fire.

Laura took it all in, but she wasn't listening to the conversation around her. All she could think about was what Mercury—if he really was Mercury—had said to her.

So the two stone sapphires were the eyes of Minerva, whatever that meant—stolen from a sacred temple by some bad emperor. Her grandfather had found one buried in some ruins, and passed it along to her, and then she—unwittingly—had turned up in Rome with it. And because of that, chaos had erupted, pretty much.

Laura gnawed on her ashy lip, trying to make sense of everything. The earthquake had begun when she held the two stones in her hand, and it stopped when she dropped them into her bag. If they really were Minerva's "eyes," then when she held them in her hands, were they *too* powerful? Was *she*, Laura, too powerful?

She tried to think calmly, to call up all she knew about Roman mythology. Who controlled earthquakes? Neptune. Who controlled volcanic eruptions? Vulcan. So did that mean Vulcan and Neptune were working together, against Minerva? Against Laura?

And how could she think about these gods and goddesses as if they were truly real, truly having influence over life in Rome?

The policeman blew his whistle at them and jabbed a finger at a street leading south—not the direction they wanted to go, if Laura had her bearings straight, but they didn't have a choice. The group carefully threaded their way past stopped cars and a toppled stoplight to the other side of the road.

Minerva, Minerva . . . Laura tried to summon up everything she'd learned in class. Minerva was the Roman version of Athena, goddess of war and wisdom. Though how those two things went together, Laura couldn't quite figure out.

Minerva must be brave and brainy and the Mercury boy had said that Minerva was "satisfied" with her. Why? Laura didn't feel particularly brave or brainy right now. Her head ached, and she was beyond jittery, uncertain of every step she took. A man walked by, slow as a zombie, bleeding from his forehead. A small boy wrapped in his mother's arms wailed and kicked, and Laura knew just how he felt. Lost and confused, not brave at all.

Am I causing this? Laura thought, looking at the scared faces of passersby. Would she cause this kind of trouble for the rest of her life? If she ever got out of Rome, would Bloomington be overtaken by earthquakes and statues that came to life?

In a piazza, they came across a parked ambulance, its back doors flung open. Guys in red jumpsuits and yellow safety vests dispensed first aid to the walking wounded. Outside a café, a waiter was handing out plastic bottles of water. While Kasper and Jack waited in line to get their injuries checked—only at

Sofie's insistence, because they both kept saying they were fine—everyone else grabbed bottles and found places to sit.

Laura realized how thirsty she was. She took her water to a doorway on the far side of the piazza and lowered herself onto the cool stone of the step. She needed to keep thinking.

You have the great goddess Minerva's protection. She has sent us here to watch over you. Who was this "us"? Mercury and his merry band of killer crows?

There'd been something written about Minerva in Ovid, she was sure: They'd read passages of his work this spring. *Goddess of a thousand things*, Laura vaguely remembered reading: Was that Minerva? And what things, exactly?

Laura took a big gulp of water and closed her eyes. Mrs. Johnson's voice floated into her mind, but not from class. Laura remembered her talking just a few days ago, when they were touring the Forum, before everyone got sick and the volcano erupted. Had that really been just a few days ago?

POTUS had been telling them something about the Capitoline Hill. They'd all been most interested in hearing how traitors were thrown off the Tarpeian Rock in ancient times; Dylan had suggested that modern-day Rome should install a bungee-jumping facility there, to re-create the experience. Mrs. Johnson had ignored him.

But there was something else, she'd told them, about a temple that was once the star attraction on that particular hill, built by the last king of Rome, long before Julius Caesar or Mark Antony or any of the emperors. A temple was built in all Roman cities, she said, to honor Rome's supreme deities: Jupiter, who was god of the sky; Juno, his wife and queen; and his favorite daughter, Minerva. They were known as the Capitoline Triad, which Jack said sounded like a bad hip-hop group. POTUS ignored that as well. These three gods, she said, were the protectors of all Romans.

Well, Laura thought, swigging some more water, Minerva wasn't doing a very good job of protecting Rome right now. First there was the erupting volcano and its ash cloud, then there were earthquakes—not to mention so many people getting sick. Ancient Romans wouldn't be surprised, Laura supposed, by what was going on right now. They'd say that everyone was sick because they hadn't prayed to Febris, the goddess who protected people from fevers. They'd say that nobody paid the correct tribute to any of the gods anymore. Nobody sacrificed bulls, or made sacred vows, beneath the big statues of the three deities. The statues were long gone, and so was the temple itself.

Once upon a time it was the largest temple in the Roman world, Mrs. Johnson had told them. Every time it burned down, an emperor rebuilt it, even bigger and grander than before, until finally, two thousand years after the first temple was built, a palace was constructed on the site by some Renaissance-era rich guy. By that time, Rome was the center of the Catholic world; the Pope was in charge. Nobody believed in the old gods anymore.

But the thing that stuck in Laura's head from Mrs. Johnson's talk that day wasn't about Minerva, or about Jupiter and Juno. It was about another god she'd never heard of before, called Terminus—kind of like Termini, the main train station near their hostel. (Ryan Banana Pants had pointed this out in a loud voice, as though it were some brilliant insight.) On the site where they were building the first temple, back in 500-something BC, there was a small, even more ancient shrine to this god, Terminus. He was the deity who presided over boundaries.

His boundary stone couldn't be moved, according to the augurs—who were priests, experts in reading omens in things like the flight of birds, or the organs of a slaughtered animal. So the stone had to be built into this great temple on the Capitoline Hill, and this was taken as a sign that some things couldn't be moved or changed or lost. Rome would last forever, POTUS said—that's what those ancient kings and emperors believed. Like the stone of Terminus, it was immovable. There would be no end to its power. ("Wrong!" Ryan had chimed, and they'd walked on to the next point in their tour.)

When she'd heard all this, Laura had thought about it the way she thought of most stories involving the ancient world, as sitting somewhere between history and myth. That old world was long gone—burnt, pillaged, built over. Over the centuries people had taken marble from the Forum to use in their houses. They'd built palaces and churches on top of temples. Some statues ended up in museums, many of them broken, and some lost forever. Now school groups like hers trailed around muse-ums and ruins trying to make sense of things, to imagine how things used to look, what they used to mean. The world of the ancient Romans was like a faded, jumbled-up puzzle with lots of missing pieces.

But the Mercury boy wasn't a statue or a fresco: He looked and sounded like a real live person, albeit one with wings on his heels. Mercury, the messenger god. This message he'd given her, that the gods had been waiting for her to return to Rome with the star sapphire, and that Minerva's decision to give her *both* stones had triggered all this chaos—well, it wasn't just weird. It was terrifying.

Laura and everyone else in this city walked around gazing at what seemed liked fragments of the past, but maybe they were all being watched by the gods. Maybe those fragments weren't quite as broken as they'd all assumed.

Laura finished her water and looked around for a trash can. Part of her hoped she was being fanciful, letting her imagination carry her away. But she couldn't help wondering: What if the world of the ancients hadn't gone away at all? What if it was still here, underground and beyond the sky and in the foundations of the city? What if those old gods were still lurking, in that separate and mysterious realm where gods lurked, feeling affronted and angry and jealous and vengeful?

After all, lots of bad things had happened to Rome over the centuries. It had been burned to the ground, attacked, invaded, left to rot into poverty, bombed. When her grandfather was here, almost seventy years ago, he was part of an invading army that had been dropping bombs on the city and killing people. Maybe the gods had been taking their revenge. Maybe they were taking their revenge all over again, right now.

"Laura!" Kasper was waving to her, his green shorts dusted with ash. His left arm was bandaged from elbow to wrist. He wandered over, holding out her pashmina, a rueful look on his face. "I tried to wash the blood out with water. I'm really sorry. I hope it won't stain."

"Don't worry about it," Laura told him. A stained scarf was the least of their problems.

Jack limped toward them. "Not broken," he announced, trying to manage a grin, though it looked more like a grimace. "Well, at least that's what they think. They said I need an X-ray when I get home."

If *we get home*, Laura thought, but she said nothing. Jack was supposed to put ice on it when he got back to the hostel, he told them, and to try to stay off it for a while.

They set off again, Jack leaning on Kasper and everyone else, gingerly picking their way along the narrow street. When Maia decided to climb over a toppled trash can rather than walk through its flowing skirt of spilled trash, Kasper held out his bad hand to help her down. Dan, walking near Laura, clucked with impatience.

"What is your problem?" Laura said to him in a low voice. "You're being really childish. Why have you got it in for Kasper?"

"I don't know what you're talking about." Dan was trying to sound breezy, but he didn't fool Laura.

"You're constantly criticizing him. And you get all annoyed when he tries to help someone else."

"I don't trust him."

"That's ridiculous."

"How do we even know he's Danish? Have you heard him speak any?"

"Well, there's no one else Danish around . . ."

"Exactly. Very convenient. And his English is way too good."

"Lots of Europeans speak really good English!" Laura protested. This was the most ridiculous conversation. She hadn't even thought about whether Kasper could be trusted or not. Besides, she had much bigger things to obsess over now, like the fact that ancient gods were talking to her. "Why would he be *pretending* to be Danish?"

"You tell me," Dan said in a low voice. "What's he got to hide?"

"I don't think he has anything to hide. You're acting really crazy."

"And what kind of name is 'Kasper,' anyway?"

"A Danish name. Obviously."

"Do we have any proof of that? He could have made it up. And why isn't he sick, like everyone else from his so-called school?"

"You're not sick, either," Laura pointed out, and then she remembered something odd that Maia had said about Dan— was it yesterday? *We might need him.* At the time it had just seemed like another strange Maia-ish thing to say. But now Laura wasn't so sure. She glanced over her shoulder to make sure nobody could hear them.

"He's always trying to help," Dan whispered, bending so his face was close to hers. "But have you ever asked yourself why? What's he trying to prove?"

"Maybe that he's more useful than you," Laura hissed. "If it weren't for Kasper, Sofie might not have made it out of that torture church this morning."

"If it weren't for Kasper," Dan said, his arm brushing Laura's, "she might not have been attacked in the first place."

"What's that supposed to mean?"

Dan didn't answer, maybe because Maia had caught up and was walking alongside them. He flashed Laura an all-knowing look, and she shook her head at him. He could be so exasperating. Strange to think that a couple of days ago they'd barely exchanged two words, and now they were arguing in the street.

"What does *what* mean?" Maia was as nosy as ever, frowning in Laura's direction.

"I was just asking Dan about Minerva," said Laura, thinking quickly. "As in, the goddess. What do you know about her?"

"Well," said Maia, as though this was the most normal question in the world, "she was part of the Capitoline Triad."

"Yeah, I know that." Laura hoped she didn't sound too snippy, but Dan had annoyed her, so it was hard to moderate her tone. "But what else? Goddess of war and of wisdom, right?"

"And arts and crafts," said Maia, who didn't seem at all offended by Laura's tone. Maybe Maia didn't notice tone of voice. It would explain why she often came across badly to other people.

"I don't suppose her signature creatures were bees," Laura said, still hoping that there was a connection with the fountain that Kasper—and her grandfather—had seen.

"Owls," said Maia. She skirted an upturned paving stone.

"And spiders," Dan added. "Or—no, hang on. I think she turned some nymph into a spider because the nymph had totally crossed her."

"Yes, Arachne!" Laura remembered it now. In class they'd translated a small passage written by Ovid from Latin to English.

"She wasn't a nymph," Maia told Dan. "She was just a maiden. She challenged Minerva to a weaving contest and lost. Hence spiders are arachnids, weaving their webs . . ."

"Yeah, yeah," Dan said quickly. "And there was something about a flute. Maybe they had a flute-playing contest?"

"No, they didn't," said Maia, her usual blunt self. "But there is a Minerva connection. She invented the flute."

"Ugh," said Dan. "My sister plays the flute, and it's so annoying when she practices."

Laura glimpsed something strange and beautiful in the rubble-strewn clearing they were approaching—another small piazza, another fountain.

"What is that?" she asked.

Although Kasper had told them that the bee fountain was near the Palazzo Barberini and nowhere remotely close by, Laura was still hoping that they'd come across it on the way to the hostel. Maybe Kasper was wrong about where he'd seen it; maybe he was disoriented after everything that had happened today.

Something Dan and Maia were just saying was still rolling around in her head, forming itself into an idea. Maia had said that Minerva had invented the flute, and Dan had complained that his sister played the flute. Laura's father sometimes played a particular classical piece, blasting the CD through the house—usually on a Saturday morning when he wanted them all to get out of bed and do something boring like rake leaves. Though she didn't know the name of the composer or performer, Laura did remember what the piece was called: "Flight of the Bumblebee." It was played on the flute.

Maybe that was the link between Minerva and the bees, she

told herself, hurrying toward the fountain up ahead. Minerva, bees, her grandfather, the star sapphires—it all had to add up somehow.

Laura had to dart around a few slow-moving groups of dusty, dazed people. On the fountain, she glimpsed dolphins, shells, plus some kind of small creatures. Not bees, though, she realized, the excitement of anticipation curdling into disappointment. The bronze creatures on the edge of the fountain's upper ring were tortoises.

Laura stopped, waiting for the others to reach her. The sky was darker now, gloomy clouds billowing high above the buildings, spitting rain. The fountain didn't seem at all affected by the earthquake. It was still firmly in place, waters still trickling into a pale stone basin. Laura pulled her map out of the pocket of her bag and found her location, Piazza Mattei, in the old Jewish Ghetto, and the name of the fountain, Fontana delle Tartarughe. Tortoises, not bees. No connection to Minerva at all.

A hooded crow squawked overhead, and Laura looked up, startled by its proximity. The bird skimmed the fountain, dipping so low its wings brushed the bronze backs of one of the tortoises. Was it trying to tell her something? Was it Mercury? Was this a sign, or a warning?

An unseen hand tugged at the bag hanging off Laura's

shoulder, and she felt it slide down her arm, the weight of it slipping away.

"No!" she cried, but it was too late. The bag was gone. The crow *had* been there to warn her, she realized. Someone had stolen the star sapphires.

CHAPTER TWELVE

My bag!" Laura cried. The wind, gusting at just that moment, seemed to carry her voice away. She spun around in a dizzying circle, looking for the mugger.

Laura's backpack was pale blue with red piping, easy to spot even though there were lots of people drifting along the street or across the small piazza. But the man carrying it was darting through the crowd, swift and sure. She ran after him, bumping into people, her chest tight, her face burning. There was no chance of catching him, but she had to try.

The crow swooped from the sky, launching itself at the man's head. Laura thudded across the cobbles of the piazza. The man cowered under the crow's onslaught, smacking at its outstretched wings. She could see a red smear in the man's dark hair, where the crow's beak had drawn blood. But still, the man was moving, slowed but not stopped by the crow's attack. She had to reach him, to grab her bag back, before he disappeared into the chaos of the street.

Laura's head was pounding, so all she could really hear was the drum of her own heartbeat. Other sounds sloshed in the periphery—the screech of the crow, the man crying out—and she could see rather than hear the shock of other people, hurrying out of the way.

"Stop!" she shouted, though it didn't sound like much of a shout. She'd always had a quiet voice; she'd never been someone anyone would describe as rowdy or raucous. *Maybe I'm too meek*, Laura thought, hurtling toward the mugger. She'd never had reason to shout at someone before. No one had ever tried to steal anything she cared about.

Someone was running next to her, and then speeding past her. It was Dan, she realized, and he was hurtling toward the mugger and tackling him to the ground. The crow flapped its wings and lifted into the air, still squawking. Laura still couldn't see the face of the man tussling with Dan. They were a blur of limbs, and she got kicked hard by a flailing leg when she approached. Laura ignored the pain. One of the handles of her bag was dangling free, and she groped for it, without any luck.

Laura had never been in a fight before. Buffy made it look easy, but it was much messier—and harder—in real life. Now she was kicking wildly at what she hoped was the mugger's leg, and, when his bleeding head rolled into view, she slammed a fist into his cheek. It hurt the side of her hand so much that Laura cried out with pain. This was why girls stuck to pulling hair, she told herself. Punching hurt.

Laura managed to grasp a small tuft of the man's hair and tugged so hard she thought she'd uproot it. His grip on the bag loosened, and Laura seized her chance. With an almighty wrench, she pulled her bag free. She had so much momentum she staggered backward several steps, only stopping when she bumped into Maia.

The man was on his feet now. Dan lay groaning on the ground, covering his face with bloodied hands. There was something familiar about the long-faced, dark-haired mugger. Maybe the intense, angry darkness of his eyes. Laura thought of the woman trying to snap the bracelet off her wrist at the Trevi Fountain. The expression was the same—ferocious and greedy, almost feral.

He was walking toward her, slowly, those angry eyes locked on hers. Laura backed away, Maia moving with her, until they bumped into the fountain's low railing. Without speaking,

Maia helped Laura climb over it. Together they clambered into the fountain, its water splashing against their legs.

They waded backward through the water as the man advanced, and Laura tried to swallow her fear. She slipped her bag onto her back, arms through both of the straps, to make it harder for the mugger. This was no ordinary thief, clearly, flitting onto a different target when one proved too difficult. Maybe he was someone sent by the rival gods, the ones who were unhappy with Minerva's "gift" to her. This man wanted her bag and wasn't going to give up. Where were Laura's protectors now, the ones that Mercury had promised?

The hooded crow returned, dipping over the fountain with a rude, ear-piercing caw, and the man—about to step into the water as they'd just done—paused to glare up at it. Someone in the distance screamed, and the crow swooped again, launching itself at the man's head.

"Climb," Maia ordered, and Laura swiveled, looking for something to grab. Her soaked sandals felt like weights on her feet, so she kicked them off. It was easier to get a grip on the fountain's smooth, wet surfaces in bare feet; it was like navigating the rocks along the river near her house in Indiana.

The top tier of the fountain was small, a toadstool-like pedestal, flanked by four bronze figures of muscular boys, each of them leaning back with one arm to grab the tail of a bronze dolphin, the other arm raised as though reaching for a tortoise. Laura could just about stretch to get one foot onto the back of a small dolphin. Maybe from there she could grab the fountain's upper rim.

Maia was behind her, pushing.

"His hand, his hand," she was saying, and Laura didn't understand what she meant.

Then she glimpsed what Maia must have seen. One of the bronze figures was no longer gripping a dolphin's tail. His hand was stretched toward *her*, palm upturned. Laura felt a shock race through her, then placed one foot in the hand, expecting to feel cold, hard bronze. But it felt like a real hand, skin against her own skin, though much steadier. And stronger as well, Laura realized, as she felt herself hoisted easily into the air.

In an instant she was facing the fountain's rounded upper lip, just inches from one of the small tortoises. They'd been sculpted at the very edge of the fountain, so they appeared to be clambering into the basin, just as Laura was trying to do now.

She flopped into the shallow water, realizing it was too perilous to try to stand up. If she knelt she could keep her bag out of the water, though her shorts would be soaked. From this new perch she could survey the tiny piazza and beyond, trying to find her group in the blurred crowd of people.

The man trying to reach her batted the crow away; he pushed Maia so hard she fell sideways into the water, her head just missing the fountain's stone rim. He was coming for her, Laura knew; she'd be easy to reach. There was nowhere else to climb or hide, no crow strong enough to carry her away on its gray wings. With her sandals gone, she didn't even have anything to throw at the thief.

A woman standing near the fountain started screaming, pointing up at Laura, crossing herself, and then other people were screaming as well. At last, she thought: Someone would try to help her! But instead of running toward the fountain, people were scrambling away. Even two policemen who'd just marched into the piazza from the other side turned around and bolted out of sight.

The crow's caws sounded in her ears; it was flying so close Laura felt the breeze from its flapping wings. And around her, close enough to touch, the tortoises were moving. *That* was why people were screaming: The four bronze tortoises had come to life.

No longer suspended half in the air, they patrolled the fountain's rim, jaws snapping. Not snapping at Laura, she was relieved to see, but at the rapidly thinning crowd.

She suppressed the urge to reach out to stroke them, their shells shiny and beaded with raindrops. They were her miniature guard dogs, summoned into action, it seemed, by the crow's incessant rallying cry. When the man below her in the fountain tried to climb up, his hands creeping over the basin's edge, a tortoise snapped at his fingers. He yelped and stopped trying to climb. Once, twice, three times it happened, Laura shrinking back, knees aching from kneeling in the water, shivering as soft rain drizzled down her face, while the tiny tortoises hissed and snapped, seeing off the intruder.

The fourth time the man's hand appeared, one of the tortoises bit so hard that Laura was sure she heard bone crunch. The offending hand slithered away, and Laura edged forward, still on her knees, anxious to see what was happening below.

"Maia!" she shouted, but all she could see was one of the bronze figurines, kicking a muscular leg at the intruder. Laura leaned farther forward, and could see one of the round dolphins writhing and spinning like a log rolling down a river, making it impossible for the man—now with bloodied fingers— to regain his foothold.

Sofie was standing in the fountain now as well; Laura could see the top of her blond head. And there was Maia, struggling to her feet in the water, and passing something to Sofie. One of Laura's sandals!

Sofie grabbed the sandal and used it to smack the intruder on the back of his head, hitting it so hard that Laura could hear every thwack. Above them the crow cawed and dipped. The tortoises formed a shimmering barricade in front of Laura, bronze jaws clanging, as though they were daring the intruder to approach again.

Rain, heavier now, splashed around them all. In the midst of all noise and movement, Laura knelt completely still, as though she were part of the original fountain, made out of bronze herself. *Girl with Backpack*, she thought, the strangest fountain in Rome. Her heart was thundering. Really, all of this was way too much. What was she doing here? She was from Bloomington, Indiana! She studied Classics!

Laura heard splashing and a roar of rage; the crow swooped again, circling the fountain. The intruder wasn't going to climb up again, she saw, and a feeling of immense relief flooded through her, so intense that she wanted to cry. He was sprinting away across the piazza. Laura watched his back disappearing down one of the narrow streets, her whole body trembling with fear.

As suddenly as it had begun, it was all over. The tortoises no longer hissed or snapped; once again they were inanimate, poised on the edge of the fountain's upper tier. She could hear police sirens in the distance, and a motorcycle revving; light rain pattered into the fountain—or perhaps it was the trickle of water from the dolphins' mouths.

The piazza had emptied. Jack was bent over Dan, who was still clutching his face. Kasper was helping Sofie and Maia, both drenched, out of the fountain.

"Need a hand?" Kasper called up to Laura. She threw her bag down to him, hands shaking, and lowered herself down from the fountain's upper tier. This time there was no bronze hand stretched out to help her, and Laura felt as though she was bumping every bone possible—knees, elbows, shoulders—on her way down.

She sloshed through the lower basin and stepped over the railing, her legs trembling. Between her wet clothes and the drizzle, she felt chilled and miserable. Kasper stood smiling at her, but Laura could see a wariness in his eyes that wasn't there before.

"Here's your bag," he said, holding out her damp backpack. "I don't know, but maybe you should . . ."

"Yes," Laura said. She took the bag from Kasper and slipped the straps over her shoulders. She needed to hang on to this, to guard it. To guard the stones.

Their group was a mess. Maia clutched the side of her head. Sofie was bent double, heaving for breath. Jack was gripping his leg in pain. Dan sat on the ground, his leg scraped and bloody, and blood clotting his upper lip. Her squabbling with him forgotten, Laura wanted to rush over to comfort him, to make sure he was fine—but her old awkwardness was back, too, and she felt almost shy around him. It was so much more complicated, she thought, when boys were involved.

"Is Dan okay?" Laura asked Jack, who was limping over to the fountain to fill a plastic bottle with water, and he nodded.

"He'll have a black eye," observed Kasper, "but he should be fine."

When Jack poured the water over Dan's bleeding leg, Dan lay back on the ground, as though he was too exhausted even to sit up anymore. They were all exhausted, Laura knew. Exhausted, beaten, confused—and still nowhere near the hostel.

"Here," said Sofie, straightening up. She handed over Laura's soggy sandals. "Sorry there is blood."

"That's okay." Laura felt too tired to smile. "Thanks. For everything."

"We should keep walking," Maia announced. Jack groaned, and Kasper offered to go back to the first piazza, to see if he could find a paramedic to take a look at Dan's nose. The others propped themselves up around the fountain, now serene and stony again.

"That lump looks painful," Laura said, noticing the grimace on Maia's face when she stroked the side of her temple.

"Could be worse." Maia sounded her usual unruffled self. "If my head had hit the rim of the fountain, I'd be concussed. Or dead, probably. I'd have drowned in the water. But that didn't happen, so . . ."

"So—good." It really was incredible, Laura thought, that Maia could be so cool about something like that. Nearby, Sofie's long legs were shaking, even though she was sitting down. Laura was huddled, clutching her knees and shivering. Rome was falling apart—the *world* was falling apart—around them, and Laura wished she could take all this in stride, the way Maia seemed to. She needed to think of something else, talk about something else, to pull herself together.

"Hey," she said, nudging Maia with one shoulder. "I know you said that owls were associated with Minerva. But what about tortoises? Could they have something to do with her as well?"

"Not with Minerva," Maia said firmly. "But remember how I was telling Dan that Minerva invented the flute? Well, Mercury invented the lyre. That's like a harp."

"Yeah, I know." The mention of Mercury's name sizzled through Laura like an electric current. "What does that have to do with tortoises?"

"Mercury used a tortoiseshell to make the first lyre," Maia reported. "So the tortoise is one of his creatures."

Tortoises are Mercury's creatures, Laura repeated to herself, trying to steady her breathing. Maybe that's why the tortoises had all come to life when the hooded crow brushed them with its wings. Maybe that's why they tried to help her, to guard her bag and its precious, dangerous, mysterious cargo.

And maybe that's what Mercury had meant when he said, *She has sent us here to watch over you.*

The trouble was, Laura thought, that dangers seemed to lurk everywhere. A dart-wielding cherub on a tomb. The Mouth of Truth. The walls of a fresco. The woman at the Trevi Fountain and the man here at the tortoise fountain. Stone horses that moved, painted snakes that slithered, bronze tortoises that crawled and snapped and bared their teeth. Rome was alive with danger, seen and unseen, real and artificial. How could she believe anyone when they told her not to be afraid?

CHAPTER THIRTEEN

It took a lot of effort from Maia to get them moving again. Nobody wanted to get up, let alone start the long trudge back to the hostel. It was possible, Laura thought, creaking to a standing position and discovering that the back of her shorts were still wet as well as incredibly dirty, that Jack was actually asleep on the ground.

Although Kasper hadn't managed to find anyone to help—the paramedic team was gone, he said, and the nearest policeman he could find just shouted at him to keep walking—Laura was relieved to see an injured Dan clamber to his feet. He was holding a balled-up wet T-shirt against his swelling eye.

"Kasper's," he told her when she approached.

"So, he's not so bad after all, right?"

"Yeah, well," said Dan. "Now he gets to walk around shirt-less, like a rock star."

He managed a rueful smile, and Laura smiled, too. But she was worried about Dan. He'd really taken a beating from the mugger. She almost wanted to hug him, but she didn't dare. There was still some kind of tension between them.

"You need to rest," she told him, in a tone that sounded more offhand than she intended. "When we get back to the hostel."

Dan reached out for her, his fingers brushing her bare forearm.

"Sorry I couldn't stop him," he said, his voice gruff. "I mean, the guy who tried to steal your bag. After he punched me in the face I just . . . I couldn't do anything. I'm glad the others helped."

"You don't have to apologize!" Dan's hand still rested on her arm, and Laura's skin tingled. She wished he didn't have that effect on her. "He would have escaped if you hadn't tackled him. I'm just really sorry about your eye, and your leg, and everything. You were really brave."

Dan shrugged, staring down at the ground. His hand was still on her arm, his fingers cool against her burning skin.

"At least you got your bag back," he said. "That's the main thing."

"Yeah, but only after—you know."

"What? Did Kasper come to the rescue?" Dan sounded disappointed. Maybe he thought he'd been trumped, yet again, by the Viking. Dan was used to being the golden boy at Riverside High, Laura knew.

"It was Maia and Sofie," she said. "And a crow. And the tortoises."

"The tortoises?" Dan seemed genuinely confused.

"You didn't see them?"

"After that punch in the face, I couldn't see anything. I still can't open my left eye. You mean the tortoises on the fountain?"

Laura nodded, not sure what to say, or whether Dan would believe her.

"I know this sounds ridiculous, but they came to life. Ask the others," she added, in case Dan thought she was imagining things again. "They were like guard dogs, biting at that guy's hand until he ran away. All of a sudden, the whole fountain just came to life. I know it doesn't make any sense, but everyone saw, I promise you."

"Okay," he said quietly, and Laura wasn't sure if that meant he believed her or if he just wasn't in the mood for another argument. Dan pulled the wet T-shirt away from his face and she winced: The skin around his left eye was dark and puffy, his eye could barely open, and there was a livid gash just above his eyebrow.

The sight of Dan's beaten face was awful, but hopefully the worst was over, as long as they could get back to the hostel safely. The teachers might be feeling better by now; they'd know what to do. Maybe the ash cloud would lift tomorrow and they could all go home. At the very least, she and Maia and Sofie could hunker down in their room, and everyone could treat their wounds with ice and antiseptics. When they got back to the hostel, everything would be fine.

Nobody could walk very quickly, and nobody had much energy to speak. Laura wondered if what they'd just seen— most of them, anyway—was too fantastical, too hard to process. Maybe nobody wanted to be the first to mention that the fountain had sprung to life, in case they thought the others would call them crazy.

A shirtless Kasper, lithe and tanned, his blond hair crusted with dirt and dust, led the way, helping poor limping Jack. Maia and Sofie flanked Laura, and Dan insisted on walking right behind her, to make sure nobody tried to steal her backpack again. Every time she slowed down he bumped into her, and after the first five times they stopped apologizing to each other.

By the time they stumbled down the lane toward the hostel's front door, they were all even more tired and dirty and aching. At least their clothes were dry, though Laura's sandals still felt gritty and damp. She'd never been so pleased to see the hostel's glass sliding door, still miraculously intact, though they had to step over smashed flowerpots from some high-up windowsill or roof terrace.

"Everyone!" Kasper swung around to face them all and stopped just shy of the door. He waited until they'd all ambled up, everyone sweaty and breathing heavily, and when he spoke again his voice was low. "This is all earthquake, okay?"

At first Laura didn't get what he was talking about, until she followed his gaze from Dan to Maia and back.

"It's too complicated to explain," said Kasper.

"What?" asked Jack, clearly dead on his feet. He swayed where he stood.

"To our teachers," Maia said, brisk as ever, one hand massaging her temple. "If we start talking about men attacking us, painted or otherwise, or about creatures on a fountain coming to life, they'll never let us outside again."

"I don't want to go outside ever again," groaned Jack.

"So all of this happened in the Internet place, right?" said Dan. Kasper nodded, his hands on his hips. Really, Laura knew that lying—or at least not telling all the truth, exactly—was the best thing to do. There was too much they couldn't explain to themselves, let alone other people, and adults tended to go crazy if words like "attack" or "mugger" entered the conversation. But when she glanced at Dan and caught his eye, she could guess what he was thinking. Why was Kasper so eager to keep what had happened on the down low?

"So we are agreed?" Kasper asked.

"Sure," said Dan, and everyone else mumbled assent. All Laura really wanted right now was a shower and clean clothes.

A hooded crow fluttered onto the flapping green awning above the door and cawed at them—just once, but enough to unnerve her. By the way everyone hurried inside, Laura suspected she wasn't the only one wondering if the crow was trying to warn them again.

The hostel was quiet—maybe too quiet, but at first that was a relief. Instead of answering questions, the girls could take lukewarm showers, get changed, and use their stash of first aid supplies to patch themselves up. Sofie's neck was still red and raw from the strangling hands of her fresco attacker, and Maia studied the bump on her head in the mirror with a detached, almost medical interest.

Above her knee Laura discovered an impressive bruise from where someone—either Dan or his attacker—had kicked her during the fight in the piazza; her knees were sore, and her wrist still ached from her tangle with the Mouth of Truth the day before.

When it was her turn to use the shower, Laura carried with her a change of clothes, along with her backpack. She needed to keep the star sapphires close by. *The eyes of Minerva, stolen from her sacred temple . . . It is her wish that you have both eyes, and take them with you, away from Rome . . .*

Before she turned the shower on, Laura checked that the door was locked and that the small frosted window was secure as well. But still, she didn't dare close the mold-spotted shower curtain, or even to turn her back on the bag for more than a second or two. Everyone in Rome—everyone and every*thing*— seemed to want to get their hands on those star sapphires. *Other gods disagree, and they now prepare for battle . . .*

Laura didn't *want* to know what that meant. There was no better feeling right now than the gush of water over her head, washing away all the dust and dirt, and the clean, minty smell of her shampoo, which reminded her of home. She wished she were home now, a breeze wafting the curtains of her bedroom, the cat leaping onto her creaky old wicker chair, a stack of books waiting on the painted stool that served as a bedside table. As long as she could remember, Laura had thought of her life as ordinary—a little too quiet, a little too calm, with everything always the same.

Everyone in the house had their hobbies and obsessions, of course, and for the past few years hers had been the Classical world, the long-ago past of the Greeks, Egyptians, Etruscans, Romans, Mesopotamians. She had a map of the ancient world tacked up over her desk, along with pictures torn from magazines, of things she could only dream of seeing—an artist's impression of the Hanging Gardens of Babylon and the Colossus of Rhodes, both gone forever—and things that she really could see in person, like the rooms of Nero's long-buried Golden House, the ruins of Ephesus in Turkey, or La Primavera of Pompeii, a patch of fresco that somehow survived the eruption of Vesuvius.

Two Christmases ago, before Laura was even old enough to take Classics at school, her parents had given her a cast-marble replica bust of Thalia, the muse of comedy. Thalia—complete with stone braids and a chipped nose—sat on Laura's desk, eyes downcast, oblivious to any pranks by annoying little brothers who liked to decorate her for Halloween.

Every week for the past two semesters, Laura had turned the pages of her book on Roman rulers—kings, tyrants, usurpers, emperors—memorizing the names of each one in turn, even though Morgan—usually slumped in the wicker chair, leafing through a magazine—would complain that it wasn't necessary to learn them *all*. As she kept reminding Laura, they wouldn't be tested on it.

But Laura had wanted to learn everything, to see everything, to know everything, whether it came up in a class test or not. Other people might think it was boring and weird to be so interested in long-ago lost civilizations, but Laura thought they were much more interesting than the fantasy worlds of her brothers' video games. She couldn't wait for this school trip, to tour ancient sites in Turkey and Greece and Italy, and to see the remnants of the past for herself.

But this wasn't quite what she'd had in mind, Laura thought, rinsing the suds out of her hair. Not Mercury taking the form of a boy with wings on his heels, telling her she'd unwittingly gotten herself entangled in some kind of god war . . .

Water coursed down her face, a combination of the shower and a sudden gush of tears. Free for a few moments from worrying about who could see or hear her, Laura gave in to her tears, her body shaking with sobs. She was tired and confused and shaken; she missed home, its calm and its comforts. She missed her ordinary life—a lucky life, Laura realized now, in that she'd never really been afraid before.

When the water turned from lukewarm to cold, Laura knew it was time to get out of the shower. Part of the problem, she thought, drying her hair with one of the hostel's sandpaper-quality towels, was not having anyone to talk to. Maybe Morgan was feeling better; maybe the quarantine would be lifted by now. But trying to explain today's events alone to Morgan . . . well, where to begin?

Laura pulled on her red vintage dress, the one she'd been planning to wear to the final-night dinner; it wasn't clean exactly, but it felt fresh and soft compared to the gritty, damp T-shirt and shorts she'd been wearing all day.

She could try talking to Maia again, she thought. Or maybe even Sofie. Unlike Dan, they'd seen the biting tortoises. Maybe they'd seen her talking to Mercury in the street— although, weirdly, no one had mentioned this to her at all. And why was Kasper so eager to keep everything a secret from their teachers? Where was he when the girls were all fighting off the mugger in the fountain? Maybe Dan was right not to trust him.

Or maybe Dan's paranoia was getting to her.

She had to talk to *someone*, she decided, shaking her damp hair. All these years she'd been fascinated with ancient worlds; she'd seen their drama, violence, and passions as stories, their beliefs as myths. Everything, bad and good, was at a safe distance, long ago. But now that it was vivid and real and happening around her, it was terrifying.

CHAPTER FOURTEEN

Laura padded down the empty corridor, her bare feet cool against the tiles, hair wrapped in a towel. Dan was like the Emperor Domitian—the emperor who was so paranoid he executed most of his senators and aides just in case they were conspiring against him. He killed so many people that his closest allies feared for their lives; they turned on him and stabbed him to death.

Not that Dan was *that* bad. He wasn't as arrogant as she'd thought earlier in the trip, when he'd just seemed smug and aloof. He looked out for her; he'd chased down that mugger by the fountain to get her bag back. Sure, he was bossy, but . . . she had to admit, she liked being around him, even if half the time they were bickering. And even with his battered face, he was still undeniably good-looking—if not quite Kasper-level handsome.

Back in the room she found the others sitting on their bunk beds, Sofie wearing the big T-shirt she slept in and complaining about her sore neck.

"I can't lie down," she was telling Maia. "It is all stiff."

"I could go and ask for some ice downstairs," Laura offered, dumping her bag on her bed. There had been no one at reception when they'd arrived, but maybe the pretty girl in the white dress was there now. Even if she wasn't, Laura had spotted a small fridge in the back room; maybe she could find some ice in there.

"Yes, I think—yes," Sofie said, managing to sound pouty rather than grateful, in Laura's opinion. She might have stepped up in the fountain fight, but the German girl was still kind of sulky.

Laura reached under her bed for a pair of flip-flops. If she was leaving the room, she should do something with her bracelet and the other star sapphire—but what? Hide them inside her pillowcase, or the inner pocket of her toilet bag?

"I don't think that Laura should go," said Maia. "Sofie, you can go downstairs yourself."

Laura was taken aback by Maia's tone: She was channeling Dan-level bossiness right now. But Sofie didn't argue: She just looked offended and annoyed. She pulled on some denim shorts and slipped on her red Converse without bothering to tie the laces.

"I will find the ice," she announced in an overdramatic voice.

"And maybe some cold drinks," Maia suggested, "if you can . . ."

But Sofie was already gone, slamming the door behind her. Laura shook off her flip-flops and settled on the bed. At least now the problem of hiding the star sapphires could be postponed. And this was the chance she'd been waiting for, to talk to Maia.

"Did you see the guy who let us out of the Internet place?" she asked. Maia, curled up like a cat on the opposite bunk, cocked her head to one side. "Did you see me talking to him?"

"The Internet place," Maia said slowly, her face a blank. "This afternoon."

"Yes," said Laura, wondering why Maia was speaking in this odd, drawly way.

"After the earthquake?"

Before Laura could reply, a sound outside the door caught her attention—soft steps, and then the door handle turning, as though someone was about to come in. Sofie always thudded around, so it didn't sound like her. And anyway, the door didn't open: whoever was turning the handle let it spring back into place.

"Hello?" Laura called. Maybe it was Dan or one of the other boys, looking for them. But still, the door didn't open. She heard a click, and then footsteps running away down the hallway.

It sounded to Laura as though someone was locking them in. Maia must have been thinking the same thing, because she was on her feet, rattling the door handle.

"Locked," she announced.

"Here," Laura said. She scrambled up and dug in her bag pocket for the room key, dangling from its wooden block, their room number scrawled on it with black marker. "We can just unlock it."

But though her key unlocked the latch the way it always did, the door didn't budge.

"What?" she said, jerking the door handle up and down in irritation.

"Look." Maia pointed to another lock, one they never used, lower down the door. "Try that one."

The lower lock needed a different key. Laura's key wouldn't turn either direction; it barely fit in the lock at all.

Someone had locked them in.

"Did Sofie do it?" Laura asked, frowning at the locked door.

"I don't think she would," said Maia, and Laura saw the logic in that. Sofie had the same key they all did, not this extra, special key. And although Sofie could be aloof and occasionally petulant, she didn't seem that spiteful—or organized.

Laura's heart was beating fast again; she didn't like this at all. Something like dread was churning up her stomach, a sensation that was more and more familiar every day she was stuck here in Rome. Rattling the door achieved nothing, nor did banging and shouting for help, though she and Maia did both.

"Maybe it's the boys playing a joke." Laura didn't really believe this, but she said it anyway, mainly to calm herself down. From the grim look on Maia's face, she could tell that Maia didn't buy that, either.

"It must be someone who has access to the second key," Maia said, peering at the low lock. "Someone who works here, maybe."

"Why would they lock us in?" Laura squeaked. She wanted her heart to stop racing, and for something practical and rational to spring into her feverish brain. It was hard to concentrate with the sound of a seagull shrieking right outside the window.

"The star sapphires," Maia announced in her most matter-of-fact voice. She stomped back to her bed and sat down.

"What?" Laura wished the stupid bird would stop flying up and down outside, making a racket.

"They're the problem, of course," said Maia, sounding almost bored with the obviousness of it. "You were carrying them in your bag when you were attacked at the Mouth of Truth. Sofie had one when she was attacked at the church. The man at the tortoise fountain tried to steal them from you. And . . ." Maia paused and bit her lip. The seagull flew past the window at top speed, so close its wing brushed the glass.

"What?" said Laura. Her stomach rumbled, and she realized it had been hours since they'd eaten.

"You had the two stones in your hand when the earthquake happened."

Laura nodded. Maia had obviously made the same connection as Dan. But Maia didn't know the rest of it. Laura already felt guilty enough about that. *You have the eyes of Minerva, stolen from her sacred temple . . .*

"The thing is," she said to Maia's back; Maia had walked to the window to peer out at the noisy gull, "I didn't want that stupid second stone. I threw it down a drain, remember? Sofie was the one who took it off the windowsill."

Laura knew she was sounding whiny, but she couldn't help it. If only she'd left her bracelet back at home, in Indiana! She could have come to Rome without setting off some kind of ancient-god alarm.

Rain was falling now, a soft drizzle pattering onto the sill. It was still only early in the evening, but it already seemed dark outside. The seagull's cry sounded more distant. Laura's stomach rumbled again, so loud she was sure that Maia could hear. If they weren't locked in right now, she would leave to go get food.

"Sofie had to take the stone off the windowsill," Maia said quietly. "If she hadn't taken it, someone else would have."

Laura stared at her.

"What?" she asked. Maia didn't meet her eye.

"You were saying something about the guy who let us out at the Internet place," Maia prompted, running a hand across her sleek dark head. "The one you were talking to."

"You saw that?" Laura was still confused about Maia's earlier comment. *If she hadn't taken it, someone else would have.*

"Oh yes," said Maia, as though it were no big deal. Laura leaned back against the window, trying to ignore the cawing seagull.

"I saw him before, in the Pantheon," Laura said, wanting to get it all out now, before Maia could interrupt or contradict her. "I talked to him there, too. And I know this sounds crazy, but I think he had wings on his heels."

"You think?"

"I know. I mean, I saw them. And they weren't, like, novelty sneakers. They were these small wings, feathery and black. On his heels."

Laura felt her face prickle with heat. It was almost embarrassing to say this out loud.

"Wings on the heels," said Maia, her voice steady, betraying no emotion.

"Like Mercury," Laura said. "As in, the messenger god."

"And," Maia continued, still with the same measured tone, "you're thinking it's the same guy who opened the door for us at the Internet place."

"I'm absolutely certain of it," Laura said, the relief of a confession washing through her. "Like I said, he spoke to me both times. In English. But I guess gods can speak whatever they want. I mean, they don't just walk around speaking Latin."

Until yesterday, Laura hadn't thought gods walked around at all, but this was a different Rome from the one she'd expected, with very different rules. Maia said nothing.

Something thumped against the window and instinctively Laura jumped away, flashing to the time back home when a cardinal flew into the glass doors that led onto the patio. It sounded exactly the same.

"Seagull," Maia told her, perched on the edge of her bed.

Laura peered out the window, trying to make sense of the ashy, rainy twilight. The seagull was swooping up and down the lane, followed—chased?—by what had to be a crow. They were moving so fast it was hard to see more than a flurry of shapes, the wild flapping of wings. It was like the aerial fight in the Protestant Cemetery all over again, except this time it looked more frantic, more violent, and there wasn't any stone Cupid to intervene.

Someone out in the hallway was rattling the door handle and banging on the door. Laura nearly jumped out of her skin.

"Hallo?" It was Sofie, sounding annoyed. "Why did you lock the door?"

"We didn't lock it," Maia called back, not bothering to get up. "Someone locked us in. Was it you?"

"No!" Now Sofie was indignant. "My key is in the room. Let me in, please."

"We can't," Laura shouted. "Someone locked the bottom lock."

She could hear Sofie muttering and complaining in German. The door handle jiggled a few more times.

"Who locked this?" Sofie demanded.

"We don't know," Maia said, scribbling something in her little book, as though being locked in was no longer of any interest or concern at all.

"Was there anyone downstairs?" Laura called.

"I don't know," said Sofie, her voice muffled. "I was upstairs talking to the boys. Kasper wants to look for some food."

Laura's stomach rumbled again on cue.

"Go downstairs," Maia ordered. "Look around the front desk for the second key."

"Okay." Sofie let out a long-suffering sigh. "I find ice and a key."

Thumping footsteps declared Sofie's retreat. Laura wondered why Maia was ordering her around this way, and why Sofie was doing Maia's bidding without protest. They'd only known each other for five minutes.

"So," said Maia, gazing at Laura. "What did he say to you?"

Laura was relieved that Maia wasn't questioning her sanity.

"He talked about Minerva," Laura said. "He said he was bringing a message from her."

"He's the messenger god, and Minerva outranks him in the pantheon," said Maia. "That's why she doesn't need to come herself."

"*I know*," Laura said, hoping she wasn't in for another of Maia's lectures. Of course Mercury was the messenger god; of course Minerva outranked him. She'd known all that when she was eight years old. She didn't need Maia to explain rudimentary things about the ancient world to her.

"He also looks after travelers," Maia continued, oblivious to Laura's tone. "He helps people crossing borders and boundaries."

A horrible thought struck Laura: Mercury also guided people from life to death. Was that why he was here—to usher Laura and her strange little group of non-friends to the underworld?

"And people transgressing boundaries," Maia continued. "You know what transgressing means? Breaking a—"

"I know what transgressing means," Laura interrupted. Transgression meant disobeying a law, breaking a rule. In Latin the word was *transgredi*, to step across a line. That's what her grandfather had done, she supposed, when he took the star sapphire—*the eye of Minerva*—from wherever it was buried.

A bird thumped against the window again, this time so hard and loud that Laura almost jumped out of her skin. She turned to the window to rap on it, the way she'd seen her mother rap on their patio doors to shoo away a raccoon that dared to venture too close to the house.

It took a moment for her eyes to adjust to the dim light outside. There was the seagull, screeching again, climbing in the air. The crow was there as well, gray-shouldered wings flapping, but this time it wasn't chasing the seagull. It was dive-bombing the seagull from on high, slamming hard into its back, pecking at its head. The seagull was shaking off the hooded crow, circling back for an attack of its own. With a screech it launched itself at the crow and dove straight into the other bird's head, so hard that the crow seemed to fall through the air.

"What's going on?" Maia asked, but all Laura could do was shake her head. The crow hadn't fallen; it looped up again, driving its beak into the seagull's white underbelly. The seagull screeched—a nasty, high-pitched sound like a child's scream— and plummeted out of sight.

The crow stayed aloft, circling. Laura watched it swoop back and forth outside the window: It was patrolling, she thought, like a feathered night watchman obscured by fog.

She wondered if this was the crow who'd woken her up last night, tapping at the window, depositing the second star sapphire on her windowsill. Maybe it was Mercury himself, in bird form.

"Birds were fighting outside," she told Maia at last. "But it's all over."

"Hallo!" Sofie was outside the door again, rattling the handle. "I have keys, many keys."

There was nothing for Laura and Maia to do but wait while Sofie tried one key after another, exclaiming and complaining in German. Finally something clicked, and there was Sofie, pushing the door open, a triumphant smile on her face. From one fist dangled a heavy-looking swag of keys.

"Thanks," Laura said, relieved that they weren't trapped anymore. She was ravenous with hunger.

"What did the girl at the desk say?" Maia asked. Sofie's eyes widened.

"At first she wasn't there, so I found the keys," Sofie announced, looking pleased with herself. "And then the girl walked in, from the street. Oh my god, she was bleeding! On her head! And holding herself here."

Sofie gripped her stomach and doubled over.

"There was blood there, too. On her dress."

"Was she okay?" Laura asked. Sofie shrugged.

"I don't know. She looked angry. I just run up the stairs to let you out."

"Good," said Maia, and Laura gazed from one to the other. Why were they both so cold and heartless? Serena, the girl in the white dress, wounded in the head, wounded in the belly, had staggered in from the street, and Sofie had just walked away? Now Maia was congratulating her? These were two of the strangest girls she'd ever met in her life.

"So," said Sofie, looking at Maia. "The crow defeats the seagull. This time, anyway."

"Sofie!" Maia shouted, and Laura started: She'd never heard Maia raise her voice, or show that much emotion. And why was Sofie talking about the bird fight? Had she seen it?

"Oh." Sofie glanced at Laura and made a face. "Sorry."

The crow defeats the seagull. Serena in her white dress, wounded in the head, wounded in the belly . . .

Laura's head swirled.

"It's time to go." Maia slid her notebook into her bag, her voice calm again. "We have to leave here. *Now.*"

CHAPTER FIFTEEN

Laura stared at Maia, not moving. She'd seen the seagull get pecked in its head and its belly, bleeding. Just like Serena. The nice girl at reception was . . . a seagull? An enemy of the crows? An enemy of *Laura*? What had Mercury told her? *Other gods disagree, and they now prepare for battle.* Was Serena another god? And did Maia and Sofie know this already, somehow?

"We have to go," Maia repeated. "Laura?"

"Why does she stop talking?" Sofie asked, looking at Laura as though she was crazy. She turned back to Maia. "And, you know, Jack cannot go anywhere. He can't walk. We must leave him here."

"Leave him?" Laura managed to squeak. Poor, injured Jack—they couldn't just abandon him and run away. And run away where, exactly?

"He'll be fine," said Maia. "We don't need him, and he's no worse off here than any of the kids who are sick. Sofie, go tell the boys to keep their door open. We don't want them getting locked in, too."

"You forget," said Sofie, jangling the bundle of keys. "I am *die Schliesserin* now. I open the doors to the jail."

"I'm not going anywhere without checking that the others are okay," said Laura. Suddenly this seemed the most important thing in the world. If Serena was some otherworldly enemy, wasn't *everyone* in the hostel at risk?

"I'll go with you." Maia started pulling on her sneakers. When Laura hoisted her battered backpack onto one shoulder, Maia and Sofie shook their heads.

"This bag is too easy to steal," Sofie told her. "You must hide the stones somewhere else."

Although it was annoying to have both Maia and Sofie telling her what to do, Laura knew this was sensible. The next time someone grabbed the bag off her, bronze tortoises might not be on hand to attack. She unzipped the inside pocket and pulled out the broken bracelet, placing it on the bed. Then she retrieved the second stone, careful not to hold the two in her hand at the same time, just in case the ground below them starting rumbling again.

"You could put them in your shoes," Maia suggested. "Unless you have a better idea?"

"No," said Sofie, shrugging, and Laura realized that Maia was looking at Sofie, asking *her opinion*, not Laura's. Suddenly they were BFFs!

Laura managed to wedge the loose stone between her toes, but it felt so uncomfortable she didn't think she could walk. She grabbed a hoodie from her bag and slipped the bracelet into the pocket, then zipped the hoodie on over her dress. Not ideal, but if would have to do for now.

"We'll meet you in the boys' room in fifteen minutes," Maia told Sofie. "If we don't turn up, come and look for us on the third floor. We'll check on the other girls."

Sofie went ahead, and then Maia and Laura left their room, locking the door behind them.

The third floor was dark, the hall's one light so dim that the walls looked a pale apricot rather than their usual dire orange. Every door was closed. Laura and Maia weren't heavy walkers like Sofie, but it still seemed to Laura that the floor creaked and complained with their every step. The silence was excruciating, she thought, and just plain wrong, given how many girls and teachers were staying on this floor. It was still early evening. Just two days since Morgan and so many of the others got sick; only one day since Woody, the last teacher standing, had left them outside the Pantheon. But surely someone was feeling better by now? Shouldn't some people be up, laughing and talking?

The room that POTUS and Woody were in was at the end of the corridor. Laura hesitated outside the room she'd shared with Morgan, Nicole, and Courtney.

"I want to check on them," she whispered to Maia.

When Maia didn't protest, Laura cracked open the unlocked door and peered in. The room was in darkness, curtains drawn, and she waited for her eyes to adjust to its gloom and for the familiar shapes of the bunk beds to emerge. Her bed was empty, covers drawn taut, but there were lumps in the three other beds. The only sound was the soft hum of regular breathing. She inched in, stubbing her toe on someone's suitcase, and groped her way to the bunk where Morgan lay. Her friend was fast asleep.

"Hey," Laura whispered, hoisting herself up on the bottom bunk until her face was close to Morgan's. POTUS would probably go nuts about her disregard for quarantine, but Laura didn't care. Something was happening in Rome now that was worse than regular old sickness. "Hey, Morgan. It's me. Are you awake?"

Morgan murmured something incoherent. Her eyes stayed closed. A water bottle, at least half full, was tucked underneath her pillow.

Maia walked over, stepping lightly. Morgan mumbled again and shifted in her sleep. Laura touched her friend's forehead; it felt clammy.

"We shouldn't wake them," Maia whispered.

"Morgan?" Laura tried again in a low voice, but still her friend didn't stir. At least she knew the girls were alive, and not in any obvious distress. She lowered herself down onto the ground, this time knocking her sore ankle on yet another suitcase, and followed Maia toward the half-light of the hallway.

"They have probably taken medication," Maia speculated, and Laura closed the door behind them. "A doctor came yesterday, remember?"

"I guess," said Laura. She wanted to hide away in that dark room and go to sleep herself. Maybe everything that was happening was just a terrible dream.

Maia tapped on the teachers' door and turned the handle when there was no reply. But this room was locked.

"We need Sofie's keys," Maia said. "There could be a master key on that chain for every room in the hostel."

"Should we go find her?" Laura whispered, annoyed that they hadn't thought to take the keys in the first place. Her stomach twisted with hunger, and her ankle throbbed in sympathy.

Before they could do anything, the door to the room opened, just a few inches—enough to reveal the gray face of Mrs. Johnson and her Riverside High Jumping Buffalos T-shirt. Her hair was disheveled and it looked as though she could barely keep her eyes open.

"Girls," she whispered, her voice groggy. "What are you doing down here? Is everything okay?"

"There was an earthquake," Maia told her, "but we're all fine."

"An earthquake?" POTUS looked confused. "We must have slept through it. The doctor came by again this morning and gave us all shots. Really, you're okay? I wish I could say I'm getting better, but all I seem to do is sleep."

"Do you have everything you need?" Maia asked her.

"Well," said POTUS, rubbing her eyes, "I went around with the doctor this morning and gave everyone water. Nobody feels much like eating, but the doctor had some minestrone soup delivered to us at some point. Maybe lunchtime, maybe later. I don't know."

The teacher stifled a yawn, and Laura felt something between relieved and disheartened. Everyone was getting medical help, water, and food. But, she realized, she'd been secretly hoping that the teachers would be better by now, and ready to take charge, to make everything okay again. Clearly, that wasn't going to happen.

"What time is it now?" POTUS asked, her eyes bleary.

"It's a little after seven at night, I think," Laura managed to say.

"You need some money for dinner?" POTUS could barely speak for yawning. There was no point in worrying her, Laura realized. No point in saying that the earthquake had messed with the city so much that normal things like grocery stores and restaurants were probably closed, or all smashed up. No point mentioning that the old gods Minerva and Mercury were taking an overactive interest in their little group. In the state she was in, Mrs. Johnson couldn't do anything to help them.

"We have money," Maia told her. "We'll be fine."

"Stay close to the hostel, all right? And stick with the boys. Make sure they don't starve. They're not sick, are they?"

"Oh, no," Laura said quickly. They were bruised and cut and limping and beaten up, but there was nothing anybody could do about that. "They're just hungry."

"Good," said POTUS, her eyes drifting closed again. She was gripping the doorframe with one hand, as though she needed it to keep herself upright. "Wait one second."

She ducked into the room, and appeared again clutching a big thermos.

"It's some of that minestrone, in case one of you wants it. But if you go out to eat, don't stay out too late, will you?"

Laura managed to nod.

"Hopefully tomorrow we'll all be better, and this ash cloud will lift, and the airport will open, and we can . . ." POTUS couldn't even finish her sentence.

"You go back to bed, Mrs. Johnson," Maia said. "Don't worry about us. We're fine."

Their teacher managed a grim half smile before she closed the door.

"We'll leave the minestrone with Jack," Maia said to Laura in a low voice.

"Where are we going?" Laura whispered back, but Maia didn't reply. There was nothing Laura could do but follow her up the endless stairs to the boys' room, and hope they could devise some kind of coherent plan—to eat, to hide, to get through the night.

The boys' room resembled a very small, very orange ER waiting room, though it still smelled like socks rather than rubbing alcohol. Dan was sitting on the ground, his head resting back on a bed, a wet towel clamped over his black eye. Jack lay on the bed behind Dan with his bad leg raised on a suitcase topped with a pillow. When Maia handed Jack the thermos of minestrone, he looked disappointed.

"It's not really hot anymore," Maia told him. "But there are no nuts in it."

"Thanks," Jack said, unscrewing the cap and peering in. Whatever he saw mustn't have been that appetizing, because he made a face.

It was no surprise to see Sofie clucking around Kasper, who'd managed to put on a new T-shirt. He was sitting on another bed, dabbing at the gash on his leg with a washcloth. It didn't look too bad, Laura thought, and it didn't seem to be causing him much pain.

"We were just thinking about coming to look for you," Dan said, sounding annoyed. "We heard about you getting locked in."

"I rescued them," said Sofie, manhandling the washcloth out of Kasper's grip so she could take over the dabbing of his wound.

"Where's your bag?" Dan asked Laura. "You didn't leave the stone things in your room, did you?"

"I'm not that stupid," she said. "One's in my shoe and the bracelet is in my pocket."

"We have to get out of here," Maia announced.

"We have to get food, that's for sure." Dan threw the wet towel onto the floor and pushed himself up. His bad eye was almost completely shut, red and puffy, with a shadowy welt smudged along his cheekbone. "Did you see POTUS?"

Laura nodded. "She's still sick. They all are."

"They can't help us," Maia said. That was such an odd turn of phrase, Laura thought. Maia kept talking about who could and couldn't "help" them.

Kasper looked equally confused. "Do we need help?" he asked. "We can go out and find food ourselves."

"I can't go anywhere," groaned Jack, clutching the thermos to his chest.

Kasper stood up. "We can bring you back something," he told Jack.

"One second." Maia held up her hand, sounding so commanding that everyone looked at her. "We're not coming back here. Not tonight, anyway."

There was silence in the room. Maia looked around at them all with that quizzical expression Laura had come to recognize as trademark Maia, somewhere between impatient and bemused.

"Laura, tell them what happened to you today," she said.

"We know—she got attacked by stuff," said Jack, leaning

back on his pillow and wincing. "We all did. This is, like, the worst school trip ever."

Laura didn't know what to say, or where to begin, so she gazed at Maia, hoping to be prompted.

"The guy who let us out of the Internet place," said Maia, nodding at her.

"I didn't see him," said Kasper. "What did he do? Did he try to steal your bag, too?"

Laura shook her head.

"He talked to me," she said, and hesitated. How much could she say? How much would they believe? "He talked to me about the star sapphires. He said that . . . that . . . they were the eyes of Minerva."

"So some weird guy says a weird thing." Dan riffled through his duffel and pulled out a sweatshirt, as though the conversation wasn't worthy of his full attention.

"Not just a weird guy," Maia continued. "It was Mercury."

No one said a word. The only sound was the patter of rain against the window, and the distant, discordant wailing of fire engines and ambulances. Sofie smiled knowingly, but the boys just looked confused.

"You mean, Mercury—the god?" Kasper asked in shock. "And Minerva—the goddess?"

"He had wings on his heels," Laura managed to say, barely believing the words herself. "And he talked about Minerva."

"Is that why you were asking about her this afternoon?" Dan asked. He still looked skeptical.

"You all probably know that Minerva's chief physical characteristic was—is—her gray eyes," said Maia.

Is? Laura thought. Did Maia really believe these gods were alive and well and living in—wherever Roman gods lived?

"Huh. Gray like Laura's," Dan said. Her cheeks started to burn again, because he was looking at her so intently. "And like the stones," he said. "The star sapphires."

"What else did this . . . this Mercury say?" Kasper asked.

Laura turned to him. "That they were stolen, hundreds of years ago, by some emperor. He took them from Minerva's sacred temple and put them somewhere else—I don't know where. But the gods destroyed him, and destroyed that place, and the stones lay buried until . . ."

"Until when?" Jack had propped himself up on his elbows.

"Until my grandfather took one," Laura said, her face still burning. She felt ashamed, though she was sure her grandfather didn't know he was stealing, exactly—and certainly not that he was stealing something so important.

"Can we see them again?" Kasper asked, and Laura nodded. She tugged off one shoe and tipped the stone onto the floor.

The bracelet she pulled from her hoodie pocket and dangled by its thin broken chain; Dan took it from her and laid it on the floor. Her hands were shaking, she realized, but she didn't know if it was from anxiety or just hunger.

She moved the second stone closer to her bracelet, bumping heads with Dan when he leaned over to adjust their positions and scoot the chain out of the way.

"Sorry," they said at the same time.

"Look," Dan added, and everyone huddled around, staring down at the floor. "Imagine them as eyes on a statue."

"Maybe not a statue," said Kasper. He nudged the stones with a fingertip. "Maybe some sort of artwork on a wall or a floor."

"A mosaic." As soon as Laura said it, the image made sense to her. She could see the star sapphires as eyes, staring up from some grand, intricate, giant mosaic set into the floor of a long-lost temple—one eye a bluish tinge, the other green, both shot through with golden veins like the sparkling trails of fireworks. "A mosaic of Minerva. And these are her eyes."

No one said anything. The rain sounded heavier now, drumming against the window. Finally Kasper sighed and rocked back on his heels.

"I don't know if I can really believe that the boy you saw was Mercury," he said. He looked up at Laura, a frown on his handsome face, and Laura understood. She wouldn't believe it herself, if she hadn't seen Mercury with her own eyes, and talked to him.

"If Laura says it's true, then it's true." Dan looked so stern that it was almost comical. She suspected that he didn't entirely believe her, either, but he just couldn't resist the chance to disagree with Kasper.

"Okay," said Kasper, holding himself steady with one hand, peering down at the stones. "Let's say it's all true. That Laura really did meet—a god. Okay. And he had a message for her from Minerva, and it was that these stones were taken, without permission. Well . . ."

He trailed off.

"What?" Sofie asked, gazing at him in her usual love-struck way. Kasper looked up, his blue eyes intent on Laura's face.

"Maybe," he said, "I'm thinking that the right thing to do is to put them back."

CHAPTER SIXTEEN

Put them back where, exactly?" Dan asked. "The elephant church?"

He had to then explain to Kasper that this was the name they'd given the church of Santa Maria sopra Minerva. They'd walked past the church their first day in Rome but hadn't gone inside. They'd all seen the statue outside, though, of a small elephant carrying an obelisk on its back.

Laura thought back to that day. The church was built hundreds of years ago over the ruins of a temple to Minerva, POTUS had mentioned as they walked past. Did that mean the remnants of a fresco to Minerva could be buried under the building? And, if so, how were they supposed to get to it?

"There's the Capitoline Triad temple thing," Jack said. "POTUS was talking about it the other day."

"But that was built over hundreds of years ago," Dan pointed out. "What are we supposed to do—tunnel our way in?"

"You have no idea where your grandfather found the stone?" Kasper asked Laura, and she shook her head, still unable to speak. She couldn't believe the boys were discussing this with so much enthusiasm and so little sense. Mercury had told her that the stones were stolen back in ancient times. And then, wherever they'd been moved to was destroyed, and they'd lain buried, underground, for centuries. Somehow her grandfather had found one during the war—maybe because the ruins had just been uncovered, or maybe because a fallen bomb had exposed it.

And now Mercury and his army of crows had gotten ahold of the second stone, and—on the orders of Minerva herself, apparently—kept throwing it at Laura, so she'd have the pair. *The eyes of Minerva.* She didn't want them; all she wanted was to keep her bracelet and get out of this city before it fell to pieces. But it seemed as though she didn't have any choice.

Sofie straightened up, sighing in a theatrical way and stretching her long, pale arms toward the ceiling. The sky was dark, and the rain kept falling. A soggy curve of ash piled up on the windowsill outside.

"So there is no Temple of Minerva in Rome," she said, as though that was the end to it. "Nowhere to put the stones back. We should go to find something to eat."

"Yes," said Maia, and Laura realized that Maia had said nothing for some time—very unusual in a conversation about the ancient world. Maia usually liked to show off her knowledge and correct other people. "Good idea. We're all hungry."

"Wait." Kasper, crouched on the ground, tapped the scratched-up floor next to the two star sapphires. "Laura said they were taken from a temple and placed somewhere else. There they lay in peace, yes? Until her grandfather took one. So that's the building we need to find. It could be an old villa or palace, a place where the person could afford mosaics on the walls and the floors and the ceiling . . ."

The ceiling.

Something dinged in Laura's brain, a floating memory. She thought of the collage of pictures—photographs torn from magazines, illustrations, maps, drawings—on the wall above her desk. There was something she could half remember and almost see, ripped from a copy of *National Geographic* her father had brought home one day, because he knew she'd be interested in one of the stories.

On one half of a page was a photograph of a vaulted ceiling above a vast empty space, everything the color of dusty clay apart from spots of faded mosaic fragments set into its soaring heights.

The other half of the page was an artist's impression of what the mosaic looked like originally, spreading its intricate net over the entire ceiling. The shape of a woman, a goddess, in a flowing robe, a shield in her hand. Minerva.

"The Golden House," said Laura. As soon as she said it, she knew this was the answer. She also wished she'd kept her mouth shut.

"What's the Golden House?" Dan asked. "Is it here in Rome?"

"Nero's palace," said Maia, nodding. "The Domus Aurea."

"It's closed," Laura said quickly. "It keeps collapsing, and nobody's been able to visit it for a couple years."

"Was it open when your grandfather was here?" Kasper asked.

"I don't think so," Laura told him, trying to remember what she'd read. The belowground ruins had been discovered sometime in the Renaissance, when painters like Raphael would lower themselves down on a rope, carrying a taper of light, so they could see the frescoes and mosaics. But it still remained romantic, vine-entangled, cavelike ruins until well into the twentieth century, and most of its hundreds of rooms were gone.

"Maybe it wasn't a museum your grandfather could tour," said Dan, trying to open his bad eye. "But he and his buddies might have gone to kick through the ruins. He might have come across whatever was left of the mosaic and just picked up the stone."

"The Golden House," Kasper mused, rocking back and forth on his haunches, his amber pendant swinging. "The emperor Nero stole the eyes of Minerva from her temple to make a big mosaic in his palace. And then the gods destroyed him as punishment."

"And the Golden House is closed," Laura said again. "Like, with scaffolding and bars, to keep people out because it's unsafe."

She didn't know if this last part was entirely true, but she wanted to stop this discussion right now, before anyone got carried away and suggested trying to break in.

"We could ask the girl at the desk downstairs if she knows," said Kasper, standing up straight. "She found a way for us to see the closed church. Maybe she can get us into the Golden House."

"No." Sofie shook her head at him, and Kasper wasn't the only one in the room looking surprised: Sofie usually agreed with everything he said. "She's not a good person. Probably she's a harpy."

"A—what?" Laura blurted.

"Sofie!" Maia exclaimed. This was the second time Laura had heard her reprimand Sofie, and it didn't make any more sense now than it had earlier. She didn't know why Maia cared what Sofie said, and why Sofie seemed to take it without complaint. Right now she looked completely unrepentant.

"What?" she asked Maia, shrugging. "They should know. She might attack them. She already tries to lock us up in our room."

"*What* are you talking about now?" Dan sounded completely exasperated. "*Serena* locked you in your room?"

"And then she fought the crow," Sofie went on, ignoring Maia's ferocious expression. "But the crow won. For now. This is why we have to go."

A harpy—Laura's mind whirred. In mythology, harpies were monsters, women in the shape of birds; Mrs. Johnson had read Virgil aloud in class. *Suddenly the harpies arrive, in a fearsome swoop from the hills, flapping their wings with a huge noise . . .*

If Serena *was* a harpy—and anything seemed possible now—maybe she had been recruited by those "other gods" Mercury had mentioned, the ones who didn't want Laura to have the star sapphires. And maybe Serena wasn't the only harpy in town. The seagull that was shot down in the cemetery; the one that swooped on her at the fountain outside the Pantheon. Maybe they were harpies as well.

Laura felt sick with fear just thinking about it. It was bad enough when she'd thought they were just aggressive birds.

And now there was one right downstairs, in this very building.

At least, if Sofie's theory proved right. And how did Sofie *know* that, anyway? And why did Maia seem to agree with her? Laura knew that there was still some piece of the puzzle she wasn't seeing.

"Okay," said Dan, sounding tired and sarcastic. "First we have Mercury chatting up Laura, and then Minerva sending her messages, and now there are harpies working in the hostel."

"Just one," Sofie corrected him. Maia's mouth was a tight line of disapproval. "We think."

"*You* think," said Dan. "Look, if we don't get something to eat soon, I think we'll all be hallucinating."

"Jack should stay here," Maia said, "with his minestrone."

"Cold minestrone," he said, looking miserable. "And a dangerous harpy at the reception desk. Thanks."

"And the rest of us will go out to eat and make some kind of plan," said Dan. "We can discuss mythical creatures later. Let's go."

"I don't want to offend anyone," Kasper said slowly, "but maybe, if people keep trying to steal the stones, Laura should not be the one to carry them. Or Sofie. Or Maia."

"You mean, any of the *girls*," Laura said, annoyed.

"I mean, if angry men attack us—or harpies," he said, nodding in Sofie's direction, "then perhaps it's better if I'm the one fighting them off. I have two inside pockets in my jacket, here. The stones will be safer."

"He's right," Maia told Laura after a minute. "You can't walk far with stones in your shoes, and carrying them in your hoodie pockets isn't safe. If Kasper's attacked, he could fight off someone more easily."

"I could take one," Dan volunteered, but Maia looked unimpressed with that idea.

"You can't see properly," she told him in her blunt way, and Laura knew she was right. Much as she'd rather hand the star sapphires—particularly her bracelet—to Dan to take care of, Laura wasn't stupid: his black eye still looked swollen and angry. And if they did get jumped again—well, one black eye a day was enough. Dan looked offended, but he didn't argue. His face had to be throbbing, Laura thought.

"Fine," she said. "Please be careful with the bracelet."

"I promise I will." Kasper held out his hand, and Laura pooled the bracelet in his palm. After he zipped it away in an inner pocket of his light jacket, she handed him the second stone. This he stowed in another inner pocket. Then, after waving good-bye to a sour-looking Jack, the five of them trooped downstairs.

Serena—the alleged harpy—was nowhere to be seen in reception. But they all still hurried out, Sofie splashing the set of keys on the counter as they raced by. Outside, the rain had stopped but the darkness felt deep and velvety, the moon hidden by the ash cloud and the streetlights in their lane not lit up, maybe because of the earthquake.

"I could have taken the stones," Dan whispered. "Europeans can't fight anyone. That's why they needed people like your grandfather to come here during the war and save their—"

"Sssh!" Laura nudged him. It was too late for sniping, and she felt hungry and afraid and unsure whether she'd done the right thing. Should she have told everyone about Mercury and his message? Should she have handed over the star sapphires to Kasper for safekeeping?

She looked at the battered little group around her. What if they really couldn't return to the hostel tonight: Where would they go? What terrible thing would happen next?

CHAPTER SEVENTEEN

They had one mission now: food. But every restaurant they reached was closed or, in one case, blackened with fire, smoke still steaming from its second-story windows.

All the handbag sellers and toy hawkers had disappeared, as though the earthquake had swept them all away, though there were a few other tourists out. Laura watched them taking pictures of damaged buildings until someone shouty and bad-tempered in a uniform ordered them away.

With every step Laura felt hungrier and hungrier. At this point, anything would do: potato chips, a candy bar, a hunk of bread. The nearest convenience store, which they'd all visited earlier in the trip to buy a cold drink or a snack, was dark, its doors boarded up. The pizza place where they'd eaten on

Sunday night had cracked windows, its sign upside down and smashed on the sidewalk.

When Dan drifted up to suggest another route to Maia, Kasper fell in step with Laura.

"Don't worry," he said, patting his jacket pocket. "Everything safe and good."

"Patting your pocket kind of gives it away," she told him. "We had the big street-smart security talk at our school before we left."

"Did they mention volcanic eruptions and earthquakes?"

Laura smiled. "Just pickpockets and con artists. You know, don't stop when anyone asks you to sign a petition. Don't fall for anyone's hard-luck story. Don't get sucked into street gambling games. Don't let your bag dangle, or your wallet show."

"Don't anger the gods."

"Something like that."

"You're too smart to fall for petty thieves," he told her. "It seems like you've traveled a lot. Not just in the US, I mean."

Laura wasn't sure, but it kind of felt as though Kasper was flirting with her. She remembered how he'd stroked her wrist at the Pantheon.

Or maybe hunger was making her light-headed.

"Mexico once," she told him. "And Montreal when I was little, so I don't really remember it. I've never been to Europe before, though I've wanted to come to Rome, like, forever. I never thought any of *this* would happen, of course. Be careful what you wish for, right?"

Kasper's pace slowed, so Laura slowed down as well, a little space opening up between them and the rest of the group.

"I want to say something," he said, his tone more earnest. Laura's arms prickled with cold, although the evening air was quite warm, and the city had that almost-fresh after-rain smell she usually liked. Now, of course, it reminded her of Mercury, and the way he smelled more like an element of nature than a person.

"What?" She tried to keep her voice steady, but she was dreading whatever Kasper had to say. When boys started talking earnestly—well, it was almost always personal and embarrassing.

"I know your bracelet has a lot of sentimental value," he said. "I understand. This piece of amber I have?"

He patted at the leather string around his neck, and its amber animal with the strange scratches.

"You said it was your father's," said Laura. "He found it in a bog in Norway, right? When he was little."

"That's right. But it's very old, we think. Not just ancient— maybe from prehistoric times. Thousands and thousands of years ago, people wore things like this, little animals carved out of amber, as magical protection."

"Wow," said Laura, wishing her bracelet offered protection. All it seemed to do was get her into trouble.

"So I understand how you feel about your bracelet," Kasper continued, and now Laura knew what he was trying to do: talk her into abandoning it. She kept her eyes fixed on the sidewalk, stepping over some broken glass and another upturned store sign. "With the stone your grandfather stole . . ."

"I don't think he *stole* anything," Laura said, her voice terse, though Kasper wasn't entirely wrong. She remembered her grandfather saying that lots of soldiers came home from the war with "souvenirs" they'd picked up in bombed-out houses or abandoned stores. He and his pals were just teenagers, not much older than Dan and Kasper.

"Sorry, I didn't mean it like that. But you know what I'm saying, yes? Maybe if we take both stones to the place he found one, we move the clock back. Then it's no more bad luck for you, no more trouble, no more people attacking us. We all leave Rome, and everything is fine again. Otherwise . . ."

"What?" Laura asked, looking up at him—Kasper with his golden hair and broad shoulders, like a god himself, come back to life.

"Otherwise maybe we'll never be able to leave." He was dead serious, she could see. He almost looked upset. "Maybe there'll be another earthquake, a worse one. Or something else—a tsunami, I don't know. Maybe the volcano will erupt even bigger, and we'll be buried like Pompeii. I know this sounds extreme, but we don't know, do we? Yesterday we had no idea of what bad things were about to happen."

"But even if I agreed to give up the bracelet," Laura said, trying not to get upset herself, "I don't know how we'd go about making things right. Like I told you before—the Golden House is all boarded up. Even if we knew the right room to look for, and even if all this earthquake-and-ash stuff wasn't going on, nobody's allowed in there. It's dangerous."

A hooded crow soared out of the shadows and settled on a striped awning on the other side of the street.

"Hey!" Dan called. "That place looks open!" The others were crossing the road now, running to get out of the way of a fire truck rumbling by.

"Food," said Kasper, grinning at her. Laura was relieved he was letting the subject of returning the bracelet drop. "At last, something good today."

The crow took flight, sailing across the street and then looping back, just visible in the darkness. When Laura reached the restaurant door, it flapped away into the sky, disappearing into the ash and the clouds.

In the restaurant, where most of the chairs were already stacked on tables, the usual menu wasn't available. They all had to have a strange salad with bits of corn in it, veal pounded thin and coated in breadcrumbs, and some soggy fried potatoes, but no one complained. They all started devouring everything, and it was the most delicious meal Laura could remember having in days.

She made sure she sat at the opposite end of the wobbly table from Kasper. He hadn't been rude to her, or insulting in any way; he was being very reasonable, not trying to bully her at all. She just didn't want to get drawn into another conversation about "giving back" the stones. It wasn't as though she could go and buy another one at a store when she got home. This one was special, because the star sapphire had been found—taken, whatever—by her grandfather, and it was the only thing of his that she had. To give it away would be worse than losing it, worse than having it stolen.

Really, if she'd left it at home, would any of this have happened? Mercury had said that Minerva was "waiting" for her to come to Rome, but maybe what he meant was that the gods were just waiting for the missing stone to return. Laura had been in Rome two wonderful, carefree, eruption-free days. Nothing had happened until the third day, when a woman—maybe another harpy, if Sofie was right—tried to steal the first stone at the Trevi Fountain, and the crow in the cemetery dropped the second stone into her bag. That was the day the volcano erupted. That was the day everyone else got sick. What was it Mercury said? *When Minerva saw you here, she was satisfied.* What would have happened, Laura wondered, if Minerva hadn't been satisfied? Maybe Laura would have been punished in some way for what her grandfather had done—a punishment even worse than what they'd gone through the past two days.

Every so often she caught Kasper looking at her from the other end of the table. He wasn't trying to get her attention. In fact, he seemed pensive, no big smile lighting up his handsome face. He barely engaged in conversation with Sofie and Maia, who were sitting closest to him.

Dan sat opposite Laura, finishing off the burned potatoes she hadn't eaten. Back at the hostel he'd changed into a red Vans 66 T-shirt, and it was pretty much the same color as the welt under his eye. He was feeling much better, he told her. He'd taken some kind of pain med that Maia had in her bag, and he insisted that his face wasn't hurting that much anymore. Certainly, he gobbled down his dinner with gusto.

"I'm sorry about before," he said to Laura softly, picking up a charred potato.

"What do you mean, before?" Laura had to bend her head toward his to hear what he was saying.

"That stuff I said about Europeans and the war and all that." Dan looked sheepish. "I guess I sounded like an ugly American. Anyway, you know what I'm saying. It's just . . ."

"Kasper. I know. You have to stop letting him get to you. He's not that bad." Although she disagreed with Kasper, Laura didn't think he was a bad guy. Maybe Dan disliked him because Kasper was tall and blond and good-looking. He would have been top dog, no doubt, at their high school. Morgan would have been besotted with him. In other circumstances, Laura could see herself falling for Kasper as well—though back at school he would be totally out of her league. Boys like Kasper and Dan usually had nothing to do with nerdy girls like Laura, a girl who wore secondhand dresses, rode her aunt's old bike to school every day, and only went to the mall when she had to work a shift as a camera elf in Winter Wonderland.

With his fork, Dan toyed with the scraps left on his plate, drawing a pattern in the grease. He started to say something, then stopped.

"What is it?" Laura prompted.

"It's . . . I mean, does he have to stare at you all the time?"

Laura glanced down the table at Kasper, just long enough to register him gazing toward her, still with that pensive expression on his face. Now she didn't know where to look— not at Kasper, and certainly not at Dan.

"He's just staring into space. You know, thinking," she mumbled. "It's nothing."

"I don't just mean tonight," Dan said, setting down his fork. "He does it all the time."

"I've never noticed," Laura told him, and this was the truth. Kasper had always been perfectly friendly and maybe a little flirtatious. But she hadn't detected anything more. Maybe she was dense about these things, because she wasn't used to boys looking at her—unless they were staring at her "mutant" eyes, or trying to copy her work in class when they thought she didn't notice.

When Dan said nothing more, Laura didn't, either, but inside she was fizzing and churning. *Was* Kasper staring at her all the time? Why did Dan care so much if he did? And what, exactly, was she supposed to do now—smile, argue, change the subject?

"I'm just going to the bathroom," she mumbled, scraping

her chair away from the table. She followed the pointing hand of their flustered waiter and headed toward the back of the restaurant. Down a narrow corridor, Laura spotted a scrawled sign and followed its arrow outside, through a heavy metal door and into a small courtyard. The bathrooms seemed to be set into the next building, though in the dark it was hard to make out which door was which.

Someone stepped out of the shadows and Laura gasped, staggering back until she bumped into the brick wall. It was a man, a dark man—no, a boy, around her age. It was Mercury, smelling like a fresh, cold breeze, a rain shower. He seemed as dark as the night itself: dark clothes, dark hair, dark eyes.

"Laura," he said, and she could barely breathe, her heart pounding. For the first time she noticed that the gray of his shirt was a feathery down rather than fabric.

"The crow we saw outside just now," she said, conscious that her voice was shaking, "was that you?"

Mercury twitched his head.

"You take the form of a bird?" Laura really wanted to get this straight, once and for all. Mercury twitched again, something between a bow and a nod. "And that was you at the hostel, fighting the seagull? And at the fountain, attacking the guy who tried to mug me?"

"No," he said. "I do not fight: I am a messenger only. But Apollo commands the crows of Rome, and they carry out his wishes. And his wish now is to please his sister, the great goddess Minerva. The crows protect you, as you have seen. And they delivered the second stone to you, Minerva's other eye."

Apollo, Minerva, Mercury. The crow flying in the cemetery, the crow tapping on her window, the crow attacking the mugger at the fountain. All of them watching Laura. She could barely breathe.

A breeze wafted a drift of ash across the enclosed yard and she shivered, though it wasn't really cold. Her hands scraped the brick of the wall behind her and she felt fixed to the spot, watching the ash swirl like mist, transfixed by Mercury's dark eyes.

"The creatures of this place still hear the gods," Mercury said. "They do as we wish."

"Even—even creatures carved out of stone?" Laura managed to ask. "Even things painted on walls?"

"We command them all," he said, his head twitching forward again. He was so close that if she reached her hand out, she could stroke the gray feathers on his chest.

"So the . . . the *things* that attacked me?"

"Commanded by *other* gods." Mercury bowed. "Minerva wishes to bestow on you a great honor, to be her representative on earth. Her handmaiden. But not everyone wishes it. You understand?"

Laura felt miserable. Great honors were fine, but she'd rather win, say, a Pulitzer Prize one day than serve the rest of her life as the handmaiden—whatever that meant—of an ancient goddess. The old gods were notoriously vengeful, capricious, and touchy. And violent—they were superviolent. People who crossed them or let them down in some way ended up beheaded, buried alive, or condemned to some brutal eternal punishment.

"The thing is," she spoke, her voice still shaky, "I'm an American, not a Roman. No disrespect at all, but . . . but we don't believe in the old gods. Nobody does anymore. Not even here in Rome."

This sounded more insolent than she'd intended; Laura didn't want to offend Mercury, or, worse, bring Minerva's wrath down on her head. While she was talking, his head twitched to one side, his short dark hair ruffled by the breeze and dusted with silvery ash. Luckily, he seemed to be intently listening rather than looking enraged.

"Just because Romans have deserted their gods," he said at

last, "doesn't mean that the gods have deserted Rome. This you must see, from everything going on around you. You must persevere until the battle is over, and Vulcan and Mars are vanquished. Then you will be able to leave with the sacred stones."

Vulcan. Mars. A battle. Mercury might think he was passing on some upbeat message about hanging tough, but from Laura's point of view, the news just got worse and worse. A helicopter's blades chattered close by, stirring up a storm of ash and drowning out the wail of a passing fire engine. Above the rooftops she could see flames shoot into the cloudy sky. She didn't want honor and glory and special attention from the great goddess. She just wanted all this to stop.

"Remember, you are to keep the sacred stones," Mercury went on. "The eyes of the great goddess. You have let them leave your possession, and that is unwise."

The door to the restaurant began to creak open; it was heavy, and squeaked as though it hadn't been oiled in years. Suddenly, Mercury sprang into the air and was transformed in an instant into a hooded crow that flew off, in a shadowy blur, into the night sky.

Sofie emerged from the bright lights of the restaurant, tripping over the doorstep and staring at Laura with wild eyes.

"You must come!" she said, holding the heavy door ajar. "Quick!"

"What's wrong?" Laura asked, her heart still thumping from the conversation with Mercury, with all its strange and unwelcome information.

"The stones are gone," said Sofie. "Kasper has taken them and run away to the House of Gold."

CHAPTER EIGHTEEN

What?" Laura couldn't believe her ears. "He ran off to the *Golden House?*"

"Yes, yes. That's what I said to you." Sofie sounded annoyed. "This is where we think he goes, anyway. He tells us he goes to the bathroom, but instead he walks out the front door. And now Dan runs after him."

Laura pushed herself off the wall and squeezed past Sofie. This was insane: It was nighttime, and the Golden House was closed, and the city was a jumble of roadblocks, rubble, and fires. By now there were probably roving bands of looters as well, clambering through the wreckage of stores and homes, not to mention the people—or harpies or spirits or other vicious minions of the gods—who were after the star sapphires. Kasper had no idea what he was letting himself in for.

At the table, Maia was calmly counting euros into the waiter's outstretched hand.

"We must go at once," Sofie said, practically bouncing with impatience. "Hurry, hurry!"

"This is your fault," Maia said to Sofie, without acknowledging Laura at all. "You were supposed to be watching him."

"I cannot go to the bathroom with him," Sofie complained. "You are the one who says—yes, Kasper, please put the stones in your pockets. They will be *so* safe."

Maia had nothing to say to this.

"Let's go," Laura said. This was no time for one of their confusing arguments, and the Golden House was a long walk from here, beyond the Colosseum. It would be hard to catch the boys if they were running. And it would be hard for Dan to catch Kasper, if Kasper had any sort of a head start. Dan was a really strong runner, but he'd taken quite a beating today, and the city was dark and confusing.

When she and the other two girls stepped out into the street, Rome was a jumble of shapes and shadows, lit up here and there by shooting flames. The air felt so warm and smoky, Laura felt as though they walking toward fire.

By the time they skirted the hulking skeleton of the Colosseum, Laura had worked herself up into a fear-fueled anger. Kasper was so arrogant, to steal something that didn't belong to him. And how he imagined he'd "return" the star sapphires was beyond Laura. The ruins were closed to the public. What did he really think he could do?

Silently, she, Maia, and Sofie managed to wend their way into the hilly park that now enclosed the ruins. Laura was exhausted and disoriented. In the smoky dark, any light blocked by tall trees, she could barely see her map, and the twisting paths were confusing.

Her only clue was the tall chain link fences, the kind erected by building contractors, curtained with mesh. Warning signs depicting a large hand, and the words *Vietato L'Ingresso*— entry forbidden—dangled at regular intervals. These fences had to be protecting the perimeter of the ruins, to stop any visitors wandering in. At least now they had something to follow.

The search for the main entrance—any entrance—seemed endless. Maia kept peering through gashes in the fence's mesh coverings but must have seen nothing worth reporting on. Finally, after Laura jogged past a clump of trees that smelled of damp pine and woodsmoke, the fence gave way to more substantial iron gates topped by spikes.

"This is it," Laura hissed at Maia, running up to a sign that told her, in six different languages, that the Domus Aurea was closed indefinitely because it was unsafe. The structure of the ruined palace itself was hard to make out in the dark, and Laura had to peer through the bars of the gate to see its two stories of brick colonnades, patched with weedy growth. A park bench and a trash can sat at peace outside the main door, as though they were waiting for the tourists currently banned from visiting.

This wasn't exactly what Laura had been expecting. This looked more like a crumbling barn than an ancient villa. There were only pieces left of Nero's great pleasure palace, she knew; it had been pillaged and dismantled, and most of it had been buried under Trajan's baths, not to mention a more modern park, where the trees had sunk their roots into what was left of the roof. That root system was letting in dangerous amounts of soil and damp, which was why the ruins had been closed for years.

"We will have to get over the gates," said Maia.

Laura pressed against the bars, gazing up at the forbidding spikes. "How?" she muttered.

"Hey," Sofie shouted, pointing into the air. "Can you see them? Hey!"

It took a moment or two for Laura to work out what she was supposed to be seeing. She followed Sofie's flapping hand, looking above the brick facade. There was another fence up there, marking the ridge of the hill where the ruins had been dug out. Shadowy figures moved along the fence, one pausing to try to scale it but sliding back down almost immediately. Two figures—the boys!

"Hey!" Sofie shouted again. "Kasper! Dan!"

One of the boys on the ridge above them lifted a hand to wave.

"Hey!" he called, his voice faint, swallowed up by the night. It sounded sort of like Dan, though it was hard to tell.

"Is he stopping Kasper or helping him?" Laura asked the others. It was so hard to see. She wanted to scream at them to come down from the ridge, but they would never hear. The other figure—was it Kasper?—had bent over. Now, moments later, he was staggering back, holding what looked like a big manhole cover.

Oh no. Had he found a place to drop the stones?

"We have to get up there," she said.

"Impossible," Sofie replied. "We must walk and walk up the hill, and even then we might not find the place they are."

"We can still catch them." Laura was trying to talk herself into this. No way was she just standing here doing nothing while Kasper threw the star sapphires into some cavernous ruins, thinking it would solve everyone's problems. Who knew what would happen next? What if some harpy got her claws on the stones—what would she do with them? And what would Minerva do if the stones fell into the wrong hands? Maybe she'd take revenge on Laura, for betraying her sacred mission or whatever it was.

"We need to go over this." Maia waved a hand at the security fence and its spiky gateposts.

"Yes," said Laura. She looked at the park bench, and then at the weedy trees growing out between the bricks of the building. They could tip the bench on one end and use it as a ladder, maybe. There had to be a way.

A crow flapped overhead; Laura heard the whir of its wings before she could see it. It landed on one of the branches growing out of the building—a sign, Laura decided. The hooded crows, Apollo's creatures, were there to look out for them. Maybe it was even Mercury in crow form, watching and waiting.

"Okay," said Maia, sounding as though the task ahead was the easiest thing in the world. "Let's do it."

To their right a part of the gate was embedded in a low brick wall, and Maia hauled herself onto the lowest rung of railing. If they pushed her, she could reach the top of the iron fence, and if she was really careful, Laura thought she could elude the spikes.

She and Sofie both followed Maia's lead, reaching for the rails and dragging themselves up the short brick wall. Laura had just enough of a foothold to help push Maia up. Although Maia was heavier than she looked, she managed to claw her way to the top, Sofie helping to keep her steady.

"Got it!" Maia shouted, but whatever she'd gotten didn't last long, because she slithered down the gate again, almost knocking Sofie off the wall.

"I am the tallest," Sofie pointed out. "I should go first."

She and Maia managed, with some difficulty, to trade places, and then the girls tried their hoist maneuver again. It worked better this time, because Sofie's long arms could easily reach the top rung of the gate, though it was still a huge effort to get the rest of her up there. Maia and Laura each took hold of one of her feet, and Laura managed to get kicked on the chin and in the shoulder before Sofie, amid much squealing and what sounded like swearing in German, wedged herself into a sitting position between two spikes.

"Now you push, I reach," panted Sofie, her long legs dangling, one hand gripping a spike for balance. Laura pushed as hard as she could. Maia felt like a lump of concrete, but she had strong arms and managed to pull herself up pretty well, grabbing a low-hanging branch from the nearest tree to help.

Only Laura was left now.

She really didn't know if she could climb the iron gate herself without someone pushing her from behind. Sofie was leaning over, waiting to grab her, but Sofie wasn't *that* strong, not strong enough to hold Laura's entire body weight with one hand. Sofie needed the other hand to hang on to the nearest spike, otherwise they'd both fall.

Maia slid, bumping all the way, onto the ground on the other side of the gate, ready to push through the bars. For the first time in her life, Laura wished she'd made more effort in gym class, and worked on pull-ups rather than joking around with Morgan.

The hooded crow was circling overhead now, calling out what might be a warning, or possibly encouragement.

"Why can't you be something useful, like a griffon?" Laura said under her breath, glancing at the swooping bird. She wedged a foot onto the low bar of the gate and stretched to reach the top with her left hand; Sofie grabbed her right, almost dragging her arm out of her socket. Laura could feel Maia's hands gripping her legs as her sneakers scrabbled against the iron railings.

Her sore ankle bashed the iron, and there was searing pain in her bruised wrist when she managed to grab a spike, but it didn't matter: She was up there, with Sofie pulling her over, and Sofie and Maia catching her—more or less—when she tumbled down the other side.

The crow whooped and wheeled overhead. Long-legged Sofie slid down the other side without any help. Laura strode toward the park bench, rubbing her aching wrist. The three of them made easy work of turning the bench on one end, and again Sofie led the way. She climbed up the first story, using two branches to pull herself up while Maia, precariously balanced, pushed from below. Laura hadn't seen Sofie so enthusiastic about anything the past two days. Breaking and entering was clearly her thing.

When it was Laura's turn, she felt like a toddler compared to Sofie's effortless climb. Maia boosted her, but it took several attempts before Laura could catch a branch, and she bashed her face and knees on multiple bricks. While Maia climbed, Laura lay prone on the walkway above, bark stuck under her fingernails and her forehead moist with blood.

"You are still alive?" Sofie asked her, with disdain rather than sympathy, and Laura nodded, dragging herself onto her knees.

The next level was trickier without the park bench to use as a ladder, but there was a rough stone wall here with more footholds. Sofie, stretching as far as she could, managed to haul herself onto what was left of a buttress. Maia was next, crying out when her bare legs dragged against the stone on her way up. Was that the first time she'd *ever* complained? Laura wondered.

"Throw me your hoodie, Laura," Maia shouted down. "I'll make a rope."

It sounded like a good idea. Laura unzipped, glad to be rid of the warm outer layer, and tossed the hoodie to Maia. But actually going up took forever. Laura squirmed and dangled on the makeshift rope, swinging like a pendulum and bouncing off the stone wall. Finally, though, after a couple of tries, Maia was able to grab her. Sofie lunged for her, and Laura thought they might both topple off the ledge.

Too exhausted to speak, the girls lay in a heap, breathing hard. When Laura looked up, she was relieved to see the hillside and its long fence, obscured by some pungent flowering bush, only a few feet above them. They still had to get over that fence, but it was nothing as high as the gate they'd climbed, and, thankfully, didn't have spikes.

Sofie climbed over easily, then Laura, then Maia—they were getting good at this, Laura thought, even though every part of her ached, and what might be sweat or might be blood was dribbling into her left eyebrow.

"So now we must find the . . ." Sofie began, but if she said anything after that, Laura didn't hear it. All she could hear was a rumble deep beneath her feet. *Like a subway train*, she thought, again. Then the ground started shaking, and a tree, bouncing around as though it was on a trampoline, thudded onto the damp ground. Laura dropped to the ground as well, her face pressed to its loamy wetness, the world still shivering, the crow shrieking somewhere unseen overhead.

This time she knew exactly what it was: another earthquake.

CHAPTER NINETEEN

Maia's leg was pretty much the only thing Laura could see, apart from dirt and grass. Maia and Sofie must have been flat on the ground as well. No one spoke as the earth trembled.

This felt even longer and bigger than the last earthquake. Laura dug her fingers into the dirt and wished it would stop shaking. Now Sofie was saying something she couldn't make out, and when Laura propped herself up, the fence was shaking and dancing. And where Sofie was lying, the ground was splitting open, like a wound when stitches break.

"Get back!" Laura shouted, but she didn't know if anyone could hear her. Maia didn't budge from where she lay, but Sofie seemed to be wriggling across the ground. She was falling, Laura realized, falling headfirst into this schism in the earth.

"Sofie!" Laura cried, crawling toward her like an insect, her belly scraping the grass. She groped blindly for one of Sofie's long legs and made contact, but she couldn't see the girl's head or arms. She could feel Maia now crawling along beside her, trying to get to Sofie, too.

The ground shuddered one last time and then everything got quiet again.

Still gripping Sofie's leg, Laura pulled herself up to her knees. Sofie was on her stomach, her legs still visible, the rest of her dangling, Laura assumed, inside the hole in the ground. It reminded Laura of when Sofie had almost been swallowed by the fresco.

"Great," said Maia, who'd perched on a mound of upturned turf and was hanging on to Sofie's other leg. "Now we have to save *her*."

"Are you okay?" Laura called down, ignoring Maia's typical lack of sympathy.

"Yeah," came the muffled response. "But . . ."

"But what? Don't worry—we can pull you out." Laura wasn't sure if this were true, but there were two of them, and they could try.

"No, not me," Sofie said, and Laura realized that her voice was echoing. A chunk of turf near her shoulders dropped out of sight, collapsing into the hole, and moments later there was the unmistakable sound of a splat as it hit something—the ground?—deep below them.

"Can you see anything?" Maia called.

"A light," said Sofie's muffled voice. "Pull me up, please."

Standing felt strange to Laura, as though the ground were still shaking beneath her. But it wasn't. Every time she and Maia tugged, more of the earth around Sofie dropped away, the hole in the ground growing larger and larger. Soon, Laura worried, it might all cave in and take them with it.

It was hard to see anything clearly, because the moon and stars were all obscured behind dark clouds. Trees rustled close by, and Laura could taste clammy flakes of ash in her mouth every time the breeze stirred. She wondered where the boys were, if they'd found a way in through the grate she'd seen one of them holding. Hopefully they'd found somewhere safe to ride out the earthquake. However annoyed she was with Kasper, she didn't want anything bad to happen to him. And she couldn't even think about something bad happening to Dan. All she wanted right now was to see his beaten-up face again.

When they finally managed to pull Sofie free, she lay panting on her back for a moment, then sat up, dusting dirt off her shoulders.

"They're down there," she said. "I'm sure of it."

"Who? The boys?" Laura asked, and Sofie nodded.

"You saw them?" Maia asked.

"Kasper has a flashlight," said Sofie. "He showed it to me yesterday—it's on his penknife. He's down there, shining it around."

"And Dan?" Laura's stomach churned; she was dreading Sofie's answer. The crow took off from a tree nearby, swooping close to them before landing on another branch.

"I think I can see his legs," Sofie told her. "Maybe. I don't know."

Laura wanted to freak out and scream. *Could Sofie see Dan or not?* She crawled to the edge of the hole in the hill, and stuck her head in.

"Dan!" she called, her voice echoing. There was no reply—nothing they could hear, anyway—so she leaned in farther.

"You should really stay back from that thing," Maia observed. "It may crumble some more and you'll go straight down."

Laura recoiled and, as though on cue, another chunk of earth fell away, disappearing into the void. The crow flapped by again, even lower this time. *Help us*, Laura thought, knowing there was no way a bird could do anything tangible at this moment. Fighting harpies in seagull form was one thing. Rescuing two tall teenage boys from a cavern on a hillside was beyond the capability of any bird, even if Apollo was its boss.

The crow didn't land: It hovered, bouncing on the breeze, directly above the jagged hole in the ground.

"There's the light," Sofie said. For a moment Laura thought she meant that the flashlight—Kasper's flashlight—was shining up from belowground, wherever the boys had fallen or crawled or reached, before the earthquake hit. But the light, Laura realized, was coming from the sky. The billowing gray clouds, all they'd seen above them for days, had parted just a sliver, enough to reveal the moon. It was a sickly yellow, still clouded by shadows, but its light was strong enough to pick out the trees, a tumble of fallen branches, the fence—uprooted and askew in places—and Maia and Sofie's scratched faces.

The crow rose a little in the air and then dove into the fissure, its black wing tips the last thing to disappear belowground.

"We should follow," Maia said, as though a bird flying into a hole in the ground was totally normal and expected.

"I think maybe this is crazy." Sofie sounded doubtful. "If it's deep, then none of us can climb out. Maybe we take some of the fence, the parts on the ground over there. Then we make some kind of ladder to get in and out."

Maia had climbed to her feet while Sofie was talking and was busily tugging at one of the fallen tree's branches.

"*Now* you're thinking," she said to Sofie. "I'm going to need some help—this is heavy."

Laura walked over to see what they were doing. When the tree had been uprooted, some of its branches had snapped off, and Maia had picked out the biggest, one that sprouted potentially useful mini branches, reeking of sap. It took all three of them to drag the huge branch over to the hole in the ground. They lowered it in until it struck earth, and only a foot or so of its splintered end stuck out. Maia tried to wiggle it around, and it moved a little, but it seemed sturdy enough.

"I hope we are not dropping it on someone's leg," said Sofie. "Maybe they would scream if we did that."

"I don't hear any screaming," said Maia, unsmiling. These girls were so weird, Laura thought. How could they be so calm about everything?

"I go first," Sofie announced, and wriggled into position. Laura held her breath as she watched her disappear, bit by bit. The thick branch trembled as it took Sofie's weight, although Maia and Laura were both trying to hold it steady.

"Okay!" Sofie called up, her voice echoing.

"You go next," Maia said to Laura. "I'm smaller than you. It's not so important to have someone holding the branch up here when I go down. You guys can catch me."

"Right." It sounded more like an order than a question. Laura hesitated, not sure exactly what she was doing.

"Go," Maia told her, clearly puzzled that she was still standing there, and Laura lowered herself into the pit, grasping for the branch with her legs. Some of its smaller offshoots had already snapped off, because there wasn't much to hang on to apart from the branch itself—rough, jagged, and lumpy. Laura wished she were wearing jeans instead of a dress: Her legs were going to be scratched to pieces.

There was a little light from the moon, and as she descended, scraping and sliding her way down, Laura was aware of the pinpoint light Sofie had mentioned, possibly from Kasper's flashlight. All she could see clearly, though, was the sharp fins of bark scratching her nose and hands and shins.

When her foot finally thwacked someone's head—Sofie's, she saw, looking down; she was holding the branch steady—Laura could barely believe she'd made it down in one piece. She jumped off, shivering even though the air was really humid in this space, this cave, whatever it was.

And then Mercury stood before her, his slender, feathery form spotlit by jaundiced moonbeams. His dark eyes were wide. Laura was suddenly certain that he was the crow who'd been watching them, the one who'd flown down into the hole.

"Laura," he said softly. "You will stay here. Until the morning. This is a safe place for now."

"For now?" Laura's voice was shaking. "The boys . . ."

"You will all be safe for now," he said. "Take care of the eyes of Minerva."

He held something out toward her, and Laura saw a thin string of gold glinting in the moonlight—*her bracelet*.

Maia thudded to the ground, exclaiming on the impact, and bent over, as though she were tying her laces. She didn't seem at all fazed by the presence of Mercury here in this hot cavern, and for a moment Laura thought that Maia couldn't see him.

But when she straightened, Maia was holding something in her hand; she held it up for Mercury to see, and when he twitched his head, she passed it to Laura. The second star sapphire, Laura knew, without even looking.

"If we cut a small hole in the waistband of your dress," Maia said, peering at Laura, "then maybe we can feed the stone in, and the bracelet. There's a double-layer of fabric, right?"

Laura nodded, plucking at the material.

"Kasper's flashlight has a penknife attached," Maia continued. "I think this'll work."

"Until the morning," Mercury said to Laura, his inky eyes like pinpoints. "Don't be afraid. The sisters will watch over you."

He sprang into the air and landed on the tree branch as a bird. His feathers velvety in the moonlight, he scuttled away up the branch and out of sight.

The sisters will watch over you.

"What did he mean, the sisters?" Laura asked, but Maia was talking to Sofie about the penknife, and didn't hear her.

When Sofie pointed the little flashlight in her direction, Laura could just about make out Kasper's tall form, lying on the ground. Something leaned against him: a slab of stone, maybe, or part of a column.

"Churt," said Maia, and Laura suspected by her tone of voice that she was saying something bad in Russian. Laura stumbled over just as Maia reached for the slab. It seemed to crumble in her hands, a huge chunk coming away. She staggered back, clutching it.

"It's turf," said Maia. "From up there. Just clay and grass. It must have fallen on him when the ground caved in. It's not that heavy."

Kasper mumbled something, wincing when he tried to sit up and rubbing his head while Maia pulled the slab of turf away. He seemed okay, just dazed. But where was Dan?

"Light!" Laura cried, waving a hand at Sofie. "We need to find Dan!"

"I'm here," croaked a voice behind her. "I'm okay."

He didn't look okay. He was propped against a wall, covered in sandy dirt, looking like a dog who'd been swimming in a lake and then rolled, over and over again, on the beach.

Laura hurried over, tripping on another mound of fallen turf in her haste.

"You look terrible," she said.

"You're the one bleeding," he replied, trying to smile, then rubbing at his mouth with the back of his hand. Laura pulled a water bottle from Dan's bag and dribbled some of the water onto her balled-up hoodie, using it to clean the grit off Dan's face. Dan drank some water, and Laura felt herself relax a little: Her neck and shoulders were aching with tension, and her scrapes stung. But the boys were all right, and they had some kind of plan for transporting the star sapphires. And now, according to Mercury, they were safe here, if only for the hours of darkness.

The sisters will watch over you, whatever that meant.

"Seriously, this is the last time I'm rescuing you," Laura told Dan, half smiling.

"Sorry," he said, returning the water bottle to her. She sat down next to him, her back against what felt like stone. It was hard to see much down here, now that the shafts of moonlight were weak and intermittent. Sofie was using Kasper's flashlight to examine his wounds.

Laura cleared her throat and glanced at Dan. "Thanks for trying to—you know. Get the star sapphires back."

"I only caught up with him on the hill. He's a really, *really* fast runner. The next thing I know he's dropping into this place, and I'm following. And then I guess he must have taken the stones out of his pocket and held them together in one hand."

"Because—the earthquake," Laura said, and Dan nodded slowly.

"I guessed that's what was causing it. I shouted at him to drop them, and then stuff was falling on us, and flying around, and I got thrown over here." Dan glanced toward the section where Sofie and Maia were bending over Kasper. "Your boyfriend okay?"

"My boyfriend?"

"Kasper."

"You know he's not my boyfriend." Laura would have laughed, but it would require too much effort. She felt exhausted, bone tired, after the dash through the city and then all the climbing.

"So do you . . . do you have a boyfriend back home?" Dan asked her.

"No," she said quickly, glad now that it was dark here, and he couldn't see her face flush. "You know that."

"Why would I know that?" His voice was low. The others,

on the far side of this strange underground space, were talking, but Laura couldn't make out what they were saying.

"Well," she said, staring into the darkness, grateful for obscuring shadows, "I'm Mutant Girl, remember?"

"That's just stupid kid stuff," Dan said. "People are in awe of you, that's all. Because you're smart and pretty. And you do your own thing—you know what I mean."

Laura didn't, but she didn't trust herself to speak. Their shoulders were brushing; she was conscious of how loud her breathing sounded. Her heart was about to beat its way out of her chest. Dan was still talking, his voice low and calm.

"What I mean is," he said, leaning even closer, "you don't look the same as other girls. You don't act the same or talk the same. You're weird in a good way. You'll probably make a thousand friends at college. High school doesn't count. At college you'll meet other brainy people who value individuality and, I don't know, imagination."

Laura bit her lip. He was giving voice to thoughts Laura had had herself—thoughts and wishes, vague hopes. His hand reached for hers and grasped it, their gritty palms pressing together.

"Look how calm you've been through all this," he went on. "All these terrible things happening to you the last couple of days, and you're not freaking out."

"What?" Laura couldn't help but laugh now. "I'm *totally* freaking out," she admitted. "Half the time I just want to curl up and hide."

She didn't add *and cry*. Even though she realized that Dan, at least the Dan she was getting to know now, would understood.

"Well, nobody could tell," he said. Laura suspected he was just being nice, but she appreciated his kindness. "Anyone who gets to know you would know you're something special. I kind of knew this whole trip, but everything that's happened the past few days . . ."

He didn't finish his sentence, and Laura didn't speak, either. She didn't know what to say. Dan thought she was something special; that she was pretty and smart. The words were dancing through her brain.

"And that guy you were talking to just now, that bird guy—"

"You saw him?" Laura asked, catching her breath.

"Sure. Well, I could see his face, and then I think I saw him turn into a bird, but I may have been hallucinating. So that's . . . Mercury? Really?"

"You didn't believe me before?"

"I did," he protested. "Well, I kind of did. I wanted to believe you. But it all seems so unreal. So *surreal*, I mean."

"I know," Laura told him. She wanted to tell Dan everything, everything Mercury had ever said to her—even the latest weird news that Vulcan and Mars somehow had it in for her. If only her heart would stop thumping and her voice would stop shaking.

She did her best to remember what Mercury had said, and Dan listened as she explained. He was still holding her hand, so Laura decided he wasn't about to tell her she was crazy. She didn't leave out anything—not the crow in the cemetery dropping the second stone into her bag, or the way she'd seen Mercury descend in the rain falling into the Pantheon. She told Dan how Mercury had kept saying that Minerva had chosen her, and was pleased with her, and had decided she should have the two star sapphires—the eyes of Minerva—forever. Dan kept listening, occasionally prompting her with questions.

"So if you take the two stones home with you, what happens?" he asked.

"I don't really know," she admitted. "If I'm Minerva's handmaiden or whatever, maybe it means that I'll be brainy like her?"

Dan squeezed her hand, and Laura's heart raced again.

"But you're already smart," he said. "It's not as though you need help from the gods or whoever. You can achieve whatever you want to achieve without magic, right?"

"I hope so," Laura said slowly. Her back felt damp against the stone wall. She was all talked out. And so tired, she could fall asleep right now, sitting next to Dan, holding his hand. She hadn't even told him about the "sisters" comment yet, or how Maia had seemed completely unsurprised to see Mercury standing there in front of her.

"I think so," Dan said quietly. Then he leaned toward her, so their temples touched.

Laura held her breath. Then in the next instant, his lips touched hers—tasting of dirt and ash and sand and grass, but Laura didn't care. He let go of her hand and stretched his arm around her instead, pulling her close.

"I promise that I'll never call you Mutant Girl again," he said, his voice soft, and that was the last thing Laura remembered hearing before she fell asleep.

CHAPTER TWENTY

When Laura awoke—her head resting against Dan's shoulder, her back stiff from leaning against the stone wall—morning light filtered through the crumbling hole above them. Now that she could get more of a sense of this place, she realized it wasn't a cave at all. There were chipped frescoes barely visible on the floor, and three arched alcoves along the wall. This was a room in Nero's Golden House! The boys had entered it from above when Kasper pulled the grate away and jumped in.

Dan was still asleep, his head resting against the wall and his arm still around her, so she tried to wriggle into a slightly more comfortable position without disturbing him. Nearby, closer than she'd realized last night, Kasper sprawled, snoring.

Sofie and Maia were each curled up sleeping in separate corners, and Sofie appeared almost as catlike as Maia.

Laura took a breath. It was chilly and damp in here, and the air tasted like dust, but at least they were safe. Her bracelet and the other stone lay next to her on the dusty floor.

She'd done what Mercury told her to do—stayed in the cavern overnight, and kept the stones with her. But this wouldn't keep them safe forever; she knew that. Eventually they had to leave this hiding place and face whatever battle might be brewing. But when could they leave Rome? Should she really take the stones with her?

Last night Dan had asked her what Minerva's interest actually meant. Would Laura have some kind of special power? She wasn't sure. What if it was the power to rule the world, the power to change the world, the power to do harm as well as good? Maybe this so-called power would disappear as soon as she left Rome; maybe everything that was sacred and potent about the stones only meant something here, and other places—like, say, Bloomington, Indiana—were beyond the reach of Rome's ancient gods.

Or would she live out her life under Minerva's watchful gaze?

In the past, whenever Laura had thought about her future,

she'd thought about going to college and then maybe traveling some more, if she could save enough money to go see the world. She'd thought about learning and exploring and figuring out what she wanted to do with her life—something interesting and useful, she'd hoped—rather than obsessing about being rich or powerful. And what kind of power could you *really* have if it was bestowed and controlled from on high, dependent on something like possession of a couple of sacred stones? To her it sounded like a power that could be stolen or withdrawn at any time. You'd spend your life paranoid, always worried about what you had to lose.

Last night, right before he kissed her—*had* he really kissed her? That felt almost as surreal as everything else—Dan had said something sweet. He'd said that she didn't need help from the gods. Maybe he was right. Maybe she *was* smart enough to face the world on her own, even if right now, aged sixteen, she was still uncertain a lot of the time, blushing too much and daydreaming and not paying enough attention in gym class . . .

Much as it was an honor to be singled out by Minerva, apparently, and deemed worthy of her "eyes," Laura couldn't help feeling that it was all a big cheat in a way, like getting help on a test, or having someone write a paper for you. True, you might try hard and work hard in life, and not get everything you hoped for: Her parents had told her that. Life wasn't fair;

the world wasn't fair. But they always encouraged her to fulfill her potential and to find her own path. She wouldn't want *them* deciding everything for her: Why be beholden to some supernatural power?

Maybe, Laura thought, shifting uncomfortably on the hard ground, it was time for her to stop being so sentimental. Maybe Kasper had been right. True, he didn't know all the details, and trying to bring both stones back here, to the Golden House, was never going to work out. There'd always be potential for this kind of turmoil and danger in the world while one or both of these stones were floating around. Much safer, Laura realized now, was that she give the bracelet up. She needed to ask Mercury if he could take *both* star sapphires back with him to the other world, or wherever it was that the gods lived.

She looked up at the gray slice of sky visible through the fissure in the hillside. The tears dribbling down her face didn't dismay her: It was a natural reaction, she told herself, to deciding to give the bracelet away. After all, it could have been stolen on Monday afternoon at the Trevi Fountain, or yesterday by the tortoise fountain. At least now she was making the decision herself.

Next to her, Dan shifted, mumbling in his sleep.

Really, Laura knew, deep down, that she could face the world without wearing the bracelet every day. She didn't need a piece of jewelry—just a thing, a material possession—to remind her of her grandfather and their special relationship. Lots of people in the world lost everything they had—people who lost their homes to tornadoes and hurricanes, fires and floods and wars. Earthquakes. She thought of the destroyed shops in Rome yesterday. Things weren't important: people were.

Just looking around this cavelike room at her strange little group gave Laura all the proof she needed. The main thing was that they were all okay. If she gave Mercury the two star sapphires and he took them away from this world forever, then maybe the battle he'd talked about could be averted. There'd be no more earthquakes and fires. The ash cloud would lift, and they could all go home.

Laura heard a flapping of wings, and there was the hooded crow, soaring in through the hole in the ground and landing inches from her feet. In the blink of an eye Mercury stood over her. His downy shirt glistened with dew.

"I need to talk to you," Laura whispered, and he knelt at her side. She sat up fully, feeling resolved. "I want to give the star sapphires back."

"What?" Mercury cocked his head to one side. He looked puzzled.

"I want to give them to you, for you to take back to the other side."

"I don't understand," he said. "These are yours. It is decreed."

"I know, I know. And please know I'm very grateful and honored to be . . . to be chosen in this way. But not everyone wants me to have these. Isn't that what you told me?"

He gave one of his twitchy bows, still looking puzzled.

"And because of that, all *this* is happening," Laura went on.

Dan was stirring now, and Laura wondered if Maia was awake, and Sofie, and Kasper.

"But after the battle—" Mercury began.

"I don't want there to be a battle," she told him. "I don't want to go through my life afraid that there might be a volcanic eruption, or an earthquake. Or that everyone I know will be struck down with an illness, or that there might be some kind of *battle* taking place, just because of me having these two stones. I think they're too powerful and too dangerous to be carried around on earth by a—well, by a mortal like me." She swallowed, summoning up the nerve to continue. "They belong to Minerva, and I want you to take them back to her, where no one else can ever defile or steal or use them. Is that possible? For you to take them away, I mean? To the other side?"

"Perhaps," he said. "But you . . ."

"I mean it," she said, looking into the dark beads of Mercury's eyes. "Wouldn't Minerva think that's the wise thing to do? To take them out of the hands of mortals and rival gods and whoever else is after them?"

"You don't want the power she offers?" Mercury cocked his head to one side again and squinted at her.

"I don't think that anyone here on earth should have the power of Minerva," Laura replied.

Mercury stood there silent, considering her words. Finally he spoke.

"I will do as you ask," he said, bowing his head. "But you must carry them for me until we reach the Pantheon. Minerva wishes no one on earth but you to have the stones."

"The Pantheon—that's how you'll get back? To your world, I mean?" Laura asked, and Mercury nodded.

"It's the only way," he said. "But I must wait for Jupiter to send more rain."

"You can't just fly there?" asked Laura. She was conscious of the others all awake now, everyone sitting up, everyone listening.

"Birds can only fly so high," he told her, with the hint of a smile. "Where I must go is beyond the sky. It is another world, another sphere. It's impossible for you to understand, because no mortals will ever see it."

Dan stretched and leaned forward, pushing hair out of his eyes. His injured eye didn't seem quite so swollen today.

"Well, I guess we're going back to the Pantheon," he said, looking at the others. Everyone began getting up, stiff and awkward, still not speaking. Watching Mercury.

"I will fly ahead, if I can," Mercury said to Laura. "But there are many dangers, and you must be careful. The sisters will tell you what to do."

"The sisters?" said Laura and Dan at the same time. Mercury twitched his head, darting a glance over to the corner where Sofie and Maia were dusting themselves off.

"You two are *sisters?*" This was Kasper, sounding incredulous. Laura was in shock, too.

"There are seven of us," said Sofie, looking smug. "We hardly ever see each other. We live in different places and we usually work alone."

"Which I prefer," said Maia, flashing Mercury a hard look. "Especially when *some of us* keep changing our names all the time, and can't keep our mouths shut." Then she looked over at Sofie.

"Electra is a stupid name," Sofie complained. "Everyone

would laugh at me at school. Germany is not Russia—everyone is much more fashionable."

Maia and Electra. Seven Sisters. Laura couldn't believe she hadn't realized before. So that was why Maia had asked Sofie what she called herself. Why they were always whispering and bickering.

"The Pleiades," Laura murmured to Dan. "They're two of the Pleiades!"

"I thought they lived in the sky," he whispered. "And were, like, stars."

"These two live in Germany and Russia, apparently."

"So," Dan said to Maia. "I'm confused. Are you coming to our school next semester or not?"

Maia sighed.

"Please," said Mercury, backing toward the tree ladder in short, precise steps. "Listen to them. Do as they say. If Jupiter is willing, we will meet again at the Pantheon. Be aware of the danger outside."

"What kind of danger?" Kasper asked, his voice husky.

"The battle we spoke of," Mercury said, nodding at Laura.

"Yes?" she said.

"It's already begun."

*   *   *

From the hillside above their pit, all they could see was the roiling ash cloud, dark and angry today, and the smoke and flames of fires all over the city. *The second earthquake*, Laura thought. As the group made their way down the hill, she kept glancing at Maia and Sofie. They were sisters—and they'd been with her the whole time for a reason. To look out for her, to keep her safe. That's why Maia had been so concerned with who else could "help." Laura felt a rush of gratitude toward them.

Before they'd climbed the tree ladder, they'd borrowed the penknife from an apologetic Kasper. Maia had cut a small slit in the outer layer of Laura's waistband, and slid the bracelet in. Laura could feel it now, a little lump against her ribs. The other stone Maia wrapped in a ripped piece of tissue, and wriggled it to the other side of the waistband, so there was no chance of the stones bumping together. There was no way to close up the hole, they'd feared, until Sofie proffered a piece of chewing gum. Disgusting, Laura thought, but so far it seemed to be working.

The sisters walked side by side, with a pensive Kasper following and Dan and Laura in the very back. Occasionally, Laura's hand would brush against Dan's, and they would exchange a kind of secret smile. Laura felt grateful to him, too.

Before they reached the Colosseum, Maia turned to give them the briefest of warnings and explanations. Neptune was lined up against Minerva and her allies, she said; he controlled horses and creatures of the sea, so they had to be ready to fight them. Except for dolphins, apparently: they were part of Apollo's domain, so they could be trusted.

"Dolphins?" Kasper asked, wide-eyed. "You're saying we don't have to worry about *dolphins*?"

"They'll be fighting," Maia explained. "But they won't attack *us*. Just keep out of their way."

"Snakes and wolves won't attack us, either," Sofie added. "Apollo commands them also."

"What about the snakes in the fresco in the church, when you were getting attacked?" Laura asked.

"They were biting the leg of the man," Sofie explained. "Did you think Kasper alone saved me with his big punch?"

By the deflated look on Kasper's face, it was clear that was exactly what he'd thought.

"Remember that dogs and vultures are bad," Maia went on. "They're all under the command of Mars. And Juno commands lions and peacocks."

Laura nodded, trying to keep everything straight.

"And watch out for the mermaids," said Sofie, squeezing Kasper's arm. "They are the worst. Really, I hate them. They are just spiteful show-offs, and they are all over Rome, in almost every fountain, with all this *hair* and *tail* and thinking they are something special. Be careful, Kasper."

"Kasper will be all right," said Maia. "It's Dan I'm more worried about."

Dan looked annoyed, and started blustering about how he was superfit, ready to fight, and not scared of anything.

"I know all that." Maia looked unimpressed. "But Kasper has the protection of Odin. Around his neck."

Laura spotted Kasper's amber pendant, and another piece of the puzzle clicked into place. Kasper smiled, touching the animal with a kind of reverence.

"Odin's not a Roman god," Dan complained, still sulky. "He's, like, Norse. So now suddenly it's a pan-ancients thing?"

"Don't worry—I will help you," Sofie told Dan, and Laura wasn't sure if she was being truly helpful or snide.

"And don't forget," said Maia, "the seagulls. Some of them are harpies. And, no, I don't know which ones. So fight anything that gets too close, okay?"

"Jack was right," Dan muttered to Laura. "This *is* the worst school trip ever. If our parents knew we'd be fighting random seagulls and statues, they'd sue the Department of Education."

By the time they got to the road encircling the Colosseum, Laura felt her stomach drop with horror. She realized neither

Mercury nor Maia had been exaggerating. The streets of Rome were a battlefield.

The long avenue that ran through the Forum, so quiet and dark last night, was thronged with people fighting. But not fighting each other—fighting the *monuments*. Fighting the fountains and statues of Rome. These creatures, apparently free from their stone moorings, were all roaming the streets, ferocious and alive.

A giant stone horse galloped down the road, teeth bared: It knocked over two policemen who didn't jump out of its way in time and then trampled a line of parked motorcycles, crushing the metal under its enormous hooves.

Carved dolphins, their faces twisted in grotesque anger, squirmed along the ground, snapping at shins and ankles, taking out the tires of an abandoned ambulance with a swish of their heavy tails. *They won't hurt us*, Laura reminded herself, even as she felt a swell of fear.

Stone bees swarmed, hitting rather than stinging the scattering crowd, surging up and down the street like a tornado of hail. Four nymphs in draped robes, their faces as serene as ever, pushed a food vendor's van over and chased its terrified owner down the road.

A hooded crow—*Mercury?* Laura wondered—flew overhead, cawing at the group, doubling back to make sure they were following. Laura stumbled, distracted by a stone Cupid, perched on the back of a bucking horse. The statue was pulling arrows from a miniature quiver on his back and firing at any seagulls in close range.

"Stay together, everyone!" Dan shouted, but Kasper had grabbed onto another stubby stone horse and was trying to jump on.

"Horses bad!" Laura shouted at him, but maybe he thought he was invincible with his amber pendant.

"I'll clear a path," he yelled, clinging to the stone ridges of the horse's mane while it screeched and bucked in protest. "Follow me!"

"Give me a break," Dan said to Laura. "Seriously, this guy is delusional. He thinks *he's* the Norse god."

"Would you stop obsessing?" shouted Laura, smacking bees away from her face. Real bees were bad enough, she decided; stone ones were monsters. "Watch out for that lion!"

A stone lion, almost as big as Kasper's horse, paced toward them, back low, a great roar erupting from its carved jaws.

"I don't know how to fight a real lion," Dan said. "Let alone one made out of stone. Maybe these stupid bees will help."

He reached into the air and grabbed a handful of the bees, flinging them at the lion's head. Laura followed his lead, pelting the lion with the stone bees buzzing around her ears; they vibrated in her hand, their sharp-edged wings scraping her palms. But at least they didn't sting. The lion flinched and recoiled, and they swerved out of its path, scampering away before the great carved beast had a chance to recover.

But their path ahead was blocked by a battalion of mermaids. Sofie was right: They looked evil. Balanced on curving tails, the mermaids spun around and around like whirling dervishes, the stone locks of their hair whipping anyone who ventured too close. Armed men in uniform, sprinting up the road in a line, fired at them, but all the bullets did was make dents in the stone torsos and tails.

The mermaids kept spinning—all hair and tail, as Sofie had complained—with their line spreading until it formed a barrier across the entire expanse of the avenue. Kasper's horse reared and bucked until Kasper slid to the ground, wincing with pain. The horse galloped off, and Laura wasn't sure how any of them would get through this line.

Sofie and Maia, the sisters, stood perilously close to the mermaids. Their heads—light and dark—bent together as they conferred, and then they both dropped to the ground, sitting on the asphalt of the road as though they were settling in for a protest. It took a moment or two for Laura to register what they were doing—using their feet to kick at two of the mermaids' tails.

Sofie seemed particularly adept at this, slamming her feet over and over where the tail curved, until her mermaid toppled, crashing to the ground and scattering shards of stone across the road. Maia's mermaid took a little longer to fall; it collapsed so close to Maia that on the way down one of the stone strands of hair knocked Maia hard in the face.

Maia fell back, clutching her jaw, and Kasper dove into the fray, groping around in the bouncing spray of stones until he emerged clutching something in his fist. When Dan pulled Maia clear of the debris, she was trying—and failing—to tell him something.

"She has lost a tooth," Sofie reported, barely able to keep the glee out of her voice. "This is why I do not like the mermaids."

Kasper held the bloody tooth aloft, and Maia grimaced. One of her bottom teeth was missing, and there was blood smeared across her face.

"Are you all right?" Laura asked, but Maia nodded, waving them forward.

"Come on," said Dan, urging them all through the break in the mermaid line before the other mermaids—whirling even more furiously now—closed the gap. Kasper was already through, kicking at a strange-looking crocodile with long snapping jaws.

"This way," said a voice in Laura's ear, and she was startled to see Mercury there in the street, steering her by the elbow.

"Why aren't you flying?" she asked him. Above the fray seemed a much better option than this wild obstacle course along the Via dei Fori Imperiali.

"Now it is too dangerous," he said, jerking his head toward the sky. Dozens of birds were circling—crows, seagulls, starlings, blackbirds; their squawks and cries were audible even over the screams and roars, amid crashes of stone and popping gunshots, down here on the street. A nymph hurled herself at Laura and tore the pocket off her dress. Laura staggered back, clutching her ripped dress in horror. Thankfully, the waistband—and its chewing-gum buckle—was still intact.

"She's looking for the star sapphires," Maia told Laura, then shouted to the others. "Everyone, over here!"

Maia, Sofie, Kasper, and Dan formed a protective circle around Laura, and Mercury stayed by her side. The group walked on, managing to keep together and to avoid any major incident, though Kasper's legs were both bleeding from his encounter with the crocodile, and Dan was rubbing his arm: He'd been walloped in the elbow by another nymph trying to grab Laura's dress. Progress was slow with so many of them limping, especially with the bees swarming them and, for one terrifying moment, Kasper's abandoned horse charging toward them—stopped only by a police van reversing into its path.

The huge marble monument on Piazza Venezia, usually as stately as an oversized wedding cake, was another field of battle today. Its statues of Winged Victories were hurling broken-off pieces of columns at anyone passing, and the bronze horses galloped headlong down the flights of stairs, chariots bouncing behind them. Laura was speechless, but also, somehow, entranced by the ludicrous spectacle of it all.

Mercury directed their group down small streets, where lion-head doorknobs snapped at them. Sofie had to use a trash can to smash a persistent bull door knocker into smithereens, just as it was about to lunge at Kasper. It would be a miracle if they reached the Pantheon, Laura thought. It would be a miracle if the Pantheon was still intact.

In the Piazza della Minerva, outside the "elephant church," the elephant still stood on its plinth. But it was trumpeting and tossing its head, the obelisk on its back shaking from side to side. As they passed, the elephant gave an almighty bellow, and tossed the obelisk aside as though it were an annoying fly. The obelisk cracked and scattered over the ground, and they had to run to avoid getting hit by the debris. Laura could only hope the elephant wouldn't come charging after them.

The sky darkened to a deeper shade of charcoal, and rain began to fall. This was it, Laura knew. Jupiter was sending the rain Mercury had asked for.

Mercury could leave Rome, and take the star sapphires with him. Now all they had to do was get to the Pantheon.

CHAPTER TWENTY-ONE

The rain was persistent but still a drizzle rather than a downpour, enough to make the cobbles slithery. But not enough, Laura suspected, to create the thundering funnel of water Mercury needed to return to the other side.

The piazza in front of the Pantheon was quiet, all the shops and restaurants shuttered. It seemed months ago rather than days, Laura thought, when she'd taken the second star sapphire from her bag. She'd shown it to Maia—one of the Seven Sisters—there at the fountain, and the seagull—a harpy—had swooped down to try to steal it. Everything seemed different in retrospect, now that Laura knew the truth.

That day, the piazza had been crowded with tourists and shoppers, buskers and hawkers. Now there was no one near the fountain with its dolphins, snapping and writhing, tails flicking, defying anyone to get too close to them. Seagulls were flying overhead, their eerie cries like warning shots echoing around the empty piazza.

"Dolphins okay," Laura muttered to herself, remembering Maia's explanations. "Seagulls not."

Today no one huddled around the granite columns of the Pantheon's porch to take shelter from the rain. The vast bronze doors, the same color as today's sky, were closed. Panic made Laura's heart beat faster: What if the Pantheon was locked? She hadn't considered the possibility of not being able to get in. They might have been able to climb up the ruins of the Golden House, but the Pantheon was huge. There was no way in for them but the doors. She looked over at Dan, Maia, Sofie, and Kasper, and she could see by the looks on their faces that they were thinking the same thing.

Mercury, his downy shirt ruffled by the wind, seemed unperturbed by the closed doors. He walked resolutely toward them and, as he approached, they creaked open, as though unseen hands were pulling them from the other side. Laura hurried through, Dan at her side, the others crowding in behind them.

Inside it was empty and quiet—no tour groups, no recorded announcements, just the sound of light rain falling through the oculus and pattering onto the marble floor. The stillness felt false and almost oppressive after the noise and chaos, the unbelievable sights and sounds, they'd encountered on the way here.

After they'd all crowded in, the heavy doors clanged shut.

"Now we must wait," Mercury told them. There wasn't enough rain yet: Laura understood that. She wondered if now was the time to hand over the star sapphires, or if she should hang on to them until the last possible moment.

Maia sank onto the floor and hugged her knees; her jawline was bruised. Sofie rummaged around in her bag for some water, then sat down beside her sister.

"Laura," said Kasper, his face contrite, and still handsome despite a nasty graze on his forehead and red scratches down one cheek. "I must say sorry to you again. I was wrong to do what I did last night, taking the stones and running. I thought it was the best thing, but maybe it was the worst. Finding the mosaic was impossible, and then there was the earthquake, and now—this."

Laura nodded, remembering the sight of Kasper's stone horse coming at them.

"I think the battle today was always going to happen, one way or another," she told him.

"It should be over soon, I hope," Kasper said. "Then we can forget about what happened here today."

Laura shot him a rueful smile. "I don't think I'll ever forget what happened," she said. "Even if I wanted to."

Kasper gathered her up in a hug and Laura hugged him back. When she spotted Dan a few feet away, frowning with irritation in Kasper's direction, Laura couldn't help but smile a little.

There was nothing to do at this point but recover from the battle scene outside, and sprawl around on the cool marble floor, watching the rain create a damp circle. Dan, though, couldn't settle: He paced around, and more than once walked over to the big doors, shaking the handles to make sure they were locked. Rain was still falling, but it wasn't heavy enough yet. Mercury was walking around as well, taking small precise steps and glancing up at the circle of gray sky visible through the oculus.

Laura stood up to stretch, and Dan sidled over.

"At least he doesn't go to our school," he muttered to Laura, nodding in Kasper's direction, and she shook her head and smiled. Obviously he wasn't going to let his grudge drop, especially if Kasper insisted on hugging her. "You didn't have to let him off so easy, you know."

"It'll all be over soon," Laura told him, though she was really telling herself. All they needed was some more rain, and this could end. Maybe it was getting heavier, or maybe it was her imagination.

A familiar cry sounded overhead—seagulls crisscrossing

the sky above them, flying closer and closer. Laura's stomach dropped. Of course, seagulls. The closed door wouldn't keep them out, not when there was a gaping oculus open to the sky. She should have thought of that.

Maia was on her feet now, speaking in a slurred voice after the blow to her jaw.

"I thought this might happen," she said, frowning up at the sky.

"What?" Dan asked.

"Harpies," said Maia and Sofie in unison, exchanging grim-faced glances.

Mercury gave a strange little hop and launched himself into the air, transforming into a crow so instantly that Laura felt the way she always did when she saw it——as though her eyes were playing tricks on her. He flew in low circles around the big, echoing space, around the scant shower of rain splattering the floor. Kasper, who'd been sitting down, was standing up, rubbing his bruised knuckles. They all knew now what seagulls meant: nothing good.

"You're the one with the star sapphires," Maia told Laura. "They're *really* going to come after you."

"So you're saying: Be ready to fight," Laura said, hoping her voice sounded strong and brave, the opposite of the way she was feeling.

"Fight dirty. *They* will." Maia cast a wary eye at the oculus, where the seagulls still swooped and cried, just outside the building. "We have to get them to the ground."

"Those harpies think they are so clever," said Sofie, contempt in her voice; she was staring up at the oculus as well. "They are just stupid monsters. *We* are the daughters of a titan."

That was all very well for Sofie and Maia, thought Laura, but she and Dan just had regular American parents. And all Kasper had to protect him—aside from his height and strength— was a supposedly magical amber amulet that some monster could probably just wrench off his neck.

Sofie, Laura noticed, was brandishing Kasper's flashlight/penknife in her hand. A good idea, Laura decided, wishing she had something on hand she could use in an attack.

"Nothing but brute strength for me," said Dan, as if reading her mind. He didn't sound very confident, either. "I hope they don't decide to punch my other eye."

"We should be like Roman soldiers," Kasper suggested.

"Like, wear armor?" Dan asked snidely.

"No," Kasper said, glancing at him. "I mean we should keep together, not spread out. That's how the Romans fought, protecting each other."

"So the enemy couldn't divide and conquer," said Maia, still looking up at the sky. "We stand in a tight circle, and when people are tired, they move inside the circle, and get ready to fight again."

"We could use bags as shields," Laura suggested. She wished she'd brought her backpack. Luckily, Maia, Sofie, Dan, and Kasper all had theirs. "If we get attacked from overhead."

Dan lent her his bag and the three girls slipped on the backpacks so that they hung in the front, like rudimentary armor. They agreed that Kasper's bag would be held aloft by whoever was in the center of their circle, to protect them from aerial attack. Laura, Maia said, should stand in the middle, sheltered by the others, to begin with, because she was the main target. When Kasper suggested that Dan be the one standing in the middle, because he had no "bag armor," Dan got annoyed, and Maia had to shout over the boys to stop them from arguing.

"Be quiet!" she yelled, and everyone was startled: Maia almost never raised her voice. But it was instantly clear why she was shouting. Mercury, in his crow form, was cawing, his echoing cries raising the alarm, and two seagulls dipped into sight, entering the Pantheon through the oculus, followed by two crows.

Mercury's troops, Laura thought. If only there were more of them.

"Take your positions now," said Maia, calm again, and they all obeyed.

Another two gulls flew in, and another two, and then Laura lost count. She scuttled into the interior of their little fighting formation and hoisted Kasper's backpack above her head for extra protection. She couldn't see anything now, tucked away in the tight circle of bodies, but she could hear the rain slapping the marble floor, and, much louder, the throbbing shrieks of the seagulls. They were getting closer, their screeches ringing in her ears.

When they launched their first attacks, Laura heard rather than saw it—the whir of wings, the cries (from the gulls and from her friends on the outside of the circle), the incessant cawing of Mercury and his crows, the whack of a makeshift weapon smacking at a seagull.

Kasper's backpack, brandished above her head, absorbed some of the impact of an attacking beak, but not all. Laura braced herself, flinching every time a bird thudded into the bag. It was taking all her strength to soak up the impact without dropping to the ground. She needed a different tactic—to be more aggressive. She remembered how she'd been able to fight the mugger yesterday. Maybe she wasn't so meek after all.

Every time she sensed a bird was close, she pushed the bag hard, up into the air, trying to bat it away rather than let it get so close to her head. Hopefully she was hitting seagulls rather than crows: it was impossible to tell with all the noise they made. Her new tactic seemed to be working, and maybe, she hoped, she'd take one of those "stupid harpies," as Sofie called them, by surprise.

"Laura out, Sofie in!" Maia called, and Sofie, panting hard and bleeding from her temple, squeezed next to Laura. There was no time to think, or to fear, anymore. Laura hesitated just long enough for Sofie to get a grip on Kasper's bag, and then she wriggled into the outer circle, between Dan and Kasper. Before her eyes had even adjusted, a seagull flew at her head, its beak pecking at her skull.

"Ow!" she screamed. The pain was terrible, searing its way into her brain. How everyone else was managing to stay upright getting attacked like this was incredible.

"Tighten up," Maia ordered the group when Laura took her place. Another seagull hurled itself at her, this time smacking straight into her backpack armor. Maybe it could sense the star sapphires, she thought, swiping at it wildly and coming away with a handful of white feathers. A crow swooped low, circling their group, and when another seagull dove toward Laura, the crow intercepted, driving the screeching white bird off course.

Laura had only the vaguest sense of Dan on one side of her and Kasper on the other, arms and legs hitting out, Kasper back in possession of the flashlight; it cracked every time it made contact with a gull's beak. Another seagull soared toward her, its beady eyes fixed on her, and Laura—her legs shaking, willing herself not to duck—tried another new tactic: lifting her fist and punching it as hard as she could. The bird's body felt tough as elephant hide under its downy coat, but it recoiled and flew away.

Laura could taste blood—her own blood, dribbling down her face. The air was thick with floating feathers and drifting ash, with the rain, heavier now, splashing up from the floor. Her feet were wet, and she ground her heels against the floor, telling herself not to slip and fall. She was hot and panting hard, and couldn't make out how many gulls were still attacking them.

But she was doing it. They all were. They were staying upright, and they were fighting.

"Sofie out, Dan in," shouted Maia, her voice clear and imperious. Unfazed as ever, Laura thought, with immense relief—when Maia started to panic, she'd know they were in real trouble.

"No way!" Dan shouted back. "I'm just hitting my stride."

He grabbed a seagull's wing and tugged it so hard, dragging it toward the ground, that the seagull let out a blood-curdling scream, sounding more like an enraged woman than a bird. And then it—she?—*was* an actual woman, standing on the ground in front of them. Dark hair and eyes, in a white dress or robe; Laura could barely see. So this was a harpy, like Serena at the hostel. And also like the dark-haired woman who tried to mug Laura at the Trevi Fountain.

Face contorted with rage, the harpy leapt at Dan, clawing at his face. Laura remembered Maia's exhortation to fight dirty, and she grabbed a handful of the harpy's hair, wrenching as hard as she could. The harpy's head jerked back, and her scream was so angry and piercing, Laura almost let go. Another seagull was zooming toward her, but Kasper was reaching for it, grabbing one wing and hurling it to the ground.

"Hit it," Laura encouraged Dan, holding the harpy's hair.

Dan hesitated. "I can't hit a girl."

"They are not girls!" shouted Sofie, wriggling in next to Laura. "They are harpies, and they want to kill us."

"Okay." Dan took a breath and then swung at the harpy's pointy face, making contact.

Black and white feathers were everywhere—stuck to Laura's bleeding face, trapped under her fingernails, drifting in the air. All but one of the crows lay dead or injured on the ground. And too many of the gulls around them were turning into dark-haired harpies, each one more ferocious than the next.

Laura and the others were fighting almost back-to-back now, punching and kicking. While Dan tried to wrestle a harpy to the ground, Laura wriggled close to Maia: A sneaker in each hand, Maia was walloping the ears of another harpy who shrieked in pain and outrage.

"Get her down flat," Maia ordered, and Laura pushed on the harpy's strong shoulders. Finally, the harpy's knees buckled, and Maia leapt on her, shoving the harpy's torso onto the marble floor. At last Laura understood what Maia meant. As soon as the harpy's shoulders hit the ground, her body dissolved into nothingness. Just like the seagull that day in the cemetery, shot down by the Cupid on the gravestone. When the harpy's body hit the ground, it couldn't survive.

"Get them to the ground!" Maia shouted, and the thrill of adrenaline coursed through Laura's body. They could do this: They could defeat the harpies. They just had to get them to the ground.

In the whirlwind of ash and feathers and splattering rain, it looked as though there were still four harpies fighting. But four harpies equaled about ten normal people, Laura decided, glimpsing one bulldoze Dan to the ground. Mercury still flew around overhead, cawing: If only he *could* fight! They could do with a few dive-bomb attacks on some harpy's head right now.

Instead she had to resort to pulling the hair of the harpy pummeling Dan. Fighting like a girl, Laura thought sardonically—

well, she *was* a girl, an ordinary girl, not one of the Pleiades, or a demigod, or a monster, and anyway, it seemed to work. The harpy fell to her knees with a roar of rage, and Dan rolled free of her grip. Laura managed to jump on the harpy, pushing her until her back hit the marble and, just like that, she dissolved into nothingness.

"Three more!" shouted Laura. There was blood running down her hand as well, and her skirt was torn—but she could still feel the stones secured in her waistband, pressing against her every time she breathed out.

"Serena," Dan said, his voice cracking with exhaustion, and they both faced the woman who'd seemed so nice, so pleasant, so helpful back at the hostel. Now she was revealed in her true form, an enraged harpy: Her once-pretty face was twisted and grotesque, her eyes bulging, her nose sharp as a beak, her forehead red and scabbed from the fight outside the hostel with one of Mercury's hooded crows.

She lunged for Laura's neck, managing to make contact even as Sofie pummeled her in the belly. Serena's hand gripped Laura's neck, her twisted face so close that Laura thought for a moment the harpy might try to bite her. Although she was choking, Laura fought back, tugging at Serena's clawlike fingers, but she didn't have the strength to wrench the harpy's hands away.

Then Sofie's face loomed, shoving the small flashlight into Serena's gaping mouth until the harpy flung her head back, unable to breathe. Her grip on Laura's neck loosened, and Laura pushed her away as hard as she could. Maia was there as well, whacking at Serena until she fell back onto the marble floor.

"No!" Serena screamed, but it was too late. Her body dissolved into nothingness, her angry screech still echoing in the air.

Then there was silence—or quiet, more accurately.

Laura, on hands and knees, could hear everyone panting and heaving, completely spent. She could hear the rain falling. She could hear Mercury's caw, and the rhythmic flap of his wings, and then even that stopped; he must have landed, she thought. The fight was over. They'd beaten the harpies.

"Is everyone okay?" Maia called. The others nodded. Dan reached out a hand and squeezed Laura's shoulder.

But now she could hear footsteps approaching and her heart started thundering: not another one! She didn't have the strength left to fight anymore. She didn't think any of her friends did, even if two of them happened to be Pleiades.

"Laura," said a soft voice, and she raised her head, exhausted and relieved.

It was Mercury, no longer in bird form, holding out one of his slender hands. Laura clambered to her feet, spitting out the feathers and ash clogging her mouth. Rain poured through the oculus now, splashing down onto the marble floor in a heavy curtain of gray. She gazed into Mercury's black eyes, and he nodded: It was time.

Laura plucked the sticky piece of gum from her torn dress and retrieved the stone wrapped in tissue, placing it in Mercury's left palm. His hand closed around it. Then she squeezed her bracelet out of its hiding place, holding it by its broken chain, gazing at her grandfather's blue-gray star sapphire one last time.

"Sorry, Grandpa," she whispered. She thought of her grandfather's eyes, and his smile—things she'd always carry with her, in her heart, whether she had the stone or not. "I have to let it go."

Mercury held out his right hand, and she dropped the bracelet into it.

"The goodwill of Minerva goes with you," he said, twitching his head at her in one of his jerky bows. Then he stepped into the whorl of rain and stared straight up at the oculus, silvery water beating onto his upturned face.

Did the gods see him? Laura wondered. Was this ancient oculus still their eye on the world? *Just because Romans have deserted their gods doesn't mean that the gods have deserted Rome.*

This time when Mercury's feet left the ground, he didn't turn into a bird. He remained as he was, a boy soaring through the air, arms at his sides, drawn through that waterfall of rain to that unknown place where he and Minerva and the other ancient gods roamed. He was taking the star sapphires, Minerva's eyes, away from this world, to a place where they could no longer be stolen. Laura wondered if the stones would simply dissolve into dust, or if Minerva would cast them into the sky as a new constellation of stars.

In the blur of rain thundering through the Pantheon's oculus, Mercury disappeared. The last thing Laura saw of him was the feathered wings on his heels, jet black and glistening, soaring up to the world beyond the sky and beyond the stars, the sphere that no mortal would ever see.

EPILOGUE

When a sudden strong wind from the east blew the ash cloud into the sea, the people of Rome returned to their homes and businesses. Everyone began putting the city back together again. The earthquakes that had followed the volcano's eruption had damaged many of churches, palazzos, and ancient ruins. Outside the church of Santa Maria sopra Minerva, the stone elephant still stood on its plinth, but the ancient obelisk that had once stood on its back now lay in a hundred shattered pieces.

One of the strangest discoveries was the fragments of many of Rome's fountains and monuments, scattered across the Via dei Fori Imperiali. Bees from the Fontana delle Api, dolphins from the Fontana del Tritone, nymphs from the Fontana delle Naiadi, mermaids from the Fontana del Nettuno—shards and smashed chunks of these were found all over the great avenue that ran the length of the ancient Forums of Rome. The horses from the Trevi Fountain were discovered near the Column of Trajan, lying on their sides, as though they were sleeping in a field.

Nobody had any idea how any of these figures were ripped from their stone moorings, or how they ended up so far away from their original homes. The police and firefighters and medics, the soldiers who'd patrolled Rome after the volcanic eruption—none of them remembered anything. The city had been under a spell, some people said. The ash cloud descended and then it disappeared, and now Rome seemed to be waking up from a very bad dream.

The Fiumicino International Airport was jammed with tourists eager, after the cancellation of three days of flights, to leave. Not long after the volcano erupted, many visitors to the city had come down with a mystery virus, sleeping through the earthquakes and whatever had taken place in their violent aftermath. Everyone was recovering now, and they were eager to make their way home to their own countries, their own towns, and their own families. They crowded the airport terminals with long, snaking lines and heaped baggage carts.

The Riverside High School group was there as well. Curious observers might have noticed that some of the students herded by the three dazed-looking teachers bore the scars and bruises of recent injuries. One boy was limping so badly he could barely walk. Another boy had a black eye. And one of the girls had bandages on her arms and legs.

The girl was Laura Martin, and she was crying. Not from the pain of her injuries—things stung and ached, but everything would heal quickly, she was sure. Jack and Dan would be okay as well. She was thinking of what had happened earlier that day, their last in Rome.

She and Dan, along with Kasper, Sofie, and Maia, had crept out of the hostel as soon as the sun rose. The sky was blue, with no trace of ash cloud or rain.

This morning they had decided to make one final pilgrimage as a group to the Trevi Fountain, to throw coins into its pale blue waters, and make the wish all travelers made there: to one day return to Rome.

Maia had been skeptical, of course.

"It's just a superstition," she pointed out on the walk there, and Laura couldn't help laughing out loud: It was kind of rich for Maia to talk about "superstition" when she and Sofie were two of the Pleiades, seven sisters who were mythological beings rather than actual human girls. Or, at least, they *were* human but were also—what was it Sofie had said? Daughters of a titan?

At the fountain they lined up, five in a row, with their backs to the burbling water. As they'd approached, Laura stared hard at the fountain, to make sure nothing was moving this morning, but all of its beings and creatures, shells and seaweed, looked reassuringly frozen and carved. Several other tourists were there as well, posing for pictures, throwing coins. An old man sat on one of the broad steps, drinking coffee and squinting into the sunshine. Maybe he was happy to see the sun out again at last, Laura thought. He reminded her of her grandfather, drinking his morning coffee on the back steps of his house, smiling face raised to the sky.

The water was a serene blue, the sun glinting off the coins scattered below the surface. Two policemen patrolled, reprimanding a boy when he started climbing onto the fountain's lip, as though he were planning to jump in. That was all the police had to worry about now, Laura realized, smiling again: Someone climbing into the Trevi Fountain.

Dan squeezed in next to her, nudging Kasper out of the way.

"You think he's going to kidnap me and take me back to Denmark?" she whispered to Dan.

"I can fight harpies," Dan murmured back. "I can take *him* no problem."

"I will count to three and then we will all throw," said Sofie. She was on the other side of Kasper, of course.

"Should we sing the song?" said Maia, in what almost sounded like an impersonation of Woody, and Laura burst out laughing. She was laughing so much she didn't even hear Sofie's countdown, and only threw her coin when she saw Dan chuck his.

Maia was right, of course. It *was* just superstition. Throwing a coin into a fountain was a symbolic gesture. Laura realized she might not return to Rome until she was older; she might never return at all. Maybe none of them would.

Kasper was about to rejoin his school group and fly to Copenhagen. Though he kept telling Laura and Dan to visit him, and to bring Jack along as well, Laura suspected they wouldn't see each other any time soon. Sofie was going back to Germany, she said, and maybe she would see them again, maybe not.

"Maybe I come to America on holiday," she said, looking as though she had no intention of doing any such thing. "Maybe I get sent there, when one of my sisters needs help."

Maia raised an eyebrow.

"So, you're *not* coming to our school this fall, are you?" Laura asked her, and Maia shook her head. "Was that just a . . . I don't know what you call it. A cover story?"

"You should hope you don't see me again," said Maia. "You should hope you don't see either of us. When one of us turns up, it usually means there's some kind of trouble to deal with."

"But Denmark is very close to Germany," Sofie hurried to tell Kasper, flashing him her most winsome smile. "I can go there on the train, any time."

Back at the hostel, when they'd all brought their bags down to the lobby and handed their keys to Agent Orange, who looked grumpy about being back at work, Sofie said her good-byes. She kissed Dan and Laura good-bye, once on each cheek, and she kissed a bemused Kasper at least six times, and made him write down his address for her. Maia didn't kiss anyone. She waited until POTUS had talked to her parents—her real parents? Laura wondered—on the lobby phone, then walked outside to a car with tinted windows that had reversed down the narrow lane. It would take her to Naples, she said, where her parents would collect her.

Laura wanted to ask her if that was really going to happen, or if she'd been summoned for another mission. But there was no time to ask anything. Maia nodded her head at Laura, in a sort of brisk dismissal, and opened the car door.

"Maia!" Laura called from the doorway. "Good-bye and— thank you!"

Maia paused, one foot inside the car. She looked puzzled. Maybe nobody had ever thanked her.

"I hope I *do* see you again," Laura said. She would miss Maia, and her odd, know-it-all, capable ways. They could have been friends at Riverside High. They could have been weird together. "Anytime you need a hand, you know. Get in touch."

The beginnings of a rare smile flickered on Maia's face. "Okay," she said. "I just might do that."

Laura stood in the doorway while the car drove away, until Dan told her the rest of the kids from their school were on their way downstairs with all their bags.

"I asked Kasper to go up and help Jack," he said. "If he's the Son of Odin or whatever, he can carry Jack down with one hand."

"You are so ridiculous," Laura told him, rolling her eyes, but she didn't mind when Dan grabbed her hand and didn't let go.

She didn't cry when Sofie left, or when Maia left, or when Kasper left. But at the airport, with BOARD NOW flashing by their flight number, and Morgan dumbstruck when she saw Dan—OMG, Dan Sinclair!—holding Laura's hand, Laura felt a sudden gush of emotion, impossible to repress.

In Rome she'd met one of the ancient gods, Mercury—that crosser of boundaries, the lord of transgression and of travelers, the god of dreams. He'd called her by name, watched over her, tried to protect her. As long as she lived, Laura would never forget him—just as she would never forget her grandfather, who had done just the same, really, in a different life, a different world.

And what her teenaged grandfather had begun in Rome all those years ago, she'd finished in Rome, returning the star sapphire he'd taken, making things right again. If he were still alive, he'd know it was the right thing to do. Wherever he was now, she hoped he was watching, and that he knew that she'd always love him, even if she had to give his precious last gift away.

Laura boarded the plane as though she were walking in a dream, thinking of Sofie and Maia and Kasper off on their own adventures, and Dan staying close to her. Wherever the future took them, Laura knew they would never forget one another. How could she ever forget the past few days in Rome, when the gods raged, birds fought one another in the sky, and stone creatures came to life to do battle? After all these years of studying the ancient world, Laura had learned more than any class or book could ever teach her. At last, she thought, she knew what it meant to step into an eternal city, beyond any limits of world or time, an empire without end.

ACKNOWLEDGMENTS

Many thanks to my editor, Aimee Friedman, for her patience, guidance, and good sense. I'm very grateful to Rebecca Hill for sharing the details of her own school Classics trip (especially the orange hostel), and to Maia Churichkova for answering all my nosy questions. For style advice, I would have been lost without the generous and detailed suggestions of Anise Aiello and Will MacDonald.

Particular thanks to Lindsey Jones and Tony Pigou for their hospitality in Rome; Trev Broughton, for lending me a peaceful place to write in the Lake District; and to Kirsten Skou, Max Nicolaisen, and the board of the Brecht House in Svendborg, Denmark, for my very happy and productive residency there.

I'm also immensely grateful for the practical support of Creative New Zealand; and for all the help and encouragement of my agent, Richard Abate; and my family, especially Lynn-Elisabeth and Stephen Hill, and Tom Moody.

There are many great books on Rome, ancient and modern, but two that I found particularly gripping were *A Day in the Life of Ancient Rome* by Alberto Angela and *The Secrets of Rome: Love and Death in the Eternal City* by Corrado Augias.

PAULA MORRIS

is the author of *Ruined*, *Unbroken*, *Dark Souls*, and several award-winning novels for adults in her native New Zealand. She now lives in England with her husband. Please visit her online at www.paula-morris.com.